D1288043

ROBERT OWEN
PRINCE OF COTTON SPINNERS

ROBERT OWEN
PRINCE OF COTTON SPINNERS

A SYMPOSIUM

EDITED BY

JOHN BUTT

DAVID & CHARLES
NEWTON ABBOT

ISBN 0 7153 5164 8

COPYRIGHT NOTICE

© DAVID & CHARLES (PUBLISHERS) LIMITED AND CONTRIBUTORS 1971

All rights reserved. No part of this publication may be reproduced, stored in a retrieval system, or transmitted, in any form or by any means, electronic, mechanical, photocopying, recording, or otherwise, without the prior permission of David & Charles (Publishers) Limited

Set in 11/13 pt Times Roman
and printed in Great Britain
by Bristol Typesetting Company Limited
for David & Charles (Publishers) Limited
South Devon House Newton Abbot Devon

CONTENTS

		Page
1	INTRODUCTION *John Butt*	9
2	THE SOCIAL AND ECONOMIC THOUGHT OF ROBERT OWEN *James H. Treble*	20
3	OWEN AS AN EDUCATOR *Margery Browning*	52
4	ROBERT OWEN AND THE WORKERS *W. Hamish Fraser*	76
5	OWEN AS FACTORY REFORMER *J. T. Ward*	99
6	ORBISTON: A SCOTTISH OWENITE COMMUNITY 1825–28 *Ian Donnachie*	135
7	ROBERT OWEN AS A BUSINESSMAN *John Butt*	168
8	THE INDUSTRIAL ARCHAEOLOGY OF NEW LANARK *John R. Hume*	215
	CHRONOLOGY	254
	INDEX	257

ILLUSTRATIONS

PLATES

Page

Colour pastel of Robert Owen by Mary Ann Knight
(*Scottish National Portrait Gallery*)   17

Robert Owen from a portrait by W. H. Brooke ARHA
(*National Portrait Gallery*)   17

New Institution   18

A recent view of the School   18

Schoolroom scene   35

Robert Owen by an unknown artist   36

Robert Owen from a drawing by Smart   36

New Lanark from the Clyde   53

New Lanark showing the rural setting   53

New Buildings   54

Workers' housing   54

Nursery Buildings   71

A village of union from a drawing by R. R. Reinagle RA   71

The remains of No 1 mill   72

The north front of No 2 mill   72

Archibald James Hamilton   89

David Dale from a Tassie medallion   90

Robert Owen from a picture by W. T. Fry   90

The lade   107

Mill dam   107

Rear of No 1 mill   108

Rear of mills 2 and 3   108

The counting house   125

Detail of musicians' gallery in the School   126

Interior of No 3 mill   126

New Lanark from the end of Caithness Row   143

Headstone in New Lanark graveyard   144

The engine house   144

IN THE TEXT

View and plan of the villages of unity and co-operation   139

Plan of the Orbiston establishment 146

No 1 mill at New Lanark (*from a drawing by B. T. Danek and Miss M. K. Borland*) 219

Ground plan of mills 1 and 2 (*McGrigor, Donald & Co MSS, Glasgow City Archives*) 220

Plan of New Lanark in 1863 (*Ordnance Survey map 1863*) 222

Front elevation of No 3 mill (*drawing by B. T. Danek and Miss M. K. Borland*) 223

Ground plan of No 3 mill (*McGrigor, Donald & Co MSS*) 224

Ground plan of No 4 mill (*McGrigor, Donald & Co MSS*) 224

Ground plan of millwrights' shop and foundries (*McGrigor, Donald & Co MSS*) 226

Front elevation of Nursery Buildings, Store, Bakehouse and Post Office (*Ian G. Lindsey & Partners*) 227

Front elevation of Caithness Row (*Ian G. Lindsey & Partners*) 227

Front elevation of New Buildings (*Ian G. Lindsey & Partners*) 229

Front and rear elevations of Braxfield Row (*Ian G. Lindsey & Partners*) 230

Ground plan of New Institution (*McGrigor, Donald & Co MSS*) 231

Ground plan of School (*McGrigor, Donald & Co MSS*) 232

All illustrations not otherwise acknowledged are from the contributors' own collection.

1

INTRODUCTION
JOHN BUTT

These essays on Robert Owen have evolved from discussions over the past five years with my colleagues in the department of Economic History at Strathclyde University. As New Lanark is virtually on our doorstep, we felt that we should not allow the bicentenary of Robert Owen's birth (on 14 May 1771) to pass without a collective effort to put on record our views on aspects of his life and work.

Owen has survived the contemporary neglect of epic figures better than most nineteenth-century worthies, as a glance at the bibliographies in J. F. C. Harrison's recent volume will show.[1] But any introduction to the life and thought of Robert Owen must, unfortunately, stress that previous works – with notable exceptions – have been based more on the intellectual and philosophical positions of their authors than on Owen's own position. Historians of the Labour movement have discovered a role for him as the father of British Socialism. Overseas, he has been regarded as the herald of the 'New Moral World' of utopian communities. Early co-operators, like George Jacob Holyoake, hailed him as the founder of co-operation and secularism.

Recent scholars in the field of co-operative practice and principles have continued the trend set by Lloyd Jones and Holyoake in the nineteenth century. Paul Lambert, for instance, declares that 'Owen and Fourier are the fathers of Co-operation, mainly because they have expressed its fundamental principles: association, voluntary character, democratic

9

government, activity aiming at service . . .'² This view does less than justice to the co-operative societies in existence before Owen's time and to the later pragmatism of Owenite co-operators who were inspired by, but did not copy, Owen. A more balanced assessment of Owen's originality and significance is required, and is attempted in these essays; it is the particular concern of Dr Treble's opening essay in which he considers a whole range of Owen's social and economic ideas.

For much of his life Robert Owen regarded established religion as a singularly vicious opponent. But this is not to imply, as many have implied, that he was an atheist. Strictly, he was a deist and remained so even in his spiritualism; though he was not prepared to drink deep from the sectarian bottle, he believed in a supreme being.³ He excited the animosity of the professedly orthodox because he claimed that both the individual and society were more important than the family. Backed by a chorus of ribaldry, ministers of the church attacked him for his refusal to class Christianity before all other religions. Yet he, more than they, emphasised in his life and thought the greatest of the declared Christian virtues – charity.

The Socialist label fits Owen very uneasily, as Dr Treble, Dr Fraser and Dr Ward, in their respective essays, show. G. D. H. Cole recommended that all Owen's later writings except his *Life* should be ignored,⁴ but it is these writings that most often reveal his hierarchical political notions and his disregard for democracy. For instance, in his *Memorial to the Right Honourable the Lords of Her Majesty's Treasury* . . . dated January 1858, his ideas for the future governance of India revolve around a hereditary monarchy 'under one of our young princes', with a fixed constitution incorporating elements of British and American constitutional experience. Like many who grew to maturity during the French wars, Owen placed security before political reform. This laid him open to the charge at several periods of his life that he was in the government's pay and, more reasonably, that Owenism was intended to divert the working classes from even the peaceable achievement of reasonable political aims.

Henry Hetherington's *Poor Man's Guardian* generally recognised Owen's personal sincerity but took him to task for attempting to implement his economic schemes before the workers had achieved political emancipation:

> To attempt to establish even partially, upon independent grounds, any of Mr Owen's philanthropic views in the present state of the country, and before the working classes are politically emancipated, is only putting the cart before the horse, and will end in an abortion . . .[5]

In the same leader, written during the stirring days of the Reform Bill agitation, Hetherington attacked Owen's superficial, deferential 'Toryism':

> It is quite clear that the Association [to establish a Labour Exchange] cannot be popular with honest working men with a grain of sense in their heads, as all the public robbers of the country, from the King downwards, are requested to afford it protection.

Hetherington considered Owen to be a dilettante philanthropist lacking a sense of political reality, a view apparently supported by Edward Thompson in his *Making of the English Working Class* (1963). Hetherington, despite occasional outbursts of intemperate language, was personally well disposed to Owen:

> Mr Owen is generally esteemed, and without doubt is, a kind-hearted man – benevolently disposed to do his utmost to better the condition of mankind; but he exhibits a strange perversity of mind in expecting to realise his political millennium before working men are placed on equal footing with the other classes of the community with regard to political rights . . . he entertains an absurd idea, that with the aid of a plundering aristocracy, he shall be able to establish Co-operative principles . . .[6]

A few English and more than a few Scottish radicals – not renowned for their revolutionary or republican views – were less generous.[7] They disliked Owen's pandering to aristocrats and they were suspicious of attempts to achieve class harmony when class antagonism within the law might secure educational facilities, the vote and the secret ballot for the working classes.

In his debate with Hetherington, Owen insisted that it was the radicals who were misleading honest working men. This caused Hetherington to resort to the common journalistic convention of repeating scurrilous rumours in order to deny them:

some have gone so far as to enquire whether Mr. Owen's *diatribes* at Radicalism may not have their origin in some collusive scheme with the government, to lure us away from the assertion of our rights by an *ignis fatuus*, and to bedevil the public mind by the witcheries of co-operation.[8]

Owen's experience in the United States – and his continued interest in American working-class experience – confirmed him in his consistent opposition to political agitation. Essentially, he regarded political reform as irrelevant to the more important questions of providing rising incomes and secure jobs for the working classes in a period of sharp business fluctuations. On the eve of Chartism he was assailing the editor of the *Poor Man's Guardian* with letters that make plain his view that the political freedom of the United States had improved neither the political life of the Union nor the working man's lot. He declared, unequivocally, that 'were you to have a Parliament chosen, next year, by Universal Suffrage and Vote by Ballot, it would be most probably the least efficient, most turbulent and worst public assembly that has yet ruled this country'.[9]

In the context of the 1820s and the following two decades, Owen was probably correct to emphasise that economic change should take precedence over political reform, and that education in the use of the vote was necessary. Yet it could be reasonably argued that without political reform economic change could not occur, and without both, educational advances would be unlikely. Owen's anti-radicalism can be traced back at least to his signing of a Unitarian message of loyalty to the

Introduction

Crown in 1793 during the anti-Jacobin outrages. To the end of his days there was little sign of change.

In Mrs Browning's essay Owen's contribution to educational theory and practice is shown in better perspective than is usual – though there is now a growing interest in climate of opinion and its relationship to social dynamics. However, it is still customary to ignore the role of the teachers at New Lanark and the part they played in the making of Owen's reputation. This must have been considerable; for his many interests and activities, not to mention his trips abroad and business commitments at home, made personal continuous involvement in the social schemes at New Lanark impossible for him.

That a controlled environment was the formative influence on character was the spring-board of Owen's total philosophy. 'Heredity' and 'environment' still retain the central positions in most debates on the function of education in forming character, and this is some measure of Owen's percipience and of his calibre as a social scientist. His view that education should fit a child practically for life rather than simply provide an opportunity for intellectual hedonism is still relevant to many contemporary discussions. His emphasis on 'useful' knowledge is quintessentially the view of the business community and of the state in a number of widely differing countries today.

Intellectually ill-equipped to compromise, Robert Owen was more successful in his personal relationships than in his political activities. Dr Ward's essay on Owen as a factory reformer reveals his qualities as a human being and his weaknesses under political stresses. Owen's obsessive and imaginative conscience would not allow him to accept social reforms in stages, and this unwillingness colours many of his writings and certainly affected his actions. He impressed a diverse group of individuals with his sincerity, but for most, his refusal to accept modest and slow changes in existing practices proved an embarrassment if not an overpowering disadvantage.

Frederic Hill, brother of the more famous Rowland and Edwin, of good Midlands dissenting stock and Benthamite principles, was appointed the first Inspector of Prisons for Scotland and soon afterwards met Owen:

> He [Owen] accosted me with these words: "Now Mr Hill, 1 have one piece of advice to give you, which is, that you begin by telling the prison authorities that up to this time they have been entirely in the wrong". I need scarcely say that I did not adopt this mode of ingratiating myself with my official coadjutors.[10]

Owen was certainly good at handing down the tablets of the law, but bad at debating their validity. Much substantiation of this can be found in Dr Fraser's essay, where it is made plain that Owen's relationship with the working classes was essentially that of a paternalist.

Yet in a society where the maximum profit was commonly confused with the greatest good, Owen provided the workers with a concept of their dignity as individuals and their worth to the community – not merely at New Lanark but wherever his writings were read or discussed. In two senses Owen was indispensable to the evolution of a working-class consciousness. First, he committed his followers to the discipline of accepting industrialism – despite their communitarian attempts to escape from industrialising society – and secondly, he refused to accept the necessity for capitalist inhumanity: 'Every working man who reads Mr Owen's essays becomes a new being in his own estimation. He no longer feels himself a mere lump of living mechanism, predestined for the use and abuse of others . . .'[11]

Historians of co-operation, like Lambert, have seen in Robert Owen a progression from paternalistic capitalist to co-operative theorist. The place of Owen in the history of economic thought deserves greater attention, as Dr Treble shows, but primarily because of his interest in state adoption of full-employment policies and because of his theories on the relationship of money supply to trade cycles. Most attention hitherto has been concentrated on the theory and practice of Owenite villages of co-operation. These 'parallelograms of paupers', as Cobbett called them, depended upon paternalistic management or on the platonic guardianship of the central government; their inhabitants, Mr Donnachie points out in his essay on Orbiston, usually wanted neither. Significantly, Owen's personal interventions in the sphere of community building ultimately dissolved around his control of a workers' democracy. Even where he was not directly involved, as at Orbiston, it is clear that detailed structural proposals for workers' participation had not been reconciled with efficiency. This was no problem to Owen the businessman at New Lanark, but it was an inescapable difficulty in a less paternalistic setting.

Thus, the problem of individual participation – once the dignity of the worker was assumed – in the New Moral World of co-operation was posed but not solved by Owen and the Owenites in their communities. The world of consumer co-operation, of Rochdale and its precursors, was increasingly a product of later Owenite adaptation and compromise. This pragmatic acceptance by respectable working men that retail societies could improve their social and economic condition piecemeal was for Owen an abhorrent prelude to his ideal co-operative communities. Yet Owen remains a fascinating figure for present-day theorists on the role of co-operative ideas in society as a whole. Paul Derrick, for instance, considers it necessary for the British Labour Party 'to choose between continuing confrontation with the trade unions over incomes and the development of its commitment to industrial democracy into a movement towards a Co-operative, Owenite or Libertarian interpretation of socialism'.[12]

In my own essay on Owen as a businessman I have attempted to bring his shrewdness and sharpness to the fore. Philanthropy is inevitably a function of the rich, but it is surprising how Owen's rise to wealth over a period of twenty-five years has been very largely ignored. Similarly, there are many preconceptions about New Lanark as an embryonic village of co-operation. Except in its setting in the countryside, it was nothing of the sort. Rather it was an unusually large business unit for the day, requiring a range of management and production-control techniques beyond the needs of the owner of the small mill in a town.

Mr Hume's essay on the industrial archaeology of New Lanark is intended for all those who want the basic facts about the village and mills with which Owen associated himself until he died. We hope that it will stimulate interest in the future of this outstanding memorial to a great man and to the process that we call the Industrial Revolution.

Biography is essentially our purpose. We have concentrated on Robert Owen and not on Owenism. Hagiography has no place in our assessment. Robert Owen's reputation does not gain from unscholarly idolatry. Yet it has not been our policy to countenance an exercise in debunking. We can accept part of what the editor of the *Poor Man's Guardian* wrote of Owen:

> We are sincere admirers of Robert Owen. We admire his benevolence, his exalted views, his perfect disinterestedness. We admire the goodness of his heart, his singularly serene temper – a temper so singularly serene, that he appears to breathe an atmosphere of his own beyond the reach of human passions. But above all we admire his extraordinary moral courage, in daring . . . to array himself singlehanded against all the established prejudices of mankind.[13]

Yet we also can recognise his weaknesses and the shifts to which he had to resort in order to maintain his position in business. Essentially, we regard Robert Owen as a great inspirer of social movements of his time rather than an efficient organiser of social advances. As a truly great man, Owen does not require adulation.

Page 17 (left) Colour pastel of Robert Owen of Lanark by Mary Ann Knight. This portrait, c1800, has a special interest as practically all other known likenesses of him belong to his middle or old age. This one reproduces his vitality as a young man. Miss Knight was a sister-in-law of Andrew Plimer, a well-known painter of miniatures, who taught her to paint; *(below)* Robert Owen from an engraving after a portrait by W. H. Brooke ARHA

Page 18 (*right*) New Institution for the formation of character, opened 1 January 1816 by Robert Owen; (*below*) the school, built sometime between 1813 and 19 – a recent view

Introduction

NOTES

1 J. F. C. Harrison, *Robert Owen and the Owenites in Britain and America* (1969), 261 ff

2 P. Lambert, *Studies in the Social Philosophy of Co-operation*, translated by J. Letargez with the assistance of D. Flanagan (1963), 59. I am grateful to James Kinloch for this reference.

3 cf *A Supplementary Appendix to the First Volume of the Life of Robert Owen* Vol 1A (1858), passim but especially 'Memorial . . . Jan 1858', xviii ; and *New Moral World* No 57 (28 Nov 1835)

4 Robert Owen, *A New View of Society and Other Writings* (ed G. D. H. Cole, Everyman's Library 1927), vii

5 *Poor Man's Guardian* 24 Dec 1831

6 Ibid, 14 Jan 1832

7 cf A. Tyrrell, 'Political economy, whiggism and the education of working class adults in Scotland 1817–40', *Scottish Historical Review* Oct 1969, 151–165 ; B. Simon, *Studies in the History of Education 1780–1870* (1960), 132 ff ; H. Silver, *The Concept of Popular Education* (1965), 210 ff

8 *Poor Man's Guardian* 29 Sept 1832

9 Ibid, 7 Nov 1835

10 *Frederic Hill: an autobiography of fifty years in times of reform*, ed Constance Hill (1893), 115–116. I am grateful to John Robertson for this reference.

11 *Poor Man's Guardian* 4 Apr 1835

12 P. Derrick, *Socialism in the Seventies?* (1970), 37

13 *Poor Man's Guardian* 21 Mar 1835

As editor, I wish to express my gratitude to my colleagues and former student Margery Browning for their generous co-operation, and to thank our typists, Mrs Glen and Mrs Milne, for all their hard work.

2

THE SOCIAL AND ECONOMIC THOUGHT OF ROBERT OWEN

JAMES H. TREBLE

If there be one duty therefore more imperative than another, on the government of every country, it is, that it should adopt, without delay, the proper means to form those sentiments and habits in the people which shall give the most permanent and substantial advantages to the individuals and to the community.

Robert Owen, *A New View of Society*, Fourth Essay (1814)

The classic period of the Industrial Revolution (from 1760 to 1830) was marked by a series of profound and mutually re-inforcing changes which were ultimately to transform both the structure of the British economy and the values of British society. In view, therefore, of the radical nature of the consequences which flowed from the process of industrial-isation, it is scarcely surprising to find contemporary commentators giving a very mixed reception to the new 'manufactories'. Some writers sought to highlight the advan-tages that accrued to the whole of society through the working of the impersonal forces of an industrial market. Others, shocked by the absence of any intimate ties between employer and employee in those large urban complexes linked with the cotton industry, argued that 'King Cotton', whatever purely material benefits he may have bestowed on his servants, had contributed powerfully to their moral debasement. Those who subscribed to this latter thesis represented a broad spectrum of political belief – from the paternalistic Toryism of Southey and Coleridge to the rumbustious radicalism of William Cobbett. Yet however bitter their disagreements on specific political issues, they were with few exceptions agreed that the manufacturing system undermined the social health of the nation and that convalescence could only begin when society returned to the hierarchical and highly personalised relationships of the idealised village community. It is against this ferment of debate and discussion during the years 1805 – 25 that the early works of Robert Owen have to be set.

With a firmly established reputation behind him as one of the great entrepreneurs in the cotton-spinning world, Owen began his public career as a social critic relatively late in life. He was in his forty-first year when in 1812 he first presented to an audience in Glasgow his deterministic or environmental-ist analysis of the factors that contributed most to the formation of character. Stressing that man's outlook and pattern of behaviour were primarily fashioned by the values of the society into which he was born, he argued that it was now within the power of the human race to control and, where necessary, to change the social and cultural forces that shaped the character of the individual. By acting on this precept, 'keeping it steadily in view, much more may yet be accomplished for the improvement of society, than has been hitherto even attempted'.[1] But, apart from making a general commitment in favour of education, he neither at this time suggested a way of translating his theorising into a positive programme of reform, nor specified in any detail the nature of the malaise that afflicted the British people. These gaps were to be filled some eighteen months later when he pro-duced the first sections of *A New View of Society*.

There were three basic themes to this study of character formation. In the first place, Owen reaffirmed his belief that 'any general character, from the best to the worst, from the most ignorant to the most enlightened, may be given to any community, even to the world at large, by the application of the proper means'.[2] Secondly, he held that it was necessary

21

to abandon the doctrine of free will as an essential pre-condition of any move to ameliorate the lot of 'the masses'. Most of the evils that beset societies could be traced to the theory that individuals form their own character. Once 'this hydra of human calamity, this immolator of every principle of rationality' was destroyed, human happiness could be 'speedily established on a rock from whence it shall never more be removed'.[3] Lastly, Owen outlined how his 'grand design' should be implemented. Assuming that the motivating force of all human action is the promotion of 'the happiness of self', he tried to show that this goal could 'only be attained by conduct that must promote the happiness of the community'.[4] It was to be the government's lot to enable the individual to realise this socialised version of Bentham's 'hedonistic calculus' by active intervention in human affairs; for 'that government . . . is the best, which in practice pro-duces the greatest happiness to the greatest number'.[5] Precisely what form, then, should this intervention take?

As Owen saw it, certain immediate steps could be taken to remove some of the 'ignorant and vicious circumstances' that helped to degrade the working man. Spirit duties, he asserted, should be increased 'until the price shall exceed the means of ordinary consumption', and this measure should be accom-panied by a systematic reduction in the number of licences granted for the sale of spirits.[6] The state lottery should be abolished, because its very existence constituted a tacit approval of gambling.[7] The Poor Laws should be drastically overhauled, for as at present constituted they encouraged the indigent to acquire the worst habits and to practise every kind of crime'.[8] The Established Church should purge 'those inconsistencies from [its] system, which now create its weakness and its dangers'.[9] Such a move would promote harmony within society and consolidate the position of the Anglican Church in the state.

Owen, however, did not confine himself to pointing out those defects in existing institutions which could be speedily remedied by the *fiat* of the legislature; he accepted that the impact of such reforms on the environment of the 'poor and labouring classes' would be small until far-reaching steps had been taken to shape the characters of their members. This was to be done through the establishment of a national system of education.[10] Education was to be the philosopher's stone which would transform the existing behavioural patterns of society and produce a race of 'rational' beings.

Adequate financial support from the state was of course the *sine qua non* of any 'uniform' scheme of instruction. 'Seminaries' for the training of teachers could only meet their obligations to society if they were generously endowed with funds from the Exchequer.[11] But important as financial aid was to the long-term success of Owen's educational project, it paled into insignificance beside the blueprint itself. Owen insisted that it was vital for the teacher to have contact with his or her pupils at the earliest possible moment, since 'much of good or evil is taught to and acquired by a child at a very early period of its life'.[12] It was for this reason, 'to counteract these primary evils', that he had established a play area at New Lanark for the infant sons and daughters of his mill-workers.[13] Received into favourable surroundings at a formative period in their life (as soon, in fact, as they could walk) these young children were to a limited degree protected from 'the erroneous treatment of yet untrained and untaught parents'.[14] Education, therefore, was for Owen something of far wider dimensions than instruction in 'booklearning'. He conceived it as nothing less than an instrument of social change; but the nature of that change, in its turn, was clearly demarcated. Man was to be made 'rational'. He was to be made aware that his prejudices and those of his contemporaries were directly related to the *mores* of the society in which they lived, and, since everyone's views were moulded for them by pressures over which they had no control, there was thus no reason for animosity between man and man. Such knowledge, however, far from placing in jeopardy the 'supposed advantages' of the upper and middle echelons of society over the working classes would merely help to strengthen them. In that sense *A New View of Society* was a deeply conservative document.

How then was man to be educated into this 'rational state of society'? Here Owen drew on his experience at New Lanark, which served in many ways as his social laboratory. He had already, he claimed, brought about a striking improvement in the way of life of his adult workers during the thirteen years he had had charge of the village. Intemperance had been considerably reduced through the simple expedient of banishing 'pot-houses' from the vicinity; immorality had been discouraged through the introduction of a fining system; and discipline and honesty increased through the setting up of a 'silent monitor', or work-performance indicator, beside each factory-hand. 'Withdraw', he concluded, 'those circumstances which tend to create crime in the human character, and crime will not be created. Replace them with such as are calculated to form habits of order, regularity, temperance, industry; and these qualities will be formed'.[15]

Even in New Lanark Owen could not satisfactorily implement the main part of his great educational experiment until he had the support of business partners who were in broad sympathy with his own outlook. Not until 1814 was he to be in that happy position. Thereafter he proceeded rapidly with his plans, and in 1816 was able to present, at the opening of the Institution for the Formation of Character, a reasoned account of his own views on the educational development of the child. Asserting that the purpose of the Institution was to 'effect a complete and thorough improvement in the *internal* as well as *external* character of the whole village', he stressed that his aim was to introduce 'a practical system into society, the complete establishment of which *shall give happiness to every human being through all succeeding generations*'.[16] To reach this goal it was essential to instil into all infants (those between the ages of one and six years) the basic precept that they should make their playmates happy.[17] This simple lesson in social

24

obligation was underlined at New Lanark by the attitude of the teachers towards their charges: 'on no account' were they 'ever to beat any one of the children, or to threaten them . . . but were always to speak to them with a pleasant countenance, and in a kind manner and tone of voice'.[18] The only punishments, in fact, that the child would encounter during his or her schooling were those imposed by the immutable laws of nature. The whole curriculum of the school was orientated towards enabling children to discover the meaning of those laws and the nature of the forces that helped to shape character. Hence much more emphasis was laid on instruction through 'sensible signs – the things themselves – or models or paintings' than through 'rote learning' or the study of books.[19] Equally important, the Institution was designed to cater at night for adults. Some might merely be attracted to this focal point in village life by such social activities as dancing. But Owen entertained the hope that others would attend lectures on how to train their children 'to become rational creatures; how to expend the earnings of their own labour to advantage; and how to appropriate the surplus gains which will be left to them, in order to create a fund which will relieve them from the anxious fear of future want'.[20] In essence, the system that was ushered in at New Lanark was to be, through the power of example, the means of reducing class antagonisms, abolishing war and producing 'extensive ameliorations throughout the British dominions'.[21]

Owen, however, was not exclusively preoccupied during the immediate post-Napoleonic-War period with ensuring the success of this venture. His passionate concern for removing, or mitigating, the worst effects of 'evil circumstances' inevitably involved him in the great debate on the impact of industrialisation on the urban population.

Owen, like many of his contemporaries, was interested in evaluating the nature of the contribution that the mill had made to the quality of life of the British workman. But unlike the majority of such critics he was well placed as a mill-owner himself to comment at first hand on the adverse or favourable influences of factory-based production on the average mill-hand's pattern of existence. Significantly enough, his verdict against his fellow entrepreneurs was for the most part scathing. In his *Observations on the Cotton Trade,* published in 1815, he described cotton mills as 'receptacles, in too many instances, for living human skeletons, almost disrobed of intellect, where, as the business is often now conducted, they linger out a few years of miserable existence, acquiring every bad habit, which they disseminate throughout society'.[22] Elsewhere he dwelt at length on the tenuous nature of the cash nexus which was the sole bond between capitalist and worker:

> The employer regards the employed as mere instruments of gain, while these acquire a gross ferocity of character, which, if legislative measures shall not be judiciously devised to prevent its increase, and ameliorate the condition of this class, will sooner or later plunge the country into a formidable and perhaps inextricable state of danger.[23]

The end result, therefore, of industrialisation was that the working man was placed 'under circumstances far more unfavourable to his happiness than the serf or villain was under the feudal system, or than the slave was in any of the nations of antiquity'.[24] Up to this point Owen's *critique* had much in common with the socialist writings of Charles Hall, who had argued that industrial growth had led to the emergence of class antagonisms: 'the situation of the rich and the poor, like the algebraic terms plus and minus, are in direct opposition to, and destructive of each other'.[25] On the other side of the political spectrum ultra-Tory pamphleteers were committing identical sentiments to paper. Southey, for example, predicted that an extension of the manufacturing system, 'increasing as it necessarily does the number, the misery and the depravity of the poor', would be followed by a revolution, 'and in the most fearful shape',[26] while Coleridge deplored the decline in 'the ancient feeling of rank and ancestry' that accompanied the growth of the spirit of commercialism.[27] Where Owen differed from most of these writers was in his belief that the process of industrialisation could not be reversed and that much good might yet be realised if only the manufacturers themselves would consent to some form of social control. As early as 1813 he was stressing that spectacular benefits would accrue to his fellow manufacturers if they would devote part of their time and capital to improving their 'living machines'.[28] Even in purely selfish terms such investment in bettering the lot of their employees would be a wise move: for they 'would return you, not five, ten, or fifteen per cent for your capital so expended, but often fifty, and in many cases a hundred per cent'.[29] These appeals for altruistic action fell on deaf ears, and it was for this reason that Owen entered the arena as an advocate of factory reform. If factory owners would not voluntarily put their own houses into order, then the state should undertake the task for them.[30]

Concern with the position of the mill-hand was accompanied by a broad interest in the problems of unemployment and the plight of that portion of the population depending for its support, either wholly or in part, on poor relief. Owen had little doubt that the changing pattern of the British economy tended in the short term to increase the incidence of unemployment in society. To some extent these trends were a recurrent phenomenon, the inevitable sequel to a 'great sudden depression in the demand for, and consequent depreciation in the value of, labour'.[31] It was just this situation that obtained in the post-1815 period when, 'the war demand for the productions of labour having ceased', a sharp rise in the numbers of those without work was recorded.[32] But industrialisation and mechanisation inevitably intensified the suffering that the working man was called upon to endure at these times of economic dislocation. As Owen saw it, the inventive genius of the British people had produced what amounted to a multiplier effect on the rate and scale of innovation in the industrial sector of the economy. During the course of the conflict with France, entrepreneurs, stimulated into activity by the demands of war, had embarked on a major programme of investment – above all, of investment in power-driven machinery. The net result was that by 1815 'our country possessed . . . a productive power, which operated to the same effect as if her population had been actually increased by fifteen or twenty fold'.[33] Given, then, 'a diminished demand' in the very different conditions of the post-war world, manufacturers had little hesitation in reducing costs by laying off men. In Owen's words,

> when, therefore, it became necessary to contract the sources of supply, it soon proved that mechanical power was much cheaper than human labour; the former, in consequence, was continued at work, while the latter was superseded; and human labour may now be obtained at a price far less than is absolutely necessary for the subsistence of the individual in ordinary comfort.[34]

Thus, the basic issue facing society was what, if anything, the state should do to help those who were placed in this invidious position. Malthus, for one, believed that it should do nothing; in other words, that it should dismantle the existing apparatus of the Poor Laws simply because poor relief removed the operation of 'prudential restraints' on its recipients and thus led to acute pressure on the means of subsistence by a geometrically increasing population.[35] Although Owen had little faith in this Malthusian spectre of people outstripping food supplies – he bitingly classified it as 'hobgoblin' talk[36] – he none the less agreed with the leading prophet of 'the dismal science' that the antiquated structure of the Poor Laws constituted a positive barrier to an improvement in the lot of the pauper.

> Benevolence says, that the destitute must not starve; and to this declaration political wisdom readily assents. Yet can that system be right, which compels the industrious, temperate and comparatively virtuous to support the ignorant, the idle, and comparatively vicious? Such, however, is the effect of the present British Poor Laws, for they publicly proclaim greater encouragement to idleness, ignorance, extravagance, and intemperance, than to industry and good conduct; and

the evils which arise from a system so irrational are hourly experienced, and hourly increasing.[37]

In 1813 Owen's solution to this dilemma was in many ways as drastic as the Malthusian recipe. Both accepted that the Poor Laws should disappear from the statute book, but Owen wanted to replace them with a system for the 'prevention of crime and the formation of human character'. This scheme, he concluded, should be supplemented during the downswing of the trade cycle by a public works' programme 'in which all who apply may be immediately occupied' – although the wage rates of those thus employed were to be below 'the average rate of private labour in the district in which such public labour should be performed'.[38]

Less than four years later he returned to the same subject. Still firmly committed to the notion that the Elizabethan Poor Laws resulted in the acquisition of bad habits by the indigent, he devoted serious attention to the problem of how society could best aid that element of 'the poor and unemployed working classes' whose livelihoods had been superseded by the advent of the machine. The solution he arrived at was fundamentally an amalgam of a make-work plan – according to J. R. Poynter 'perhaps the greatest of make-work schemes' of the post-Napoleonic-War years[39] – and of his distinctive ideas on character formation. The essence of his plan, embodied in his *Report to the Committee of the Association for the Relief of the Manufacturing and Labouring Poor* (March 1817), was breathtakingly simple. Settlements of paupers, each consisting of roughly 1,200 persons, were to be made on designated sites throughout the countryside. Squares of buildings (Cobbett's 'parallelograms of paupers') were to be erected for their accommodation, and between 1,000 and 1,500 acres were to be purchased for the community's use.[40] Once this experiment in communal living had been launched, the members of these 'villages of co-operation' would become self-supporting individuals, capable 'as might be required, [of paying back] the capital expended on their establishment'.[41] Capital, however,

had still to be raised in the first instance, and here Owen be-
trayed a naïve optimism that funds for such a venture would
be quickly forthcoming. Financial backing, he believed, could
be readily obtained by consolidating the funds of certain public
charities, by borrowing on the security of the poor rate and by
offering reasonable inducements to private citizens who had
money to invest but who had been unable to find lucrative out-
lets for it.[42] But it was not so much the mechanics of fund raising that dominated Owen's thinking as the social benefits he
expected to follow in the wake of such settlements. The burden
of poor relief would be eased while at the same time the situation of the paupers would be transformed out of all recognition. More than that, the emphasis placed on communal
obligation could only promote feelings of unity among the inhabitants. Almost within one generation a race of 'rational
beings' could be formed, since the villagers would be completely removed from the taint of the bad influences of the
outside world.[43]

In March 1817, therefore, Owen was still content with
putting forward a set of proposals which had as their objective
the regeneration of the pauper. In that respect his was merely
one of many blueprints designed to tackle the vexed question
of how to prevent the pauperisation of the masses.[44] But by
September of the same year Owen had greatly enlarged the
scope of his initial vision; for he now envisaged ushering in a
'new state of society' through the formation of co-operative
settlements to cover every segment of the population.[45] No
coercive pressures were to be used to bring about this fundamental change; nor was the existing structure of class relationships to be disturbed by this new pattern of production and
organisation. Three distinct types of village were to be created,
each catering for different income groups. In terms of social
class these ranged from the paupers in the Parish Employment
Settlements, under the control of the parish authorities, to the
investors of the Voluntary Independent Associations who were
to put between £1,000 and £20,000 each in these undertak-

ings.[46] Irrespective, however, of the kind of settlement in which the individual was placed, he would be trained to become 'rational, intelligent, wise, sincere, and good'.[47] In millennialist language Owen concluded by proclaiming the reign of the 'New Religion' of charity.

> Ere long, there shall be but one action [nation ?], one language and one people. Even now the time is near at hand . . . when swords shall be turned into ploughshares, and spears into pruning hooks – when every man shall sit under his own vine and his own fig-tree, and none shall make him afraid.[48]

All this would come to pass because the sources of the 'gross errors' and evils that had inhibited the growth of harmony between all classes were now known. As Owen had announced to an audience at the City of London Tavern a fortnight earlier, these were 'the errors . . . that have been combined with the fundamental notions of every religion that has hitherto been taught' and they had prevented mankind 'from even knowing what happiness really is'. The world had therefore only 'to dismiss all its erroneous religious notions' and to assume an attitude of universal tolerance towards all beliefs for the millennium to be realised. If it were not prepared to do this, then 'it will be futile to erect villages of union and mutual co-operation; for it will be vain to look on this earth for inhabitants to occupy them, *who can understand how to live in the bond of peace and unity*'.[49] In the last analysis, therefore, the success of Owen's communal system of living was bound up with the destruction of organised religion, 'this Moloch' which had brought so much misery to society.[50]

Until the end of 1817 Owen's speeches and written works had been mainly devoted to what might be broadly termed sociological questions. In many respects his search for a science of society labelled him as a true son of the Enlightenment. Certainly most of his ideas, above all his belief that the study of human behaviour should be based on empirical analysis rather than on *a priori* reasoning, can be traced back to some

31

of the most powerful minds of eighteenth-century Europe. There was thus far – and this fact must be stressed – little in his thought that could be labelled original. Godwin, for example, had argued long before Owen that the mind of the new-born child was a *tabula rasa* and that its good or bad propensities were the product of the environment in which it was raised. The same writer had also tried to show that true happiness could only be attained when the individual pledged himself to work for the well-being of his fellow-men.[51] Again, Owen's view that the early training of the infant should be conducted through the observation of the phenomena of the external world rather than through books could be found in the pages of Rousseau's *Emile,* while the concept of the 'hedonistic calculus' stemmed directly from the pen of Jeremy Bentham. Even his attack on the churches and sectarianism contained little that had not been heard many times before. Finally, Owen's passionate advocacy of villages of co-operation had honourable antecedents, although in this case they owed less to the Enlightenment than any other aspect of his thought. In a British context John Bellers had published as long ago as 1696 his *Proposals for Raising a Colledge* [sic] *of Industry.*[52] More recently the young Coleridge and Southey, carried away by the ferment of the French Revolution and by the persuasiveness of Godwin's early writings, had proposed in 1794 to set up a 'pantisocracy', or community of absolute equality, in the United States.[53] However, the principal inspiration of the communitarian vision came not from Britain but from the sectarian settlements in America where, as Professor Bestor has argued, 'for the first century and a half of its history in America, the communitarian viewpoint was peculiarly associated with religion'.[54] In the late 1790s and early years of the nineteenth century the number of such settlements proliferated, largely as a result of an influx of European immigrants who sought to realise the kingdom of God on earth through the setting up of self-contained communities for members of their particular sects. The most widely known and soundly based of these

32

settlements were associated with the Shakers, who had emigrated from Britain, and the Rappites who had left their homes in Germany for the New World.[55]

The extent to which Owen borrowed from, or was consciously influenced by, these diverse sources is more difficult to determine. If, for instance, Robert Dale Owen's testimony is to be believed, his father was never at any stage of his life a voracious reader. Yet for a gregarious mixer in society like Owen, this was less a drawback to the acquisition of fresh knowledge than it might have been in the case of a man of a more retiring disposition. Given the wide range of his social contacts – his association with the Unitarians in Manchester, his membership of the Manchester Literary and Philosophical Society, his friendship with Bentham and with several of the professors at the University of Glasgow – it is almost certain that he imbibed many of the ideas of the Enlightenment from conversations and discussions with his contemporaries. There is also positive evidence to suggest that he knew at first hand of the nature of the communitarian experiments in the United States. In 1817 Owen published W. S. Warder's *A Brief Sketch of the Religious Society of People called Shakers*, arguing that 'the following narrative conveys a simple but convincing proof of the effects of the principle *of combined labour and expenditure*'.[56] Besides this, it is hardly likely, in view of his later contact with the Rappite community, that he was unacquainted with Thomas Evans's *Christian Policy in full practice among the people of Harmony, a town in the State of Pennsylvania,* a work that appeared in the same year.[57] Owen's idea of 'community living', though stripped of its native religious overtones, had its roots in his study of the American social scene. If Owen, therefore, has any claim to be a major innovator in the realm of ideas and social policy, that claim must rest rather on his ability to produce a synthesis of rationalist thought and sectarian communitarianism than on his regurgitation of the philosophy of the Enlightenment.

But it was exactly at this point that the Owenite structure

was at its weakest. Notwithstanding his emphasis on the virtues of experience – or empirical investigation – and on the use of reason, Owen had not constructed his system on very solid foundations. While promoting the cause of rational behaviour, he himself tried to proceed by assertion rather than argument – a course of action made even less effective by his constant use of millennialist language and a writing style which Holyoake caustically – and indeed unfairly – stigmatised as 'duller reading than the Fifth Book of Euclid'.[58] His dogmatism may have been, as some writers have asserted, the product of an inferiority complex in the face of university-educated opponents. Certainly it helped to highlight the inconsistencies in Owen's work. His major defect was that he begged too many important questions. Could, for example, any government by a process of direct intervention do anything to increase the sum-total of happiness in the state? Why could the happiness of the individual only be fully experienced in a village or community? Could it not be argued that the churches, far from adding to the burden of human misery, had done much to promote virtue? And if heredity played so small a part and circumstances so large a one in forming character, how was it that Owen had stepped outside a deterministic world and 'alone among men, had broken the iron chain of cause and consequence'?[59] The nature of his dilemma was perhaps best expressed by the Reverend J. H. Roebuck in May 1837:

> According to Mr Owen's system, we are but mere machines, impelled by a force over which we have no control, and we are the mere sport of circumstances, and move on by their influence in that precise direction in which they chance to carry us. And yet strange to say, we have the power to alter and control the constitution of the circumstances by which we ourselves are constantly surrounded and controlled . . . Mr Owen cannot explain to us consistently with his scheme, how out of the rubbish of the old irrational world, he sprang up so beautifully rational.[60]

Last but not least, it must be admitted that by concentrating

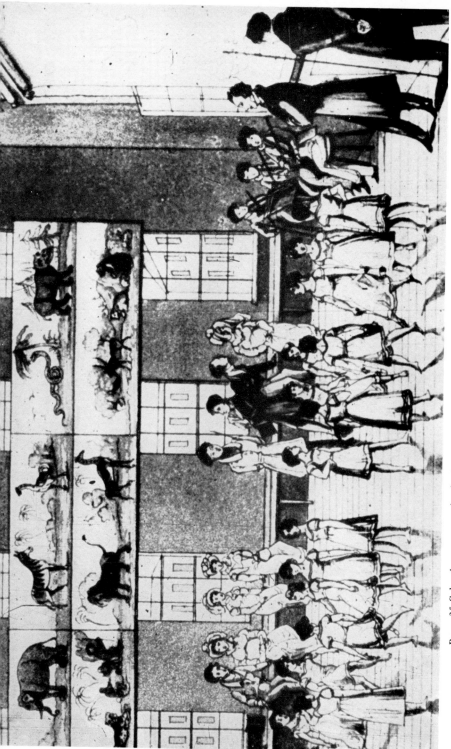

Page 35 Schoolroom scene in the New Institution. Note the musicians, dancing children and visual aids

Page 36 (*left*) Robert Owen from an early mezzotint portrait by an unknown artist; (*below*) Robert Owen from a print after a drawing by Smart published in 1822

on the social purpose of his co-operative settlements, Owen never really came to grips with the economic problems they would be called upon to face. He never clearly defined, even in the context of his original plan for dealing solely with paupers, what was to be the relationship of the community to the economy as a whole. For example, after an unconvincing discussion of the factors affecting the supply and price-level of commodities, Owen tended to dismiss the very idea of a glutted market:

> Is it possible that there can be too many productions desirable and useful to society? and is it not to the interests of all that they should be produced with the least expense and labour, and with the smallest degree of misery and moral degradation to the working classes, and, of course, in the greatest abundance to the higher classes, in return for their wealth?

Having advanced thus far, however, and having argued that villages of co-operation would help to reduce prices, he was content to leave it to the rest of society to decide whether or not such settlements should be self-supporting or be allowed to compete with 'the existing agricultural and manufacturing systems'.[61] Yet even this choice was not as straightforward as it looked, since the community would have to pay interest to the outside investor. How was such revenue to be raised in an autarkic, or self-sufficient, settlement of paupers?

There was still a blurring of these and allied issues when Owen proposed to make the village of co-operation the instrument for transforming the way of life of all ranks of society. Not surprisingly, therefore, he had to face a barrage of hostile comment from contemporary political economists. Ricardo, for one, was openly sceptical about the economic basis of Owen's 'grand design'. But by far the most trenchant criticism he was called upon to face came from Robert Torrens in the *Edinburgh Review*. Writing in October 1819, Torrens insisted that from whatever angle Owen's plans were examined, they promised far less than their author claimed for them. If the settlements were to be completely self-sufficient, then they would be faced with a considerable rise in production costs compared with the competitive market outside, since the limited size of their populations would militate against efficient use of the labour force. Alternatively, if they were to be fully integrated into the market economy, then their inhabitants would still experience considerable fluctuations in their living standards simply because they would continue to be exposed to the movements of the trade cycle.

Owen's best-known work, *Report to the County of Lanark* (1820), should in some ways be regarded as an answer to such critics. From almost the opening sentence Owen laid much more stress than hitherto on the economic forces that bred despair and unhappiness among the working classes. The most pressing problem facing society was how to remove unemployment and at the same time to ensure that the family of a working man could earn sufficient to secure a subsistence level of existence. One of the major obstacles to a satisfactory solution of this question was the failure of society to exercise any form of social control over the installation and working of machinery: 'the want of beneficial employment for the working classes, and the consequent public distress, were owing to the rapid increase of the new productive power, for the advantageous application of which, society had neglected to make the proper arrangement'.[62]

Some alleviation of the plight of the working man could of course be achieved if new markets could be opened up, but still more might be accomplished if the main cause of the existing economic dislocation were accurately diagnosed. In Owen's view, the principal barrier to letting 'prosperity loose on the country' was the existing standard of value: he maintained that the use of gold and silver as 'a standard of value altered the *intrinsic* value of all things into *artificial* values; and in consequence, they have materially retarded the general improvement of society'.[63] Thomas Attwood was at this same time fulminating against the deflationary consequences which would

38

follow a resumption of cash payments after the wars,[64] and Owen was at one with the Birmingham industrialist in deploring such a move. But he diverged sharply from his contemporary when he suggested an alternative to precious metals as the lubricants of the British economy. According to Owen, all the deficiencies in the distributive mechanism – deficiencies which were responsible for current hardships – could be overcome simply by accepting that 'the natural standard of value is, in principle, human labour, or the combined manual and mental powers of men called into action'.[65] All, then, that remained to be done in order to set in motion a system of distribution and exchange which would bestow unprecedented material benefits on the working classes was to decide how to evaluate the input of labour in any given commodity. To a very considerable degree, Owen argued,

> this [process of evaluation] is . . . already accomplished, and is denoted by what in commerce is technically termed "the prime cost", or the net value of the whole labour contained in any article of value – the material contained in or consumed by the manufacture of the article forming a part of the whole labour.[66]

Up to this point Owen had advanced a solution to the vexed question of unemployment which seemed very different from his recommendations in 1817. Then he had been concerned with placing the indigent into villages of co-operation; now, three years later, he was seeking to bring about a period of material abundance by replacing the existing standard of value with what amounted to a system of labour notes. Yet, as the concluding section of the *Report* showed, this was a change of emphasis rather than a repudiation of his earlier commitment to the communitarian ideal. Before the labour theory of value could be actively implemented, several preliminary steps were necessary. Pre-eminent among these was the establishment of village settlements, operating on 'the principle of union and mutual co-operation' and exemplifying Owen's views on character formation.[67] In other words, his villages of co-operation were to fulfil a dual purpose: not only were they to make man a rational being but they were also to be the first institutions which, in their dealings with one another, would measure the value of their products in terms of their labour content. This apart, the *Report* contained only one other major proposal which was new, and that was Owen's startling suggestion that in the arable sector of the economy the spade should ultimately replace the plough. Relying heavily on Falla's currently successful experiments with spade husbandry at Gateshead near Newcastle, he argued that if the farming community were to adopt this policy it would soon discover that crop yields per acre would spectacularly increase. But the social benefits stemming from such a switch-over were equally significant: spade husbandry would guarantee to the labouring poor 'permanent beneficial employment for many centuries to come'.[68]

If, subsequently, scarcely any attention was paid to this attempt to reverse the whole trend of agricultural innovation, the same could not be said of other sections of the *Report*. This document above all others marked the beginning of Owen's claims to be one of the founding fathers of British Socialism. After 1820 – and almost for the first time – Owenism became a creed of the working man. Some of them accepted Owen's labour theory as a useful ideological weapon with which to attack the manufacturing elements in society. Others, impressed by the contrasts which Owen had drawn between the competitive and co-operative ethic, began to organise themselves into co-operative trading associations.[69] The professed aim of all these bodies, no matter how wide the gap appeared to be between their intentions and their achievements, was to set up Owenite villages of co-operation. Significantly enough, despite the disastrous failures in the late 1820s of both the Orbiston and the New Harmony experiments, the faith of many working-class Owenites in communitarianism remained unbroken. The reason for this was not hard to find; in the words of William Lovett, 'the plodding, toiling, ill-re-

40

munerated sons and daughters of labour' found something singularly attractive in the idea 'of all the powers of machinery, of all the arts and inventions of man, being applied for the benefit of all in common, to the lightening of their toil, and the increase of their comforts'. Lovett himself, like many others, had been initially impressed by the view that co-operative 'associations formed the first step towards the social independence of the labouring classes', but in his case disillusionment with the Owenite vision occurred very quickly.[70]

Down to 1824, however, whatever the working classes may have thought to the contrary, the main corpus of Owenite thought was profoundly conservative in its emphasis and tone. In the first place, the labour theory as enunciated by Owen fell very far short of its later refinements at the hands of the Ricardian Socialists – Thompson, Hodgskin, Gray[71] – and of Marx and Engels. Whether or not Owen borrowed the idea itself from Ricardo or Adam Smith – for in one form it was to be found in the pages of the *Wealth of Nations*[72] – it contained few revolutionary implications. For even if Owen had begun by announcing that 'manual labour, properly directed, is the source of all wealth',[73] he had ended by implying – and thereby creating ambiguity and confusion – that capital was in its own right a factor of production and could justly claim a share in any profits that were made.[74] All, it seemed, the labourer was entitled to enjoy was a 'fair proportion' of the new wealth which had been created through his endeavours.[75] This viewpoint contrasted strongly with the assertion of his contemporary Thomas Hodgskin that 'the landlord and the capitalist produce nothing. Capital is the product of labour, profit is nothing but a portion of that produce, uncharitably exacted for permitting the labourer to consume a part of what he himself has produced'.[76] If, then, capital was, as Hodgskin believed, merely the product of past labour, the working classes could legitimately seek to redress existing property and class relationships. Although Hodgskin himself refused to endorse in any way such a resort to violence, it is significant that this conclusion could be drawn from his *Labour Defended against the Claims of Capital* (1825). A similar verdict could not be passed on Owen's treatment of the labour theory in the *Report to the County of Lanark*. But perhaps a better indication than this of the essential conservatism of Owen's early works was the type of audience he was catering for.

In a sense, before 1824 he obtained a working-class audience in spite of himself, for his real message was beamed almost exclusively at the upper echelons of society. One of the four 'Essays on the Formation of Human Character', which together comprised *A New View of Society,* was originally dedicated to the Prince Regent and another to William Wilberforce, while a third was addressed to his fellow manufacturers. Furthermore, as his *Autobiography* shows, he was almost morbidly anxious that this work should be well received by Sidmouth and Liverpool, the two leading figures in the ultra-Tory administration of the day.[77] Again, he was at pains to show that the privileged classes could and should co-operate in forwarding his 'grand design' since there would be no attempt 'to touch one iota of the supposed advantages which they now possess'.[78] Even his scheme for villages of co-operation would have no effect on the existing class structure of society: 'no one will envy them their [the 'upper classes'] privileges, whatever they may be, and every hair of their heads will be securely guarded by the rapidly improving condition of the great mass of the people'.[79] Elsewhere he proclaimed that all change, to be effective, should be gradual. The new system was only to be introduced slowly[80] and the principal instrument of effecting such a transformation was to be the Tory government of Liverpool. 'The whole frame of society', Owen concluded, 'may remain as it is. The British constitution will readily admit of every improvement requisite to ensure the interest and happiness of the empire'.[81] Owen's faith in the efficacy of this strategy stemmed partly from his own political beliefs. As Holyoake and other writers have pointed out, Owen was in many of his attitudes a Tory.[82] Thus he could un-

42

critically seek the support of an administration that had done much to suppress working-class rumblings of political and social discontent. Partly, too, Owen pursued this distinctly conservative line simply because he believed – in Miliband's striking phrase – in 'the benevolent despot as the agent of social change'.[83] To put it another way, 'he held with the government of the few, but, being a philanthropist, he meant that the government of the few should be the government of the good'.[84] It was precisely for this reason that Owen, despite the pleas of Bronterre O'Brien, was completely indifferent to the 1830–32 Reform agitation and the later campaign to secure the National Charter.[85] Political reform, in Owen's eyes, would not advance the millennium in the slightest degree.

But his 'Toryism' did not solely manifest itself in his defence of the status quo or in his anti-Whig sentiments. It was equally apparent in his treatment of three inter-related politico-social themes. In the first place Owen was at heart a paternalist who believed in the basic structural unity of society. At New Lanark he had demonstrated that the industrial village could, if properly organised, reproduce the same patterns of mutual obligation and duty which had been characteristic of the rigidly hierarchical society of rural Britain. The cash nexus and the restless mob were not the inevitable concomitants of industrialisation. Secondly, he regarded the working classes – except during his brief involvement in trade unionism in the early 1830s – as fundamentally unenlightened. Their enlightenment was to be left to middle-class leaders – above all to Owen himself – who could show them the error of their ways and instruct them in the basic principles of rationality and communitarianism. As Lovett and other working-class co-operators were to experience to their cost, this view could be used by Owen as a justification for ignoring the wishes of the majority.[86] Thirdly, the village of co-operation, with its stress on class harmony and its recognition of rank, could to some extent be identified with the type of society in which the Tory squire moved and had his being.

With these views, it is hardly surprising that Owen secured a measure of sympathy from unimpeachably orthodox sources. If he came under fire from the supporters of the received doctrines of political economy and if he was assiduously ignored by the 1817 Select Committee on the Poor Laws, he was none the less powerfully supported by the Duke of Kent, who presided in 1819 over a committee dedicated to raising £100,000 to enable a trial Owenite settlement to be established. Although only some £8,000 was in the end advanced for this project, it is interesting to observe how the members of this body interpreted the central doctrines of the Owenite canon. Villages of co-operation, it was recorded, 'are not only practicable, but as sure as human institutions can be sure, of producing the results which Mr Owen anticipates'. Moreover they would not interfere with property rights; 'there would be no community of goods nor any deviation from the laws of property'.[87] The failure of this body to achieve its financial target may indeed show that Owen's attack on organised religion two years earlier had cost him his standing among those whom he was anxious to cultivate. Men like Wilberforce were not prepared to forget Owen's broadside, especially against the Established Church. But amongst the gentry, as his reception in Scotland and Ireland in the early 1820s demonstrated, Owen still retained a substantial degree of support.[88] What mattered to them was not so much his age-of-Enlightenment views on the nature of Christianity, as his concern for bettering the lot of the working man 'by means of agriculturally orientated philanthropy'.[89] Even Southey, although he was appalled by Owen's rejection of the Christian revelation, continued to make a sharp distinction between Owen's religious opinions and his social ideas, and believed that villages of co-operation might play a useful role, within the context of a general programme of self help, in raising the living standards of the labouring classes.[90]

Between 1824 and 1835, however, Owen's social views became noticeably more radical. Several factors contributed to the perceptible change of emphasis which for the best part of the next decade was to mark both his speeches and his writings. Firstly, as Professor Bestor has pointed out, Owen was consciously influenced by the work of the Ricardian Socialists. Above all he seems to have been impressed by William Thompson's indictment of capitalist society and all its works.[91] In the second place Owen's wholehearted commitment to the New Harmony settlement in Indiana intensified his dislike of the values of the old society which he was trying to destroy. By 1826, therefore – and before the ultimate collapse of his American experiment in communitarian living – he was prepared to denounce both the institution of marriage and the very existence of private property. The human race, he informed the New Harmony colonists, had to be liberated from 'a TRINITY of the most monstrous evils that could be combined to inflict mental and physical evil'. The forces against which they should contend were 'PRIVILEGE OR INDIVIDUAL PROPERTY – absurd and irrational SYSTEMS OF RELIGION – AND MARRIAGE, founded on individual property combined with some of these irrational systems of religion'.[92]

During the course of the next decade he elaborated on these themes. In 1830 he produced his *Lectures on an entire New State of Society* which contained a strong denunciation of inequality of rank, coupled with an attack on the competitive ethic and on private property. 'Private property is entirely the child of the existing system of the world; it emanates from ignorant selfishness, and perpetuates it.'[93] Five years later Owen focused his attention on the evils which were, in his mind, indissolubly linked with matrimony. Marriage, he proclaimed, was an

. . . unnatural crime [which] destroys the finest feelings and best powers of the species, by changing sincerity, kindness, affection, sympathy and pure love into deception, envy, jealousy, hatred, and revenge. It is a Satanic device of the Priesthood to place and keep mankind within their slavish superstitions, and to render them subservient to all purposes.[94]

Above all it bred unhappiness through its stress on the family unit; for the very concept of the family, rooted as it was in the values of the 'old world', constituted a serious stumbling-block to man's achievement of the 'social state'.[95]

After such a comprehensive onslaught on those institutions which the British middle classes held most dear, it is scarcely surprising to find that by the early 1830s Owen was deprived of almost all socially influential support. Such middle-class followers as he did retain – men, for example, like John Finch of Liverpool – remained loyal to him largely because Owenism had become for them a new secularised religion. The attitude of the working classes towards these developments was on the other hand more ambivalent. Many, like James Hole and the members of the Leeds Redemptionist Society, sought to extract from Owen's teaching social lessons on the virtues of communitarianism while repudiating, because of their divisive results, his anti-religious sentiments.[96] Others – and they constituted a very small minority – were attracted by the totality of a vision which threatened to undermine so completely the 'corrupt' world in which they toiled. Last but not least, there were the working-class co-operators who, notwithstanding Owen's disapproval, saw in the co-operative stores a means of improving their lot through combining with their fellow workmen. Whatever Owen may have thought about the dividend principle which, after the foundation of the Rochdale Pioneers in 1844, became the cornerstone of the co-operative movement, working-class co-operators continued to trace their origin back to the *Report to the County of Lanark*.

By the mid-1830s, therefore, the historian must distinguish between the cluster of ideas which together comprised Owenism and the movements with which Owen was associated. Owen himself, after his brief honeymoon with the British trade union movement during the years 1832–4, became increasingly involved after 1835 in the organisation of his Association of All Classes of All Nations, a body which, notwithstanding its grandiose title, had scarcely any impact on the social scene. Dedicated to propagating Owen's social message, it was quickly to assume the characteristics of a sect.[97] With its change of title in 1839 to the Universal Community Society of Rational Religionists, its metamorphosis into a secularised version of early nineteenth-century sectarianism was complete.[98] Owenism, on the other hand, reached a much wider audience. As we have seen, many of Owen's concepts, sometimes misunderstood or reinterpreted, quickly found their way into the broad stream of working-class culture and life.

Part of the Owenite message, then, survived into the second half of the nineteenth century, in spite of the evolution of 'scientific Socialism' and of the slow but sure increase in real wages which eroded much of the appeal that the village of co-operation had had in the harsher economic climate of the 1820s and 1830s. The part that did survive, albeit in an emaciated and drastically altered form, was on the whole the most positive and the least millennialist segment of Owen's work. His stress on education, his belief that man does not live by bread alone, and his profound dislike of the atomising effects of an unregulated market have became an integral element in the empirical tradition of British Socialism. His crude outpourings on religion, his total failure to come to grips with the existence of class antagonisms, and his inability to see that changes in economic organisation could only be followed by parallel changes in the social structure of any given society – all this and much more has long been forgotten. And perhaps rightly so; for if Owen deserves a place in the list of the founding fathers of British Socialism he does so by virtue of his generalised challenge to the whole competitive ethic. In that sense at least Owen still has, in this the 200th year of his birth, something relevant to say to the Britain of the 1970s.

NOTES

1 'Owen's 1812 Speech at a Glasgow Dinner to Joseph Lancaster' in *The Life of Robert Owen Written by Himself,* Vol 1 (1857), 250 [hereafter *Life* 1]
2 'A New View of Society', First Essay, *Life* 1, 266
3 Fourth Essay, ibid, 310
4 First Essay, ibid, 268
5 Fourth Essay, ibid 308
6 Ibid, 312. At the same time consumption of malt liquor should be encouraged
7 Ibid, 313
8 Ibid, 314
9 Ibid, 322
10 First Essay, ibid, 271 ; Fourth Essay, ibid, 324–5
11 Fourth Essay, ibid, 325
12 Third Essay, ibid, 288
13 Ibid
14 Ibid, 289
15 Second Essay, ibid, 283
16 'An Address Delivered to the Inhabitants of New Lanark on the 1st January 1816 at the Opening of the Institution for the Formation of Character', ibid, 339, 341
17 'Autobiography', ibid, 139
18 Ibid
19 Ibid, 135. When 'the best means of instruction or forming character shall be known, I doubt whether books will be ever used before children attain their tenth year', ibid, 140
20 'A New View of Society', Third Essay, ibid, 297
21 'An Address Delivered to the Inhabitants of New Lanark on the 1st January 1816 at the Opening of the Institution for the Formation of Character', ibid, 337
22 'Observations on the Cotton Trade . . . January 1815', *A Supplementary Appendix to the First Volume of the Life of Robert Owen,* Vol 1A (1858), 17 [hereafter *Life* 1A]
23 'Observations on the Effect of the Manufacturing Systems (1815)' ibid, 41
24 'Letter to the Earl of Liverpool on the Employment of Children in Manufactories, 30 March 1818', ibid, 187
25 C. Hall, *Effects of Civilisation* (1805), quoted M. Beer, *A History of British Socialism* 1 (1919), 128
26 R. Southey, *Letters from England* (1807), quoted M. Beer, op cit, 133

The Social and Economic Thought of Robert Owen

²⁷ S. T. Coleridge, 'A Lay Sermon' (1817) in *Political Tracts of Wordsworth, Coleridge and Shelley* (ed R. J. White 1953), 82

²⁸ 'A New View of Society', Preface to Third Essay, *Life* 1, 260

²⁹ Ibid, 261

³⁰ Among other places in 'Observations on the Effect of the Manufacturing System (1815)', *Life* 1A, 41

³¹ 'A New View of Society', Fourth Essay, *Life* 1, 328

³² 'Report to the Committee of the Association for the Relief of the Manufacturing and Labouring Poor (March 1817)', *Life* 1A, 55

³³ Ibid, 54–5

³⁴ Ibid, 55

³⁵ J. R. Poynter, *Society and Pauperism* (1969), 152–8

³⁶ Fear of a population explosion 'has no better foundation than exists for the nursery terrors of ghosts and hobgoblins', 'Letter to the Earl of Liverpool on the Employment of Children in Manufactories, 30 March 1818', *Life* 1A, 192–3

³⁷ 'A New View of Society', Fourth Essay, *Life* 1, 314

³⁸ Ibid, 328–9

³⁹ Poynter, op cit, 257

⁴⁰ 'Report to the Committee of the Association for the Relief of the Manufacturing and Labouring Poor (March, 1817), *Life* 1A, 58

⁴¹ Ibid, 61

⁴² Ibid, 62–3

⁴³ Ibid, 63–4

⁴⁴ Poynter, op cit, 254–7

⁴⁵ 'Fourth Letter 6 September 1817', *Life* 1A, 122–6, 132–3

⁴⁶ Ibid, 122–5

⁴⁷ Ibid, 136

⁴⁸ Ibid, 132–3

⁴⁹ The quotations in this section on religion are taken from 'Second Address [at the City of London Tavern] 21 August 1817', *Life* 1A, 115–16

⁵⁰ Owen asserted that if he had ten thousand lives, he would sacrifice them to 'destroy this Moloch [organised religion], which in every generation destroys the rationality and happiness of about a thousand million of my poor suffering fellow men and women'. 'Autobiography', *Life* 1, 207

⁵¹ Beer, op cit, 116–18

⁵² Republished in 1817 by Owen. See *Life* 1A

⁵³ Beer, op cit, 121. Both Coleridge and Southey later abandoned their youthful radicalism for their own distinctive type of high Toryism

⁵⁴ A. E. Bestor, jr, *Backwoods Utopias* (1950), 4

⁵⁵ Ibid, 31–3, 35

⁵⁶ *Life* 1A, 146

⁵⁷ Beer, op cit, 141
⁵⁸ G. J. Holyoake, *Life and Last Days of Robert Owen of New Lanark* (2nd ed 1859), 18
⁵⁹ Bestor, op cit, 61
⁶⁰ F. Podmore, *Robert Owen* 2 (1906), 500
⁶¹ 'Letter published in London Newspaper of 30 July 1817', *Life* 1A, 74
⁶² 'Report to the County of Lanark (1820)', *Life* 1A, 265
⁶³ Ibid, 265–6
⁶⁴ Beer, op cit, 157–8
⁶⁵ 'Report to the County of Lanark (1820)', *Life* 1A, 268
⁶⁶ Ibid, 278
⁶⁷ Ibid, 281–310
⁶⁸ Ibid, 271–7
⁶⁹ S. Pollard, 'Nineteenth Century Co-operation. From Community Building to Shopkeeping', *Essays in Labour History*, ed A. Briggs and J. Saville (1967), 79–87
⁷⁰ William Lovett, *The Life and Struggles of William Lovett* (1876), 41, 43
⁷¹ See E. Lowenthal, *The Ricardian Socialists* (1911)
⁷² A. Smith, *An Inquiry into the Nature and Causes of the Wealth of Nations* 1, (Henry Frowde, University of Oxford Press, 1908), 71–2
⁷³ 'Report to the County of Lanark (1820)', *Life* 1A, 264
⁷⁴ Ibid, 278
⁷⁵ Ibid
⁷⁶ T. Hodgskin, *Labour Defended against the Claims of Capital* (1825), quoted E. Lowenthal, op cit, 72
⁷⁷ 'Autobiography', *Life* 1, 108–11
⁷⁸ 'A New View of Society', First Essay, ibid, 270
⁷⁹ 'Second Address [at the City of London Tavern]', *Life* 1A, 117
⁸⁰ 'Fourth Letter 6 September 1817', ibid, 137
⁸¹ Ibid
⁸² G. Holyoake, *Sixty Years of an Agitator's Life* 1 (1892), 117
⁸³ R. Miliband, 'The Politics of Robert Owen', *Journal of the History of Ideas*, 15 (1954), 235
⁸⁴ Holyoake, loc cit
⁸⁵ Miliband, loc cit, 237 ; E. P. Thompson, *The Making of the English Working Class* (Pelican Books 1968), 861
⁸⁶ In reply to a working-class delegation's protest that he had unilaterally added his own printed amendment to the agenda of a Co-operative Congress, Owen acknowledged that his proceedings were 'despotic ; but as we, as well as the [organising] committee that sent us, were all ignorant of his plans, and of the objects he had in view, we must consent to be ruled by despots till we had acquired sufficient knowledge to know ourselves'. Lovett, op cit, 49

50

87 *Life* 1A, 242, 244, 246, 249
88 J. F. C. Harrison, *Robert Owen and the Owenites in Britain and America* (1969), 28–30
89 Ibid, 30
90 R. Williams, *Culture and Society 1780–1950* (Penguin Books 1961), 43
91 Bestor, op cit, 86
92 Ibid, 222, speech of Robert Owen at New Harmony, 4 July 1826
93 Quoted ibid, 86
94 *Lectures on the Marriages of the Priesthood of the Old Immoral World* (1840 edition), quoted F. Podmore, op cit, 2, 489–90 [The first edition of this work was produced in 1835.]
95 Ibid, 490–92
96 J. F. C. Harrison, 'James Hole and Social Reform in Leeds', *The Publications of the Thoresby Society* Monograph III (1954), 4–5
97 Podmore 2, op cit, 463–6
98 Ibid, 469–73. 'Social hymns' were sung at Sunday services in Halls of Science. The 'naming' of children could also be likened to a secularisation of the baptismal service. Significantly enough Owen in 1853 accepted the claims of spiritualism, ibid 604–5

In the preparation of this article the author is greatly indebted to the staff of the Reading Room of the British Museum for the courteous and efficient way in which they dealt with all his queries.

3

OWEN AS AN EDUCATOR
MARGERY BROWNING

*. . . children can be trained to acquire any language, senti-
ments, belief, or any bodily habits and manners, not contrary
to human nature, even to make them, to a great extent, either
imbecile or energetic characters.*
    Robert Owen, *A New View of Society*, First Essay (1813)

In *A New View of Society*, the most famous of his extensive
writings, Robert Owen called for the reform of mankind
through a planned scheme of education. The utopian plan there
put forward has caused these four essays to be regarded as a
general treatise on education.[1] Throughout his life Owen remained consistently committed to the cause of education, and
his propagandist inspiration earned him the right to the title
'educator', for much the same reasons as his most loyal disciples called him 'Social Father'. His schemes for education
were not the ephemeral day-dreams of a philosopher, but a
concrete set of principles, aims and values on which he based
his educational system at New Lanark. Many of these principles
were to influence not only the foundation of schools in Owenite
communities but more especially the whole infant school
movement.
    Owen has not generally been awarded a prominent place in
the textbook history of educational thought, but he is now
being recognised as the man who made education a 'mass
issue'.[2] In the *laissez-faire* conditions of the early nineteenth
century British education presented a confused pattern. For

Page 53 (above) New Lanark from west bank of river Clyde c1825, showing mills in the foreground with workers' housing behind; (below) a print of New Lanark, looking from the north-west c1818, clearly illustrating the magnificent rural setting of the mills and the village

Page 54 (above) New Buildings originally planned to free No 4 mill for production; *(below)* workers' housing in Rosedale Street built in the 1790s with the Long Row on the left and Broad Row on the right. The New Buildings may be seen in the distance

the rich there was a choice extending from the nine great public schools, in which the standard of education was generally deplorable, to the great dissenting academies such as New College, Manchester, where John Dalton (mathematician, chemist and natural philosopher) taught, and in which a high level of scientific and classical learning was achieved. There was also the system of grammar schools, which had become schools not for the poor for whom they had been endowed but for the children of the lower middle class. Private tutors were still commonly employed – indeed Owen engaged tutors for his own children.[3]

In Scotland even the children of the poor had, theoretically, the chance of a good education through the parish-school system set up under the influence of John Knox; but with the increase in population in the latter half of the eighteenth century the system had largely ossified, especially in the new industrial centres. After the Jacobite risings, the Society for the Propagation of Christian Knowledge and government commissioners established spinning schools on Scottish estates declared forfeit, using the rents for this purpose.[4] By 1800 there were twelve such schools, educating 2,350 'young females'. However, these schools were confined to the teaching of the skills of spinning and weaving, and reading and learning passages from the Bible.

For the working-class child in England, whose parents were interested in and able to afford the rudiments of learning, there was little choice or even opportunity. Dame schools of the meanest kind were set up in cramped conditions by old ladies intent on supplementing their incomes by childminding. Pitifully ignorant – many were unable to write or count – the dames became objects of satire and ridicule. The primitive curriculum of these schools consisted of reading, learning the catechism and biblical texts and, for girls, sewing. Discipline and learning were together instilled by the rod. On a much higher level were the schools of Hannah More and Sarah Trimmer. These schools emphasised the religious aspects of the curriculum, primarily because their founders were intent on rescuing young girls from moral degradation and turning them into respectable domestic servants. During the social ferment of the 1790s Hannah More's influence became suspect and unpopular in official circles because her schools were used, unknown to her, as meeting places by dissenting ministers. It was also felt that her insistence on the importance of writing was politically dangerous.

One other alternative for the poor was the Sunday School movement begun in Gloucester in 1780 by Robert Raikes. His intention was to remove children from the vices of the street in industrial towns on the Sabbath and to provide them with the rudiments of learning and Christian knowledge. The success of the Sunday Schools was limited. Attendance was often irregular; meetings were commonly held in damp, unheated churches; religious services punctuated education.[5]

One reason for the dearth of schools for the working classes was that there was a feeling among the middle and upper classes that their positions as leaders of society and employers might be threatened if the workers were educated. James Mill blamed the clergy and members of the Church of England who feared that the tenets of the Established Church would be undermined by the extension of education to the lower orders.[6] William Lovett referred to the 'hawks and owls' of society who were 'seeking to perpetuate the state of mental darkness most favourable to their prey'.[7] Samuel Wilderspin and other promulgators of popular education showed that they were all too well aware of this opposition.[8] One indication of the extent of it is found in the Manchester rule of 1786, that no writing was to be taught in the Sunday Schools of that town.

A new method of teaching, however, made it possible to tackle the problems of working-class education; this was the monitorial system, developed at roughly the same time by the Reverend Andrew Bell and Joseph Lancaster, a nonconformist. The latter set up a model school at Borough Road, London, and demonstrated how education could be conducted cheaply through the medium of child teachers. He was so successful that in 1807 the British and Foreign School Society was formed to direct his schools on the principle that 'education might not be subservient to the propagation of the peculiar tenets of any sect'.[9] Bell, on returning from India where he had devised his Madras system, fostered its adoption in this country and in 1811 was encouraged to form the National Society for the Education of the Poor, with the avowed aim of upholding the teachings of the Church of England. In both Bell and Lancaster schools the curriculum was limited to reading, writing and arithmetic, and great emphasis was placed on rote learning.

Robert Owen was at first impressed by the efforts of his precursors. He gave £1,000 to Lancaster, but only £500 to Bell, who would not make his schools undenominational. However, by 1816, he had decided that their aims were too narrow. Through his early work on Dr Percival's board of inquiry into the evils of the factory system and from his own fact-finding tours of industrial areas for Sir Robert Peel's Factory Act, Owen was convinced that the educational needs of the industrial masses needed to be planned in conjunction with a new social system. In what Harrison has called his most splendid period,[10] 1800–24, Owen devised his own system of education.

His ideas were not entirely original. He was influenced, often at second-hand, by the philosophers of the Enlightenment, and was clearly affected by discussions with his many prominent friends in the Manchester Literary and Philosophical Society where the ideas of Rousseau, Helvétius, Godwin, Wollstonecraft, Paine and Bentham were subjects of considerable debate and analysis.[11] Later, he was also influenced by Francis Place and James Mill who helped him correct his Fourth Essay in *A New View of Society*. There have been arguments about the respective influences of these thinkers on Owen, but elements of all their philosophies can be found embedded in his writings. Owen was not himself a great educationist in terms of original philosophy, but, in welding together what he considered to be the best of all that had been thought and said, he produced a theory of education the influence of which is still evident today in government reports on education in Britain.[12]

Owen's definition of education was not the limited one of the monitorial schools, but was concerned with the full development of each man and woman. This was one of his major contributions to the history of educational thought. He was one of the first to attack the narrow concept of education as the learning of the rudiments of reading, writing, arithmetic and religion. But he himself also tended to confuse indoctrination and education when he was proclaiming his social methods.

The importance of the influence of environment on the mind and growth of man was paramount in Owen's scheme of education, and his message was vital:

> Any character, from the best to the worst, from the most ignorant to the most enlightened may be given to any community, even to the world at large, by the application of proper means; which means are to a great extent at the command and under the control of those who have influence in the affairs of men.[13]

Owen had seen the vice, crime and degradation bred in slums of cities; he believed with Rousseau that 'God makes all things good; man meddles with them and they become evil',[14] but he also believed that the man is created by the physical and educational environment of the child. Thus Owen brought an optimistic humanity into his concept of popular education, since he rejected the idea of original sin – what the Wesleyans called 'innate evil' – within the child.

Owen subscribed partially to Locke's theory of *tabula rasa*, that the mind of the child is blank at birth and that education and experience form the concepts which the child will hold, although he also believed that nature has given different qualities to each person. For Owen a nature/nurture controversy did not exist, for in the modern manner he reconciled both. Thus, he believed that if all contaminating influences were removed from the child's surroundings, the child would develop into a moral reasoning adult. Owen, in his early writings, realised that education must begin at birth and that society could be changed slowly and gradually, because the child could be moulded by education. He was paraphrasing Godwin when he described young children as being 'passive and wonderfully contrived compounds'[15] and as containing a 'plastic quality' which could be moulded at will. This theory gained Owen much support since he was suggesting that education would provide the solution to the law-and-order problems which troubled Lord Liverpool's Tory government.

Owen did not fully subscribe to the thesis of Helvétius, 'l'éducation peut tout', but he believed that education correctly directed would create the ideal society. 'Train any population rationally and they will be rational' was for him a self-evident proposition.[16] Men have natural differences, but Owen believed that these could be subordinated to the requirements of society. For him education was a means to national moral re-generation, as his Fourth Essay indicates, and essentially he aimed at developing collectivists not individualists. The child, therefore, had to be educated away from the contaminating in-fluence of unenlightened parents – or at least to be as much as possible in a rational environment. Since learning begins at birth, schooling also should be provided as early as possible, as soon as the child could walk:

> It must be evident to those who have been in the practice of observing children with attention, that much of good or evil is taught to or acquired by a child at a very early period in its life; that much of temper or disposition is correctly or incorrectly formed before he attains his second year; and that many durable impressions are made at the termination of the first twelve or even six months of his existence.[17]

It was important, therefore, that the child's first lessons should teach him to be kind to his fellows and to learn to love all.

French society had been shocked when Helvétius expounded his theory that humans were motivated by the principle of self-interest. Owen adopted this principle to the exclusion of all others though he modified it in a Benthamite fashion. His son wrote of him that he 'regarded self-love or man's longing for happiness, rationally educated, as the most trustworthy foundation for morals'.[18] Owen rejected belief in any supernatural power, the product, he thought, of man's conscience or spiritual needs (although ultimately he turned to spiritualism), yet he always accepted the ethical content of the higher religions, the distillate of which he saw as absolute tolerance of, and regard for, others. His association with the Manchester unitarians and with David Dale – whom he considered the most liberal Christian he ever met – was certainly influential in the formation of his moral code. Lessons, therefore, were to be directed towards the amusement and delight of the child, and the child would gradually come to associate learning and delight. Then, as the child grew older, he would learn to defer immediate enjoyment to the future greater good and rejoice instead in the future use of knowledge.[19]

Following logically from this belief was Owen's rejection of all methods of 'irrational rewards and punishments' such as the badges which were used in monitorial schools to encourage children to become monitors. Samuel Wilderspin declared that he could find no means of controlling children without rewards and punishments, although he rejected corporal punishment.[20] Owen's pupils were to be rewarded by the satisfaction they would find in obtaining knowledge. This principle is being re-expressed today in nursery and primary schools, through the influence of John Dewey.

Owen realised that the child could take no interest in the acquisition of knowledge, unless he fully understood the concepts involved. It was on this issue that he came to criticise the monitorial system. Rousseau had ridiculed the learning of catechisms when he wrote, 'If I had to deplore the most heartbreaking stupidity, I would paint a pedant teaching children the catechisms; if I wanted to drive a child crazy, I would set him to explain what he learned in his catechism.'[21] Owen echoed these sentiments in his criticism of learning by rote; it was, he said, a 'mockery of learning' in which memory was all that was required.[22] He himself accepted the importance of educating the senses in the tradition of Rousseau. Eye, ear and hand were to be trained in appreciation. Music teaching, for example, was to begin in the nursery school so that the child should learn to distinguish sounds and to develop his musical talents. Owen also developed a method of teaching, which he called the object lesson, to train the child's power of observation and judgement. The chosen object – it might perhaps be an animal, or some physical feature of the landscape – was presented to the child either in the form of a picture or in its natural state, and by answering a series of key questions put by the teacher, the pupil was to provide all the information required. This method of training was adopted by followers of Owen in the belief that through increasing awareness of a good environment the child would learn to perceive all that was good.

From Helvétius Owen adopted the idea of association as an important element in the theory of learning. In *De l'Esprit* Helvétius described the human mind as having the faculty of receiving and retaining impressions, and active thought took place because the mind had the power to associate and compare these different impressions.[23] Owen stated that man was born with 'faculties, which, in their growth, receive, convey, compare and become conscious of receiving and comparing ideas'.[24] Individuals reacted differently to external stimuli because of individual preferences, but these differences could be checked by education and by a controlled environment and, consequently, disparities within society would be minimised.

Owen's aims in education, however, were in many ways limited, for he rejected any kind of higher learning or understanding. Godwin had premised that popular education would result in the gradual acceptance of a higher culture, but for Owen there was no higher culture than the happiness of all members of a society living harmoniously together. Owen himself, although he claimed to have read much in his youth,[25] was no great student. His son wrote of him that he read only two dailies and other periodicals, and that though he had an extensive library and perused books he did not master them.[26] The main aim of Owenite education was to produce a man able to accept his role in a community, carrying out whatever was required of him, 'intimately connected with the employment of the association'.[27] While some children from New Lanark did eventually attend university, Owen did not consider such higher education necessary because it did not have a practical application. Education had to be utilitarian. The children were to enter the factory or take up the plough and be happy because they were contributing to the general good. There was a dichotomy in Owen's own role in the community, for while he told the people of New Lanark that he wished to be regarded as a simple cotton spinner going about his daily and necessary avocations, he was also the paternalistic employer who expected to be obeyed by those under him.

Owen rejected the attitude of the Enlightenment towards government interference in education and, like Mary Wollstonecraft and the Utilitarians, placed responsibility for education on the state. He opposed the power of ministers of religion in education, and put his faith in a Board of Education manned by the rationally educated. He demanded, in effect, a centralised system of education in which all schools would use the same methods, follow the same curriculum and employ teachers trained in state seminaries.

The Godwinian doctrine of perfectibility dominated Owen's conception of the moral improvement of man, but while Godwin tempered this sweeping generalisation – 'by perfectible . . . is not meant . . . capable of being brought to perfection'[28] – Owen believed that with the correct education and environment man could be brought to perfection in a single generation. Education was to be suited to the growth and development of the child's mind and body. From two to six years the child would attend the nursery school; this would be followed by elementary education from six to ten or twelve years, and adult education thereafter. Owen believed that all were capable of learning and he failed to recognise or appreciate any intellectual differences. In all, therefore, Owen brought a new dimension of humanitarian concern to the growth and development of the individual. He admonished the wealthier classes:

> Either give the poor a rational and useful training or mock not their ignorance, their poverty and their misery, by merely instructing them to become conscious of the extent of the degradation under which they exist.[29]

At New Lanark there were two schools, the more famous being the new Institution for the Formation of Character, opened in January 1816.[30] This new school was interesting, not only because Owen's educational theory was put into practice in an environment planned by him – as his earlier school was not – but also because the British infant school movements had their origins here. Like many Owenite institutions, this new school arose as a result of practical considerations: Owen saw that if the children of two years and over were cared for in a school, then their mothers 'would be enabled to earn a better maintenance or support' for them and they would have 'less care and anxiety about them'. Thus, Owen the industrialist acquired more female labour, and Owen the educator felt that the children were being instructed and formed according to his theories. The New Lanark schools were Owen's work uniquely, as no other later school was.

Robert Owen's claim to be the founder of the infant school was strongly contested in his time. For the first infant school in western Europe credit must go to Father Oberlin, the pastor of Waldbach, but his school did not have a great impact on educational development in Britain. It was the system of education at New Lanark that impressed reformers here, and Owen's methods, through the agency of James Buchanan his infants master, became the basis for infant education in Britain. Samuel Wilderspin, the master of the Spitalfield Infant School, first supported Owen's and then Buchanan's claims in the second edition of his book on infant school instruction, *The Importance of Educating the Infant Poor*. However, in some subsequent editions, he erased all references to Owen as the founder of the infant school, and later gained a pension from the government in recognition of his own work in this respect. However, Lord Brougham and *The Westminster and Foreign Quarterly Review* repeatedly supported Owen's and Buchanan's claims, as did many contemporary pamphlets.

There has also been much acrimony in dispute over the qualities of James Buchanan, a poor cotton weaver who came to New Lanark in 1815 and was chosen by Owen to take over the Infant School. Buchanan had great charm and a deep compassion for and understanding of infants and, after his experience at New Lanark, he was sent by Owen to help in the setting up of a school at Westminster. Owen referred to his work at Westminster in scathing terms, and letters of the Leigh family largely substantiate Owen's opinion of Buchanan's unsettled temperament in later years, when he became absorbed in Swedenborgian theology. However, there can be little doubt that Buchanan had both responsibility and influence at New Lanark, for Owen was absent a great deal on business in 1816 and 1817 and Buchanan was left to devise the curriculum for the school.

The New Lanark Infant School consisted of one room on the ground floor of the 1816 Institution for the Formation of Character and a playground laid out in front of it, where the children were to spend the greater part of their time. They were supervised by Buchanan and Molly Young, a young woman of seventeen who had been selected for this task by Owen on account of her good sense and kindliness. William Rathbone, a Liverpool merchant and philanthropist, testified to the happy state of these infants on the basis of a questionnaire he sent to Owen concerning the school.[31]

Owen as an Educator

Owen instructed the teachers that the children were to receive no formal teaching, but Buchanan worked out a programme for their amusement, centred round singing, dancing and an appreciation of natural objects. It is said that he was able to control the children by playing his flute. The day probably began with a march round the playground, followed by short prayers – for Buchanan believed that young children should have some knowledge of God. The Buchanan family records show that Buchanan was in the habit of teaching the children by means of rhymes, and that before the age of six the children were introduced to counting and grammar. Owen encouraged Buchanan to develop the children's powers of observation, and so they were taken for short walks by their schoolmaster, in the course of which he drew their attention to the beauty and uses of nature. Again, he devised rhymes to reinforce the lessons, and the simplicity of the man shines through the following account of the sheep:

> Hark to me and silence keep,
> And you will hear about the sheep;
> For sheep are useful and you know
> That on their backs the wool does grow.
> The sheep are taken once a year,
> And plunged in water cool and clear
> And there they swim and never bite
> While men do wash them clean and white.

The parents demanded – and they were supported by Owen's partners – that some form of religious instruction should be given, and the manuscript account book of the Institution reveals that hymn books and Bibles were purchased for the schools.[32] Although he thought violence could corrupt, Buchanan seems to have had the children enact Bible stories such as the casting of Daniel into the lions' den.

In the elementary stage of the school, children attended for five and a half hours per day, the actual hours depending on the season of the year and allowing time for breakfast and lunch. No lesson lasted longer than three-quarters of an hour.

There were about 300 pupils attending this school, and boys and girls were educated together. The upper storey of the Institution was divided into two apartments. One was the principal schoolroom, planned on the lines of a Lancastrian school, with desks and forms laid out in long rows. There were galleries around the room and a pulpit for the speaker at one end. The other room was cleared for dancing and singing, with space for an orchestra, and the walls were hung with pictures. In the two smaller rooms on the ground floor, pupils learned reading, writing, arithmetic and sewing.

The curriculum for the elementary school was very modern in that all lessons were co-ordinated. Owen's son described this school in great detail and outlined his father's principles clearly.[33] The criteria of knowledge were utility and understanding of the world. Owen did not wish the young children to 'be annoyed' with books and he would have deferred the formal teaching of reading until the age of ten had the parents not objected. No doubt he felt that he would have little control over the influences a child might receive from the written page.

Owen devised his own methods of teaching social studies, but in the teaching of arithmetic he borrowed Pestalozzi's method of using tables of units. The account book also indicates that small blocks of wood were used to help the child appreciate the workings of addition and subtraction. Brass letters were employed to teach the children their alphabet. They learned to form simple syllables by the methods used in the monitorial schools and to recognise words with the help of word-and-picture cards. Slates were used for the teaching of writing, and as the children grew older they learned to acquire a useful business style and even copied accounts from the offices.

Apart from learning the basic skills, the children were also given an introduction to natural history, geography, ancient and modern history, geology and botany. The schools were furnished with a very large number of visual aids and materials. Travel books and histories were the main printed works used, because of the dearth of suitable texts; but Miss Edgeworth's books were acceptable for they had a high moral content. As late as 1852 Matthew Arnold was complaining of this lack of adequate textbooks and reading books for children.

When visual aids could not be purchased, Owen employed Miss Whitwell, a London headmistress who later became a teacher at Orbiston, to paint large canvases depicting subjects of natural history and events in the history of nations on the stream-of-time principle. These were hung on rollers in the recreation room. She was aided by a young man, probably an employee at the mill, but she did not teach the children how to draw or paint. To help the children understand grammatical principles she showed the parts of speech pictorially as members of an army: General Noun, Colonel Verb, Corporal Adverb, and so on. George Combe, the Edinburgh phrenologist, reported that Owen ordered transparent pictures of natural objects from London at a cost of £500. An entry in the account book shows that £251 10s 0d was spent on paintings from London in July 1822. Other aids are enumerated in this book: a phrenologist's head, various maps and spheres and an 'arithmetick machine'.

Not only were visual aids provided to stimulate the imagination of the pupils but there is also evidence that the children were taken out on visits. The account book shows that £2 0s 0d was paid to 'James Earl Exhibiting Wild Beast to the children', and five shillings was also paid for the exhibition of a crocodile. However, some of Owen's own descriptions of lessons he enjoyed seeing suggest that they were not as promising educationally as one might expect. The lessons on geography, for instance, seem to have degenerated into a game of guessing the names of physical features.

The part of the curriculum that won Owen much acclaim was the execution of dances of many nations and the singing of country airs by the children. The emphasis Owen laid on popular music and dancing is again indicated in the account book, where it is recorded that David Budge the dancing master was paid at the same rate as the master in charge of the more academic subjects. The son of the dancing master was also trained in Edinburgh at the expense of the Institution.

Owen intended that the new Institution should be a centre for adult education in the evenings, but apart from the regular attendance after work of children from ten to twelve years, there is little evidence of more than winter lectures as far as the adults were concerned. The rooms on the ground floor were heated and lighted for any adult who might care to read books from the small library. In the account book there are only a few references to expenditure on adults, one relating to a recital by a Mr Rwolta and the other to expenses of port for a ball.

The teachers in the school seem to have been drawn from the village population and they were trained and instructed by Owen himself. They were not allowed to use any form of corporal punishment and at all times had to show tolerance and understanding. The teacher-pupil ratio varied. In 1816 there were 274 children at the day school, and in October of that year there were 14 teachers. Two of these teachers were solely for the Infant School in which there were 80 children – a teacher-pupil ratio of 1:40. In the elementary school the ratio was 1:18. The second figure compares favourably with modern ratios; in 1967 the ratio in nursery schools was 1:23 and in primary schools 1:27.8. In evidence to the Select Committee of 1816 Owen stated that he considered a great number of masters necessary 'to do justice to the children'.[34] He claimed that a superior master should be employed at a salary of £250 per annum, but during 1822, 1823 and 1824 the account book shows that there were two principal masters employed at a rate of one guinea per week, and some of the ladies received only six shillings per week. Robert Owen's children also taught in the schools; Anne Owen seems to have attended every day, and Robert Dale Owen took the children out on trips. There was also a superannuated soldier paid to drill the children.

Clothes were an important part of the educational environment at New Lanark. Owen decreed that the schoolchildren's clothes should be simply designed in the style of Roman or Highland dress, in order to allow the body to move freely. He also believed that such dress would increase sexual delicacy,[35] but his partners, who firmly held to the opposite opinion, later banned the kilt for boys of six and over.

Because of the extent of his innovations, Owen's schools cost a great deal more than other popular schools of the time. The criterion for setting up a school was usually cost per pupil. When William Allen, Owen's partner, gave evidence to the 1816 Committee in his capacity as Treasurer to the British and Foreign School Society, he estimated that the annual cost of educating a child should be five or six shillings.[36] Samuel Wilderspin calculated the cost at ten shillings per annum, while Andrew Bell thought that the cost could be reduced to four shillings per annum. Owen, however, stated that the cost of educating a child in his school was £1 0s 0d, assuming that the capital cost had been covered. By 1823 this figure had risen to £2 14s 0d for each day-pupil and 16s 0d for each pupil attending night school. The largest part of the school budget was, then as now, the cost of the teachers' salaries and in 1823 this item was 57 per cent of the total, while the cost of the clothing was 18 per cent of the total. The children were encouraged to pay for their education at the rate of threepence per month, but this was a tiny part of the total income necessary.

Owen, however, was not a benevolent philanthropist as far as the school was concerned, because it was financed from the profits of the village co-operative store. Since the amount in the village store's favour was very large, standing at £8,595 2s 9d on 30 September 1823,[37]. Owen did not have to acquire money as did other educators of the time – and he could afford to encourage an ambitious syllabus. Apart from these running costs which were borne by the community, the cost of building the Institution, £3,000, was paid out of the profits of the company since the partners insisted only on a 5 per cent return on their capital invested, although they often received much more.[38]

The high cost of running a school of this type was a deterrent in an age when men were thinking in terms of lowest costs. On grounds of cost alone, the Owenite school system at New Lanark could not have been fully copied throughout the rest of Britain without a drastic change in government attitudes to education and public expenditure.

Owen's connection with the school came to an end in 1825 because of the opposition of his partner William Allen and the clergy of New Lanark to the Owenite curriculum, where dancing and music took precedence over religion. In 1825 the partners made Owen sign an agreement whereby religious instruction was to be introduced, dancing and singing were to be abolished and the boys were to wear trousers. John Daniel, a master trained in monitorial methods, was engaged to become head teacher at a salary of £150 per annum and he introduced a course of science lessons in place of dancing. Owen by this time, however, had turned his attention to the social experiment at New Harmony.

Owen's educational methods spread from this small industrial village round the world, first of all through James Buchanan's work at the Westminster Infant School, London (set up under the aegis of Lord Brougham), and later from South Africa where the Buchanan family finally settled and set up infant schools. Other Owenites took their enthusiasm for education to the United States and Canada. Samuel Wilderspin learned a great deal from both Owen and Buchanan and many of the methods popularised in his writings stemmed from the New Lanark and Westminster Infant Schools. The very rhymes he used were Buchanan's in origin. Barbara Bodichon (1827–91), founder of Portman Hall School, London and co-founder of Girton College, based her infant school

Page 71 (above) Nursery Buildings built c1810, immediately after reconstruction for the New Lanark Association. This was probably Owen's only exercise in the construction of new housing; *(below)* a view of one of Mr Owen's villages of union. Note the resemblance to plan of Orbiston on page 146

Page 72 (*above*) The cut-down remains of No 1 mill, the oldest surviving built by Dale c1786; (*below*) the north front of No 2 mill reconstructed c1905. Note the contrast with the older and more elegant No 3 mill on the left

methods on Owen's. In Glasgow, the First Infant School Report of 1829 bore no reference to Owen, but many of the methods, especially the object lessons, set out in the Glasgow Infant School Instructor were based on those of the Infant School in New Lanark. David Stowe (1793–1864), educationist and first inspector of Scottish schools, though primarily concerned with educating a Christian child, was also inspired by Owen. The Infant School Society, formed in 1825, was instrumental in spreading Owen's ideas and methods.

However, even by 1852 not much progress had been made and Matthew Arnold was deploring the lack of infant schools in Britain. When infant schools were next actively encouraged again, the influence came largely from the continental reformers Pestalozzi, Fellenberg and Froebel, through the work of Dr Elton Mayo. In 1871, on the occasion of the centenary of Owen's birth, Huxley assessed Owen's contribution to the history of education: he thought that without Owen's preliminary propaganda and example infant schools might not have become an accepted part of the national system in the 1870 Education Act. Owen brought to popular education a feeling of humanity and established the right of the poor to be educated. He also began the technical revolution within education which has led to experimentation with all kinds of 'educational hardware'.

In the community at New Harmony, Indiana, Owen's influence on the education system was not great, for with the arrival there of William Maclure and Joseph Neef, education passed from Owen's control. Joseph Neef and his family had been pupils of Pestalozzi at Yverdun and they brought his methods with them. Maclure, unlike Owen, required the school to be a centre for learning and publication, and by 1827 he had set up his own school on the land of the Education Society.

After Owen returned to Britain he became involved in the working-class movements of the 1830s, and was chiefly concerned with the education of workers in social co-operation. His influence was reflected in the emphasis placed on education by co-operative societies, but he never achieved the same success in adult education as in the education of children. His association with workers' movements was too short-lived to make any significant impact. It is to Lord Brougham, to individual co-operative societies and to the Mechanics Institutes that credit must go for the development of adult education in Britain. In the Owenite Halls of Science Owen preached the gospel of the New Moral World, but his influence was in decline. Workers in the late 1840s and 1850s had become interested in other, more limited and less grandiose social and political objectives.

When Owen died in 1858, he was appropriately in the midst of negotiations for setting up a new school system in his birthplace, Newtown. To the end he remained the energetic propagandist for mass education.

NOTES

1. J. F. C. Harrison, *Robert Owen and the Owenites in Britain and America* (1969), 139 ; cf also his article 'The Steam Engine of the New Moral World: Owenism and Education 1817–1829', *Journal of British Studies* 6 (May 1967), 2
2. Harold Silver, *Robert Owen and the Concept of Popular Education* (1964), 67
3. Robert Dale Owen, *Threading My Way* (1874), 64
4. Irene F. M. Dean, *Scottish Spinning Schools* (Edinburgh 1930)
5. *Central Society For Education, Second Publication* (1838), 365–6
6. James Mill, 'Schools For All, In Preference to Schools for Churchmen Only', *James Mill On Education,* ed W. H. Burston (1969), 120 ff
7. Silver, op cit, 31
8. Samuel Wilderspin, *On the Importance of Educating the Infant Poor* (2nd edition 1824), 175
9. Joseph Lancaster, *Improvements In Education* (6th edition 1806), vii
10. J. F. C. Harrison, op cit, 6

[11] E. M. Fraser, 'Robert Owen in Manchester 1787–1800', *Memoirs and Proceedings of the Manchester Literary and Philosophical Society* 82 (1937–38), 29, 37

[12] Central Advisory Council for Education (England), *Children in their Primary Schools Vol 1 ; Report* ('Plowden Report' 1967) ; Scottish Education Department *Primary Education in Scotland* (1965)

[13] Robert Owen, *A New View of Society and Other Writings* (ed G. D. H. Cole, Everyman's Library 1927), 16 [hereafter *A New View*]

[14] J. J. Rousseau, *Emile* (Everyman's Library 1963), 5

[15] *A New View*, 22

[16] Ibid, 14

[17] Ibid, 40

[18] R. D. Owen, *Threading My Way* (1874), 169

[19] Robert Owen, 'Report to the County of Lanark', *A New View*, 272

[20] Wilderspin, op cit, 22

[21] Rousseau, op cit, 220

[22] *A New View*, 75

[23] Ian Cumming, *Helvétius His Life and Place in the History of Economic Thought* (1955), 74

[24] *A New View*, 54

[25] *Robert Owen on Education*, ed Harold Silver (1969), 42

[26] Robert Dale Owen, op cit, 67

[27] *A New View*, 63

[28] B. R. Pollin, *Education and the Enlightenment in the Works of William Godwin* (New York 1962), 62

[29] *A New View*, 75

[30] vide infra, 230 ff

[31] James Murphy, 'Robert Owen in Liverpool', *Transactions of the Historical Society of Lancashire and Cheshire* (1961), 10

[32] Edinburgh University Library, Account Book of the New Lanark Institution 1816–25

[33] R. D. Owen, *Outlines of Education at New Lanark* (Glasgow 1824)

[34] 'Report of the Parliamentary Committees on the Education of the Lower Orders in the Metropolis and Beyond 1816–18', *Educational Documents England and Wales 1816–1963*, ed J. Stuart Maclure (1965), 26

[35] 'Report to the County of Lanark', *A New View*, 277

[36] J. Stuart Maclure, ed, op cit, 22

[37] Gourock Ropework Company MSS, Balance Sheets 1818–23

[38] vide infra 199 ff

75

4

ROBERT OWEN AND THE WORKERS
W. HAMISH FRASER

And when it was perceived that inanimate mechanism was greatly improved by being made firm and substantial; that it was the essence of economy to keep it neat, clean, regularly supplied with the best substance to prevent unnecessary friction, and by proper provision for the purpose to preserve it in good repair; it was natural to conclude that the more delicate, complex, living mechanism, would be equally improved by being trained to strength and activity; and that it would prove true economy to keep it neat and clean; to treat it with kindness, that its mental movements might not experience too much irritating friction; to endeavour by every means to make it more perfect; to supply it regularly with a sufficient quantity of wholesome food and other necessaries of life, that the body might be preserved in good working condition, and prevented from being out of repair, or falling prematurely to decay.

Robert Owen, *A New View of Society*, Preface to the Third Essay (1814)

Security can now be found only in that system of policy which regards the proper training, education and advantageous employment of the working classes as the primary object of government.

Robert Owen, *On the Employment of Children in Manufactories* (1818)

Robert Owen now seems to fit quite comfortably into most

histories of socialism as 'the father of British Socialism', and
to find an honoured place in the history of the working class
as one of the 'makers of the labour movement'. He has even
found a less comfortable place in the history of radicalism,
somewhere between Tom Paine and Lloyd George.[1] Yet many
contemporary working-class leaders regarded Owen with a
considerable amount of suspicion and treated his views with
caution. William Cobbett's rejection of the villages of co-
operation as 'parallelograms of paupers' is well known, and
another radical editor, T. Sherwin, considered them to be no
better than workhouses, creating 'a community of slaves'. But
others went further: Jonathan Wooler, the editor of the *Black
Dwarf*, suggested that some of Owen's money came from the
government, and that government ministers gave their backing
to Owen's plan as a solution to the discontent that existed in
the years after Waterloo. Another declared that 'Mr Owen . . .
will find that the lower classes are pretty well convinced that he
is a tool to the land-holders and Ministers'. There were other
similar accusations and they persisted into the 1830s.[2]

Among many radical leaders a suspicion of Owen continued
particularly because of his persistent rejection of political
action at a time when other working-class leaders were joining
in the demand for parliamentary reform. None the less, by
1833 enough of his ideas had been absorbed and accepted by
the working class for the term Owenite to be attached to the
tremendous outburst of trade unionism and working-class
activity that took place between 1832 and 1834. The purpose
of this essay is to consider the evolution of Owen's relationship with the working class and his changing, and often ambivalent, attitude towards them.

1

Owen came into contact with the working class first and fore-
most as an employer of labour: first as a manager for Peter
Drinkwater in Manchester and then on his own account. His

arrival at New Lanark gave him charge of nearly 2,000 workers. As an employer, Owen was faced with the major problem of all early industrialists: he was concerned to achieve a stable, disciplined and efficient workforce. He was dealing largely with a displaced highland peasantry who took ill to the restrictions of factory life and who had no commitment to industrialism. Owen set himself the task of getting such a commitment.[3]

The workers that Owen found at New Lanark, according to his own account, were indolent, drunken and rebellious, hostile to his new management – 'a very inferior class of workpeople, very dirty in their habits and houses, very intemperate and demoralised'.[4] He blamed their opposition to his management on the 'strong prejudices' of the Scots against an Englishman, but the situation he found at New Lanark was typical of one where a formerly largely independent peasantry was making the adjustment to factory-based existence and protesting against the new disciplines which that change imposed.

Owen's response to this situation was not so different from that of other employers, except perhaps in its humaneness. He removed opportunities for drunkenness by excluding public houses from the vicinity of the village. He eliminated the widespread stealing that had prevailed by a system of checks which ensured detection. His 'silent monitor' attached to each machine brought communal pressure on the undisciplined worker, and careful record-keeping of the daily conduct shown on the monitor allowed for the pinpointing of slackers. A stable workforce was achieved by encouraging families to settle at New Lanark; housing was provided, and employment given to all the family. By making a weekly deduction from wages to finance a fund for workers in sickness and old age, Owen cut down the major problem of high labour turnover (presumably the deductions were not refundable if the worker left New Lanark). The efficiency of his workforce was ensured by keeping his workers clean and healthy and reasonably well-educated. Owen made no secret of his belief that investment in the care of 'living machines' would bring a high return.[5] The result was a contented workforce, 'sensible that our circumstances are much superior to those of all cotton spinners'.[6]

As an employer Owen differed from many of his contemporaries in that he achieved the disciplining of his workforce without resorting to violence. However, neither his problems nor his solutions were particularly unusual. Even the use of the 'silent monitor' and the careful compilation of individual records were ideas borrowed fom Samuel Oldknow (1756–1828), cotton-master at Mellor and Marple, Cheshire.

2

The second stage in Robert Owen's relationship with the working class came when he offered to the world the ideas that he had worked out during his first decade at New Lanark. Early in 1813 he published his *First Essay on the Formation of Human Character,* propounding 'A New View of Society'. For the next decade he was elucidating and elaborating his scheme with growing urgency in speeches, letters and papers. He saw imminent danger in the ill-condition of the 'poor and working classes'. These he regarded as 'the worst and most dangerous subjects in the empire' and he warned that if there was not an improvement in their conditions 'great disorder must ensue'.[7]

A fear of impending violence and disorder hovers behind almost all of Owen's early writings. Employers and statesmen are urged to take measures to avert trouble. In 1813 he was pressing the 'privileged class' to make concessions on the lines he indicated, to procure social harmony 'without domestic revolution – without war or bloodshed – nay, without prematurely disturbing anything which exists'.[8] In 1818 he was still on the same theme: the continuing misery of the workers 'will annihilate every proper feeling between the governed and their rulers'. Therefore, he tells Lord Liverpool, 'a truly enlightened statesman will avert by wise ameliorating measures, those increasing evils, which, if permitted to proceed un-remedied, will inevitably derange the social system which it is his duty to direct and control.'[9] All around him Owen saw evils threatening 'forcibly to dissolve all existing Governments and institutions'[10] and far from welcoming this he was greatly concerned in trying to prevent it.

This concern about the potential violence of the working class is perfectly understandable when set against the outbreaks of disorder which did in fact occur in the second decade of the century. The year in which Owen was first formulating his ideas for publication, 1812, was one of extreme disorder. Luddism, beginning among the stocking-makers of Nottinghamshire, spread to Lancashire, Cheshire and Yorkshire. Nearer home, in Edinburgh and Montrose, there were food riots against the steady and extensive rise in the price of foodstuffs. The worst trouble of all was, however, right on Owen's doorstep, with the national strike of handloom weavers.

Having failed to persuade Parliament to fix a minimum rate, the General Association of Operative Weavers in Scotland, a union formed in 1809, asked the Justices of the Peace of Lanarkshire, of whom Owen was one, to fix their wages by approving a table of prices. This the JPs did, and the Court of Session upheld their right to do so under an Act of 1617. When, however, the employers refused to pay the agreed rates, the Justices declined to enforce them. The result was a strike, beginning in November 1812, which brought out most of the handloom weavers between Aberdeen and Carlisle.

It is true that the Scottish weavers, unlike their fellow workers in the Midlands, rejected Luddism. But the particular concern of the government was the linking of political unrest with economic distress. There had been a revival of Jacobin agitations, assisted by the presence of French prisoners of war who seem to have been making a favourable impression on the common people.[11] Not the least cause of worry to Lord Sidmouth and his Scottish colleague Alexander Colquhoun, the Lord Advocate, was the presence in Scotland of Maurice Margarot, the former chairman of the London Corresponding Society, who in 1793 had been arrested as one of the delegates at the Scottish Convention, and sentenced by the notorious Lord Braxfield to fourteen years' transportation.[12]

It was during this period of social and political unrest that Owen was completing his *First Essay*. As one of the Lanarkshire magistrates he was well aware of the extent of discontent among the weavers and other groups of workers. Hence his concern and his call for concessions that would bring improvement in working-class conditions.

After 1815 there was almost continuous unrest in different parts of the country as food riots developed into demands for political reform.[13] The political clubs occasionally merged into revolutionary cadres. Hence the greater urgency that enters Owen's writings after 1817, when, for the first time, he was coming into contact with the most militant of radicals, such as Thistlewood and his associates.[14]

Inevitably the question arises of just how far Owen's concern to prevent working-class disorder governed his ideas and actions. Were there any grounds for Wooler and others to be suspicious of his association with the authorities? Apart from the general tone of some of his writings of these years, there are a number of items giving circumstantial evidence of a more than literary involvement with Lord Sidmouth and his ilk. As Mr E. P. Thompson has pointed out, a fortnight after the sad fiasco of the 'Pentrich Rebellion' in the summer of 1817, and the exposure of Oliver as spy and *agent provocateur* employed by the Home Secretary, Owen was writing of Lord Sidmouth's 'mild and amiable' disposition.[15] That same summer, in an address delivered at the City of London Tavern, Owen went further than he had previously done in condemning the radicals: 'Should greater liberty be now given than the British Constitution can with safety afford to all its subjects, the lives and properties of the well-disposed, and the safety of the State would be put to imminent hazard'.[16]

By far the most intriguing sidelight on Owen's position during these radical years comes from his relations with Alexander Richmond. Richmond was a member of the central committee of the General Association of Operative Weavers in 1812. He seems to have been reasonably well-educated and articulate, and acted as chief spokesman for the weavers when they conferred with the manufacturers and JPs. It may have been at this time that Owen first came across him. When the weavers' leaders were arrested in December 1812, Richmond was one of those indicted, but he jumped bail on the advice, so he said, of the Whig lawyers Francis Jeffrey and Henry Cockburn who acted as the weavers' counsel. He fled to Lancashire where he remained for fifteen months. On returning to Scotland he gave himself up and received the comparatively light sentence of one month in gaol.

It was soon after his return to Scotland that Richmond made contact with Scotland's leading cotton-master, Kirkman Finlay, who was Lord Provost of Glasgow and also MP for the city. Finlay was greatly concerned at the dangers to public order from radical agitations among the working class and he had a number of informants investigating activities, particularly among the large weaving community. Alexander Richmond is reputed to have been one of these informants – in fact the chief of them. At the end of 1816, thanks to an introduction by Finlay, Richmond obtained a position with Robert Owen at New Lanark. According to Richmond, it was as a manager; according to Owen, it was as an assistant schoolmaster.[17] Owen later denied that he knew anything of the arrangement between Richmond and Finlay, but Richmond's testimony ran thus: 'I informed Mr Owen what Mr Finlay had requested me to do at Glasgow, and what I had learned was going forward, and Mr Owen highly approved of the views I had taken'.

One historian has written of Owen that he 'had a vacant place in his mind where most men have political responses'. It may be that this explains his attitudes in the campaign for parliamentary reform in 1831 and 1832, but it seems likely that during his sojourn in Scotland his political attitudes were very positively those of an anti-radical. His concern for the poor and his plan for communities have to be seen in this context. He believed that without some measures to relieve distress there was likely to be violent protest, but like others among his contemporaries he regarded any extension of outdoor relief as likely 'to shake the foundation of civil society'.[18] Therefore he offered an alternative to both those possibilities in his communities of the unemployed. These communities would be self-sufficient, bringing relief to the poor, but 'without violently or prematurely interfering with the existing institutions of society'.[19]

Owen was clearly not offering a scheme for the redistribution of wealth. On the contrary, he argued that improvements in the condition of the working classes can only 'yield to the higher classes a still larger proportion of wealth',[20] and he very perceptively realised the importance of the workers as customers.[21]

3

The first time that Owen addressed his remarks directly to the working class was in 1819. Previous publications had been dedicated to William Wilberforce and the Prince Regent and addressed to manufacturers and the Prime Minister. His own workers at New Lanark had been harangued at the opening of the Institution for the Formation of Character in 1816, when he held out to them the prospect of the millennium – a society 'without crime, without poverty, with health greatly improved, with little, if any, misery, and with intelligence and happiness increased a hundred-fold'[22] – largely to be achieved through education. His *Address to the Working Classes* at the beginning of 1819 widened the scope of his propaganda, but there was no essential change in his message. When radical agitations revived in the months before Peterloo, Owen was urging the workers to abandon class hatred, to reject violence and to

'heed not what men with fanciful theories and without practical knowledge may say to you'.[23] He asked them to accept
the premise 'that the rich and the poor, the governors and the
governed, have really but one interest'.[24]

In other words, there was not, as G. D. H. Cole suggested,
at that stage any alteration in the direction of Owen's appeal
when he addressed the working classes in 1819. His attitude
to them was still that of the conservative paternalist, seeking to
turn the workers away from their misguided radical and
revolutionary ways. It is true that by his denunciation of all
religions in August 1817, Owen had alienated some of the
more respectable figures who had earlier given him a sym-
pathetic ear. But there is no evidence that Owen was in any
sense concerned in seeking a new area of support. He was,
after all, still acceptable to the royal dukes of Kent and
Sussex, even if Lord Sidmouth had given up the search for
an alternative to repression. There was in fact a new urgency
in Owen's warnings of impending revolution:

> already are the seeds of revolution sown in our country and
> quickly must produce a sanguinary harvest, unless the con-
> dition of the lower orders is greatly ameliorated.[25]

And again,

> We resemble individuals standing on the narrow causeway of
> a surrounding abyss. We have yet a short period left for
> extricating ourselves from the perilous situation into which
> we have been brought by the use of machinery.[26]

A new relationship between Owen and the working classes
did not develop until after 1820, and it seems probable that
Owen was far from being aware of it. The change came with
the publication of *The Report to the County of Lanark,* in
which he turned from ethical to economic considerations. He
started with the premise that 'manual labour, properly
directed, is the source of all wealth'[27] and went on to propose
that labour be the 'natural standard of value'. If this were to
be accepted then the wage system could be abolished, and

Owen went further than he had ever gone in condemning this system as 'more cruel in its effects than any slavery ever practised by society, either barbarous or civilised'. It was this that made Owen's views dangerous and no longer respectable. The progeny of eighteenth-century rationalism could accept attacks on religion without turning a hair; it was an altogether different matter when the relationship between worker and employer was questioned. By rejecting the wage system and by advocating a community of property, Owen was pointing the way to an overturning of society. One wonders if Owen himself was aware of the implications of what he was saying, for, as so often in his writings, he gives an impression of dealing in second-hand ideas that have been only half-digested.

However, others certainly saw the far-reaching significance of the *Report to the County of Lanark*. It was after 1820 that Owen lost the last of his influential friends, because this was really the first time that Owen's ideas had threatened the established order. And it was only after 1820 that his ideas, refined and developed by other more consciously anti-capitalist writers, began to seem relevant to groups of workers. These writers enlarged on the idea that labour was the source of all wealth and insisted that the whole product of labour, therefore, was due to the workers.

During the 1820s it was others who were leading 'Owenism'. Robert Owen himself was still by far the best-known figure, but there was hardly any development in his thinking during the decade. He was moving around, mouthing the old catch-phrases, first in Ireland and then in America. In 1824 he bought New Harmony in Indiana, thus opting out of any of the developments that were taking place in Britain. Not until the end of 1829 did he return to Britain – in this case, London – permanently. In the interim, however, his whole position vis-à-vis the working class had altered.

Evidence that Owen's ideas were having an impact upon the working class came in 1821 with the establishment of *The Economist* by the Edinburgh printer George Mudie, and the formation, under Mudie's leadership, of a Co-operative and Economical Society 'to establish a village of unity and mutual co-operation'. The concept of a community of property, as an alternative to the competitive system, particularly appealed to the increasing number of craftsmen who were finding themselves displaced, partly by machinery but mainly by increased competition for jobs resulting from an influx of 'dishonourable' elements into trades.[28] Thus, Mudie's community consisted of people who were skilled in carving, gilding, umbrella-making, painting on velvet, and making 'transparent landscape window-blinds' as well as in some of the more mundane jobs such as shoemaking and millinery.[29] The group that formed the core of the first major Owenite community in Britain at Orbiston,[30] near Motherwell in Scotland, was not dissimilar in composition.

The first abortive communities and other would-be communitarian groups, such as the London co-operative society formed in 1824, looked towards wealthy patrons to provide the necessary initial capital for community building. But, after 1828, there came suggestions from a number of directions that the future lay with the working classes themselves. Alexander Campbell (the later social missionary), who had been schoolmaster at Orbiston, wrote on these lines to Owen in October 1828 from Hamilton jail where he was detained as one of those responsible for the debts of the failed community. He argued that, as a result of the failure of Orbiston, it was unlikely that capitalists would wish to speculate on further schemes and that, therefore, the hope of future communities lay with 'the Labouring Class'. Lack of capital among this class could be overcome 'by Union Society's [sic] raising funds for such purposes as friendly societies and gradually increasing their premises and numbers'.[31] That same month Dr William King of Brighton, in the pages of *The Co-operator,* was outlining his scheme for raising capital for community building by means of co-operative trading.[32]

It was this same 'Brighton system' that spread to most of

the main centres of population during 1829 and 1830. By August 1830 there were 300 such co-operative societies up and down the country. They looked to Owen as their prophet and mentor, but, as William Lovett declared in a much-quoted passage,

> When Mr Owen first came over from America he looked somewhat coolly on those "Trading Associations", and very candidly declared that mere buying and selling formed no part of his grand "co-operative scheme"; but when he found that great numbers among them were disposed to entertain his views, he took them more in favour, and ultimately took an active part among them.[33]

The 'great numbers' came largely from the working classes, particularly from the trade unionism emerging after the economic depression of the years 1825 to 1828. A number of key figures formed a link between co-operative groups and trade union groups: in London there was the Deptford shipwright John Gast and the cabinetmaker William Lovett; in Lancashire there was the fiery Irishman John Doherty; in Glasgow there was the joiner Alexander Campbell; in Yorkshire there was Lawrence Pitkeithly; in Liverpool, John Finch. This is not to say that there were no differences between co-operators and trade unionists on the best methods of obtaining social improvement, but generally there was an overlapping of personnel and, as Professor J. F. C. Harrison has shown, 'the idea of a co-operative store was not clearly demarcated from a trade union or a friendly benefit society'.[34]

It seems clear that it took some time before Owen accepted or became attuned to his eponymous movement. He started off on the wrong foot by his rejection of co-operative stores. In 1830 he was so out of touch as to be found advocating emigration in *The Times*, for which he was reprimanded by John Minter Morgan.[35] And he showed no particular enthusiasm for the labour exchange (a depot for the exchange of products on a labour-note basis) which was opened in the spring of 1832.[36] In fact, Owen was still very much concerned with the danger of violent unrest. His first journal *The Crisis,* which came out in April 1832, saw crises all around. It saw society as presented with a straight choice between 'either reason or physical violence of the worst kind'.[37] He was once again searching for some way to avoid violence, short of achieving the millennium. What he sought was 'a rational and therefore beneficial compromise between . . . the producers of real wealth on the one part, and the non-producers and governors of society, on the other part'.[38] He seems to have thought that this could be achieved by education and propaganda, but gradually he came to see labour exchanges as pointing the way to such a compromise.

In September 1832 the National Equitable Labour Exchange was opened. However, even then, Owen did not bring in the workers; his Exchange was run by shopkeepers, and artisans came in only slowly.[39] But the early success of the Exchange attracted groups of handicraftsmen, 'the industrious and sober-minded portion of the Working Classes', and it was through such artisans that Owen made his first contact with trade unionism. By March 1833 there was a United Trades Association consisting of societies of craftsmen who brought their goods to the Exchange.[40] Not all these societies were strictly trade unions, but in time of strike they were in a position to convert themselves into unions. Owen recognised the new growth and hoped to incorporate it into his movement. *The Crisis* added to its title *National Co-operative Trades Union, and Equitable Labour Exchange Gazette.*

The labour-exchange movement also brought Owen into contact with the provinces where some of the most important trade union developments were taking place. In March 1833 he was off to Birmingham 'to put the working classes in the way of taking their own affairs into their own hands'.[41] He found the trade unions in the Midlands and North of England 'business-like and encouraging' and with considerable effect he set out in the summer and autumn of 1853 to woo them. He was thoroughly enraptured by the potential power he saw in

Page 89 Archibald James Hamilton, younger, of Dalzell, co-founder of Orbiston

Page 90 (*left*) David Dale (1739–1806), founder of New Lanark, from a Tassie medallion of 1791; (*below*) Robert Owen Esquire from an engraving after a picture by W. T. Fry published in 1821. Note the angel (presumably secular but clearly an advocate of spade husbandry)

the working class, 'greatly more numerous and powerful than the other two combined'.[42] For a brief time he seems to have seen the possibility of a change in society coming from below. His greatest success was with the Operative Builders' Union which transformed itself under Owen's guidance into 'a National Building Guild of Brothers', with the intention of eliminating building contractors and becoming a self-employing organisation. He sought to link labour exchanges with the unions by proposing a plan for a Grand Moral Union which envisaged a pyramid of production with trade union lodges at the base, provincial exchanges in the middle, and a national exchange at the top; but it did not come about. It failed because trade unionism was getting too much out of hand for Owen's taste.

Perhaps it can be taken as a sign of impending disillusionment with unionism that Owen involved himself in factory reform once again in November 1833 by joining with John Fielden in the Society for Promoting Moral Regeneration, and demanding an eight-hour working day. Once again he was looking to employers and government to ameliorate the condition of the workers. A clear sign of unhappiness at the direction events were taking came early in 1834 when he expressed his concern to James Morrison, the militant editor of *The Pioneer*, the organ of the Builders' Union, at the loss of 'the spirit of peace and charity by which alone the regeneration of mankind can ever be effected'.

> You have drawn a line of opposition of feelings and of interests between the employers and employed in the production of wealth, which if it were continued would tend to delay the progress of this great cause . . .

And to the trade unions he declared:

> Your friends are afraid you have scarcely sufficient experience and wisdom to assert [the rights of industry] in a proper spirit, and to maintain them without throwing society into confusion.[43]

Owen was right to be concerned, because the unions were moving in a direction different from that which he had laid down. They were increasingly concerned with short-term industrial gains, and co-operative goals tended to be pushed into the background. Strikes spread throughout the North and Midlands, and the employers retaliated with considerable ferocity. In the most bitter of these strikes, at Derby at the end of 1833, it seems that the co-operative goal was not forgotten: the Derby unionists 'declared their aim to be the establishment of co-operative factories and self-employment',[44] but this was to be achieved by driving the capitalists out of business. Owen had no concept of the bitterness of the struggle going on there and kept hoping that 'before the end of another week a Union would be formed amongst the masters and men'.[45] As the struggle for survival progressed, Owen's role in unionism became increasingly irrelevant. Even the Owenite press, under the editorships of James Elishma Smith and James Morrison, was preaching a different message from Owen. They, too, were concerned with the immediate practical goals sought by the unionists and, like the unionists, used the language of class war rather than of class co-operation.

By the time the Grand National Consolidated Trades Union emerged in February 1834, the signs of a parting of the ways between Owen and the trade unionists could be detected. He did not immediately associate with the Grand National but came forward only after the conviction of the Tolpuddle labourers and, once again, the motive may have been to try to calm some of the more violent reactions to the sentences.[46] Promptings from the Home Secretary, Lord Melbourne, on the dangers of such 'displays of force' may not have gone unheeded.[47]

As trade unionism crumbled in the summer of 1834, Owen finally broke with it. *The Pioneer* and *The Crisis* were closed down and gave way to the milder *Official Gazette of the Trades' Unions* and to the innocuous *New Moral World*. By August it was all over: the Grand National had been rather arbitrarily transformed into the British and Foreign Consolidated Association of Industry, Humanity and Knowledge, and Owen's short-lived attempt to bring about his new moral world from below was abandoned. He reverted to the position of 1830, preferring an educating, moralising, but largely ineffective propaganda organisation to a militant and potentially violent one.

4

Robert Owen's involvement with the working class and in particular with the trade unions was never a happy one. The basic flaw in the relationship was that Owen in no way identified with working-class aspirations nor, indeed, did he understand them. He saw in the co-operatives and then in the trade unions a possible base for his movement. For a moment, during the crisis years of the early 1830s he had a vision of the tremendous dynamism of the workers in these years being harnessed to achieve his new moral world. He failed, however, to consider the workers' own aspirations for immediate improvement in the condition of their lives. He failed also to appreciate the specific class attitudes which some of his ideas, as refined by other people, had encouraged, and he was not at all responsive to the nuances of working-class attitudes. As a result he was not able to control the movement. Accepting this, in August 1834 he pulled out and from then until his death in 1858 made no further attempt to create a mass movement, but concentrated on keeping alive an ever-diminishing sect.

But what of the workers' attitude to Robert Owen? The suspicions of him that existed in 1817 were never entirely dissipated. Bronterre O'Brien in 1832 still felt it necessary to defend Owen from accusations of being in collusion with the government. His persistent refusal to involve himself in working-class political demands, especially during the agitation of 1831–2, did nothing to quieten such accusations. Many of the working class who adopted Owen's ideas on co-operation, and who probably regarded themselves as Owenites, did link up political and social demands, particularly during the chartist years, and it was in this link-up that the real danger to authority lay. Owen himself was not considered a danger. He was not singled out for vilification in the contemporary press, in spite of his association with trade unionism, and even Lord Melbourne saw no harm in continuing to correspond with him.

The workers took up some of Robert Owen's ideas: they used those of his rather vague notions that seemed relevant to their position. Co-operation appealed to the craftsmen, for instance, because it was for them an immediate, practical possibility. Owen was also able to make an impact on the building workers, because they were searching for some means of eliminating the general building contractors who were steadily encroaching on the former independence of builders, and his schemes seemed to offer an alternative. There were, of course, certain factors in Owenism that had a broader appeal. For example, the millennial element in the writings of Owen and his followers did find an answering chord among a substantial section of the working class.[48] Owen's enthusiasm and the certitude of his own rightness gave him at times a messianic appeal to those who heard him. But he was never wholeheartedly accepted. Always there was some reservation and a rejection of his *leadership*. It was, however, *leadership* on which the despotic, if 'benevolent', man insisted and so he parted from his thankless associates.

One major obstacle to a complete rapport between Owen and the workers was his attitude to religion. In his later years, Owen saw his denunciation of all religions, made in 1817, as a turning point in his career, because it brought a breach with his respectable upper-class patrons. Some historians believe that it was this breach that caused him to look to the working classes for support. Yet, Owen's attitude to religion proved just as great a stumbling block for his working-class followers. William Lovett, in his autobiography, recalled how Owen's Sunday Morning Lectures on his return from America had stirred up dissension among the members of the London co-operative societies and contributed to their collapse.[49] And his views continued to cause dissension. A strongly methodist element among the pottery workers of Staffordshire prevented the important Potters' Union from fully associating with Owenism, and there was hostility to Owen's religious views among the Glasgow trades.[50] Finally, religion was a major cause of the differences between Owen and the two editors, Smith and Morrison. Owen wished to press his views, but his editors refused to co-operate, and as long as they were in charge of the press his religious views were kept well in the background.

Paradoxically, however, it was the secularist, anti-religious side of Owenism that held together the Owenite movement in the years after 1834. The Social Institutions, or Halls of Science, which sprang up in most of the main towns attracted to them a number of working-class secularists. The pseudo-religious format of these halls, with their marriage and baptismal ceremonies, gave expression to an element of Owenism that had until 1834 been kept in the background, overshadowed by co-operative and trade-union activities.

The post-1834 situation was probably much more to Owen's liking than the near-revolutionary mass movement he had found himself involved in during the crisis years. He clearly revelled in his role as the greatly respected 'social father' of the Association of All Classes of All Nations, surrounded by a rather sycophantic group of disciples. The Association, with its social missionaries preaching throughout the country, was an organisation acceptable to Owen: it was sectarian; it had not a class basis; and it was concerned with educating society. As Owen consistently argued, the first step to the millennium was by eliminating ignorance and by creating rational human beings through education. The attempt to by-pass this stage in the heady months of 1833 was, on Owen's part, an aberration.

It would be quite wrong, however, to give the impression that the Owenite involvement with the working class was irrelevant. Owenites had provided leadership of trade unionism at crucial moments. The chiliasm of Owenism had inspired the working class with enthusiasm and an expectation of change. Indeed, perhaps, its main contribution was towards the creation of a working-class consciousness in the early years of the 1830s.[51] But all these were the products of a movement, and its importance for the working class did not end in 1834. Individual Owenites like Alexander Campbell, James Hole and George Jacob Holyoake retained contact with and were influential among working-class co-operators and trade unionists. But, as had been true since the 1820s, the Owenite movement and its ideas was rather different from Robert Owen and his ideas.

NOTES

[1] Max Beer, *A History of British Socialism* (1919); Margaret Cole, *Makers of the Labour Movement* (1948); J. W. Derry, *The Radical Tradition. Tom Paine to Lloyd George* (1967)
[2] F. Podmore, *Robert Owen* (1906) Vol 1, 238; Vol 2, 432; E. P. Thompson, *The Making of the English Working Class* (1965), 782–3, 806
[3] For a general discussion of industrialism and the process of commitment see C. Kerr et al, *Industrialism and Industrial Man* (1962)
[4] *The Life of Robert Owen Written by Himself*, Vol 1 (1857), xxvi
[5] Robert Owen, *A New View of Society and Other Writings* (ed G. D. H. Cole, Everyman's Library 1927), 9 [hereafter *A New View*]
[6] *A Supplementary Appendix to the First Volume of the Life of Robert Owen* Vol 1A (1858), Appendix W, 329
[7] *A New View*, 14–15
[8] Ibid, 19
[9] 'On the Employment of Children in Manufactories', ibid 133–4
[10] Ibid, 136
[11] Home Office Papers 102–22
[12] Thompson, op cit, 123–4; M. Roe, 'Maurice Margarot: A Radical in Two Hemispheres, 1792–1815', *Bulletin of the Institute of Historical Research* 31 (1958), 68
[13] S. Bamford, *Passages in the Life of a Radical* 1 (1844), 6–7
[14] Podmore 1, op cit, 241

[15] 'Letters on Poor Relief', *A New View,* 187 ; Thompson, op cit, 782 ; for the Pentrich Rebellion see R. J. White, *From Waterloo to Peterloo* (1968 edition), 170–83

[16] 'Letters on Poor Relief', *A New View,* 209

[17] *A. B. Richmond v Simpkin & Marshall, and others. Trial for Libel in the Court of Exchequer, Guildhall, London, on Saturday and Monday the 20th and 22nd Dec 1834, before the Hon Baron Park and a Special Jury* (1834), 6, 43–44. In 1832 Peter Mackenzie, a leading Glasgow radical editor, published an exposé of Richmond in a pamphlet – 'An Exposure of the Spy System pursued in Glasgow during the years 1816–17–18–19 and 20'. Richmond was accused of having been not only a spy but an *agent provocateur.* Tait's *Edinburgh Magazine* published an extensive review of the pamphlet, and Richmond, by then a parliamentary agent in London, sued the distributors of the magazine. There was an impressive array of witnesses against Richmond, while he called no witnesses to contradict the evidence and allowed the case to be non-suited. Richmond's version of events is in A. Richmond, *Narrative on the Conditions of the Manufacturing Population* (2nd edition, 1835)

[18] 'To the British Master Manufacturers', *A New View,* 145

[19] 'Report to the Committee for the Relief of the Manufacturing Poor', ibid, 169

[20] 'On the Employment of Children in Manufactories', ibid, 133

[21] 'To the British Master Manufacturers', ibid, 144

[22] 'Address to the Inhabitants at New Lanark', ibid, 106

[23] 'An Address to the Working Classes', ibid, 153

[24] Ibid, 154

[25] *Mr Owen's proposed arrangements for the Distressed Working Classes shown to be consistent with sound principles of political economy in three letters addressed to David Ricardo* (1819), 31

[26] Ibid, 7

[27] 'Report to the County of Lanark', *A New View,* 246

[28] For the problems facing craftsmen in these years, see Thompson op cit, particularly 234–68

[29] Podmore 2, op cit, 352

[30] vide infra, 164-7

[31] Co-operative Union Manchester, Owen Coll, Alexander Campbell, Hamilton Jail, to Owen 3 Oct 1828

[32] S. Pollard, 'Nineteenth-Century Co-operation: From Community Building to Shopkeeping', *Essays in Labour History,* ed A. Briggs and J. Saville (1967), 83

[33] W. Lovett, *Life and Struggles of William Lovett* (1967 edition), 35

[34] J. F. C. Harrison, *Robert Owen and the Owenites in Britain and America* (1969), 200

[35] Co-operative Union, Owen Coll, J. M. Morgan to Owen 18 June 1830
[36] Owen Coll, W. King, Gothic Hall to Owen 10 May 1832
[37] *The Crisis,* 14 Apr 1832
[38] Ibid, 21 July 1832
[39] W. H. Oliver, 'The Labour Exchange Phase of the Co-operative Movement', *Oxford Economic Papers* 10 (1958), 357
[40] Ibid, 358
[41] *The Crisis* 16 Mar 1833
[42] Ibid, 7 Sept 1833
[43] Ibid, 11 Jan 1834
[44] W. H. Oliver, 'Robert Owen and the English Working Class Movements', *History Today* 8 (1958), 795
[45] *The Crisis* 18 Jan 1834
[46] W. H. Oliver, 'Organizations and Ideas Behind the Efforts to Achieve a General Union of the Working Classes in England in the Early 1830's' (unpublished D.Phil. thesis, Oxford University 1954), 281
[47] Podmore 2, op cit, 447
[48] For this see Thompson, op cit, 798–806 ; Harrison, op cit, 91–139
[49] Lovett, op cit, 35
[50] Owen Coll, H. L. Pratt, Stoke-on-Trent, to Owen 12 Nov 1833 ; *The Herald to the Trades Advocate* (Glasgow) 19 Mar 1891
[51] See Thompson, op cit, 779–806

5

OWEN AS FACTORY REFORMER
J. T. WARD

To relieve us from the dangerous and critical situation in which we are now placed, we must devise effectual measures to ameliorate the condition of the millions employed in this manufacture, which has already changed almost all the good habits of our ancestors.

    Robert Owen, *Observations on the Cotton Trade* (Glasgow 1815)

'No government that is incompetent to find good perpetual employment for the working classes in such manner that in return for it they shall be well-placed, fed, clothed, lodged, trained, educated, amused, and governed, ought any longer to be allowed by the people to govern them'. So wrote Owen in 1857.[1] On this matter at least he was reasonably consistent over the years, although his solutions for industrial and social problems varied from time to time. One of his first reformist concerns was, of course, his development of new managerial techniques at Manchester and New Lanark.[2] Another was his involvement in the cause of factory reform. Many writers have commented on this aspect of Owen's career, but it deserves further examination.

1

Owen's reputation as a factory reformer rests primarily upon his activities between 1815 and 1819. It was not until 1815, after twenty-five years in the cotton industry, that he seriously investigated factory conditions. 'I visited most of them from north to south', he recalled in 1857,

> to enable me to form a correct judgment of the condition of the children and workpeople employed in them. I thus saw the importance of the machinery employed in these manufactories and its rapid annual improvements. I also became vividly alive to the deteriorating condition of the young children and others who were made the slaves of these new mechanical powers. And whatever may be said to the contrary, bad and unwise as American slavery is and must continue to be, the white slavery in the manufactories of England was at this unrestricted period far worse than the house slaves whom I afterwards saw in the West Indies and in the United States, and in many respects, especially as regards health, food, and clothing, the latter were much better provided for than were these oppressed and degraded children and workpeople in the home manufactories of Great Britain.[3]

Owen thus adopted views similar to those already advanced by some Lancashire merchants and clergymen. And certainly, he took up the issue at a crucial time.

As the French wars ended in 1815, the only legislative restriction on factory labour was the Health and Morals of Apprentices Act, secured by the first Sir Robert Peel in 1802. Peel, himself the greatest calico printer in Britain, had been concerned to protect the so-called 'apprentices' in remote rural spinning mills. His Act provided that factories and mills should be washed twice a year and have adequate ventilation. Apprentice children were limited to twelve hours' actual work daily (excluding mealtimes) and nightwork (between 9 pm and 6 am) was forbidden. They were to have two sets of clothes, to be visited by physicians in the event of infectious disease, to be segregated in male and female dormitories, and to receive some elementary education. The local magistrates were to ensure the observance of the Act.[4]

In a sense, the 1802 measure was not strictly a Factory Act. It was planned mainly to protect pauper apprentices, sent from parochial workhouses to distant rural mills, 'where they served unknown, unprotected and forgotten by those to whose care nature or the laws had consigned them'.[5] It was thus, arguably, a reform of Poor Law arrangements. The Act was also passed in response to concern over the danger of epidemic diseases spreading from the mills – a concern initially aroused by an outbreak at Peel's own mills and publicised by Dr Thomas Percival's Manchester Board of Health.[6] It was, therefore, also a piece of health legislation. But in any case it was soon rendered inoperative, as the magistrates largely forgot or ignored the unwelcome new task and technological innovation changed the nature of the problem. The increased use of steam power allowed and encouraged the movement of factories from rural riversides to urban sites. Local children, who lived at home and were unaffected by Peel's Act, might freely be employed in the new and larger establishments. 'Owing to the present use of steam power in factories, the Forty-second of the King is likely to become a dead letter', Peel told the House of Commons on 6 June 1815:

> Large buildings are now erected, not only as formerly on the banks of streams, but in the midst of populous towns, and instead of parish apprentices being sought after, the children of the surrounding poor are preferred, whose masters being free from the operation of the former Act of Parliament are subjected to no limitation of time in the prosecution of their business, though children are frequently admitted there to work 13 to 14 hours per day, at the tender age of 7 years, and even in some cases still younger.[7]

Owen's later explanation of the late development of his own concern with the problem was reasonable (and typical):

> As employer and master manufacturer in Lancashire and Lanarkshire, I had done all I could to lighten the evils of those whom I employed; yet with all I could do under our most irrational system for creating wealth, forming character, and conducting all human affairs, I could only to a limited extent alleviate the wretchedness of their condition, while I knew that society, even at this period, possessed the most ample means to educate, employ, place, and govern, the

whole population of the British Empire, so as to make all into fully-formed, highly intelligent, united, and permanently prosperous and happy men and women, superior in all physical and mental qualities . . .

. . . I thought previous to experience, that the simple, plain, honest enunciation of truth, and of its beautiful application to all the real business of life, would attract the attention and engage the warm interest of all parties; and that the reformation of the population of the world would be comparatively an easy task. But, promising as many things appeared at first, as I advanced I found superstitions and mistaken self-interest so deeply rooted and ramified throughout society, that they resisted the *coup de grâce* which I now began to prepare to give to them when matters could be adapted to promise success.[8]

He now sought to secure further legislative protection for child-workers in the textile factories. This work brought him, for the first time, onto a national stage.[9]

2

On 25 January 1815, the confident, 44-year-old master of New Lanark attended a 'meeting of cotton spinners, cotton manufacturers, and others interested in the trade and manufacture of cotton wool', in Glasgow. The Lord Provost, Henry Monteith, presided, and Owen (who later claimed to have called the meeting) used the opportunity to make a major speech to the assembled Scottish industrialists. He made two principal points. First he reverted to a theme which he had originally developed in a paper to the Glasgow cotton masters in 1803, condemning the duties on imports of raw cotton.[10] He went on to call for industrial reform, on the grounds that 'the main pillar and prop of the political greatness and prosperity of our country is a manufacture which, as it is now carried on, is destructive of the health, morals, and social comforts of the mass of the people engaged in it'. The cotton industry had driven children into mills – 'those receptacles, in too many instances, for living human skeletons, almost disrobed of in-

tellect, where, as the business is often now conducted, they
linger out a few years of miserable existence, acquiring every
bad habit, which they disseminate throughout society'. Owen
maintained (with some inaccuracy) that

> It is only since the introduction of this trade, that children,
> and even grown people, were required to labour more than
> twelve hours in the day, including the time allotted for meals.
> It is only since the introduction of this trade, that the sole
> recreation of the labourer is to be found in the pot-house or
> gin-shop. It is only since the introduction of this baneful
> trade, that poverty, crime, and misery, have made rapid and
> fearful strides throughout the community.

Owen's remedy for industrial distress was a three-point Bill.
Children should be prohibited from employment in 'cotton or
other mills of machinery' under the age of twelve; hours of
labour should not exceed twelve per day (including an hour
and a half for meals and recreation); and no children should
be employed without passing an educational test. Owen proposed that his fellow-employers should consider his two proposals for a week and then meet again. He circulated and
published his observations widely, but the result was – not
surprisingly – disappointing. 'Although all were enthusiastic-
ally in favour of asking for the remission of the tax', he recalled
forty-two years later, 'not one would second my motion for
the relief of those whom they employed.'[11] He consequently
decided to act independently.

From New Lanark Owen sent revised copies of his address
to every peer and MP, which, he claimed, 'made me yet better
known to the government, and was afterwards a passport for
me to all the members of both Houses of Parliament, and
created a considerable sensation among the upper classes and
the manufacturing interest over the kingdom'. Thus encouraged, he visited London and (by his own account) quickly converted the Chancellor of the Exchequer, Nicholas Vansittart,
by his superior knowledge on the cotton tax. 'The government
was also favourable to my views for the relief of the children

and others employed in the growing manufactures of the kingdom, if I could induce the members of both Houses to pass a
bill for the purpose.' Thus began Owen's brief connection with
the Earl of Liverpool's Tory government.

Owen's pamphlet for Parliamentary readers expanded his
Glasgow address. Again, the rapid break-through in industrial
and technological achievements was stressed, but again the
'accompanying evils' – 'the political and moral effects' – were
raised. Industry was quickly effecting 'an essential change in
the general character of the mass of the people', and 'ere long
the comparatively happy simplicity of the agricultural peasant
would be wholly lost'. The desire to acquire wealth and the
resultant competition had carried 'the lower orders'

> to a point of real oppression, reducing them by successive
> changes, as the spirit of competition increased and the ease
> of acquiring wealth diminished, to a state more wretched
> than can be imagined by those who have not attentively ob-
> served the changes as they have gradually occurred. In con-
> sequence, they are at present in a situation infinitely more
> degraded and miserable than they were before the introduc-
> tion of these manufactories, upon the success of which their
> bare subsistence now depends.

Exports were now essential 'to support the additional population which this increased demand for labour had produced',
but Owen thought that British export trade would probably
'now gradually diminish', partly as a result of the new Corn
Law. Laisser-faire economics had destroyed 'that open, honest
sincerity, without which man cannot make others happy, nor
enjoy happiness himself' and had particularly harmed 'the
working classes'. Again, Owen maintained (against much
evidence) that it was only in the last thirty years that parents
had permitted children under the age of fourteen to work
regularly – and that twelve hours daily, including 'time for
regular rest and meals', had been thought sufficient for 'the
most robust adult'. Furthermore, workers 'were generally
trained by the example of some landed proprietor, and in such

habits as created a mutual interest between the parties, by which means even the lowest peasant was generally considered as belonging to, and forming somewhat of a member of, a respectable family'.[12]

Owen contrasted the imagined idyllic existence of the eighteenth-century rural peasantry with the bleak realities of contemporary factory life, when children toiled from 6 am to 8 pm 'for their bare subsistence'. The legislative proposals were now amended: children should not be employed under the age of ten, or should work a maximum of six hours daily until they were twelve. Owen's experience had taught him that 'in a national view, the labour which is exerted twelve hours per day will be obtained more economically than if stretched to a longer period.'[13] He prepared a draft Bill incorporating his proposed reforms.

Even Owen realised that he faced 'a formidable task' in converting Parliament. Characteristically, he later gave a mistaken explanation of the difficulty, ascribing it to his belief that 'by this time the manufacturing interest had become strong in the House of Commons, and yet stronger in its influence with the members, whose election was much under its control'. Yet Owen was 'generally well received' at Westminster and in particular the Tory Viscount Lascelles helped him to organise a series of meetings at the King's Arms Hotel in New Palace Yard with members of both Houses. During these sessions the draft Bill was amended and the Parliamentary leadership of the proposal was settled on Sir Robert Peel.

3

Owen's Bill of June 1815, as amended during discussions with the politicians, would apply to 'all Cotton, Woollen, Flax, *and other* Mills, Manufactories, or Buildings, in which *Twenty or more Persons* shall be employed *under* the age of *Eighteen years*'. No child under ten should be employed and none under eighteen should work over ten and a half hours (to which two hours were added for meals and instruction), such labour being performed between 5 am and 9 pm. Teachers were to report quarterly to the local Clerk of the Peace, who, with other paid inspectors, should visit local mills regularly to ensure observance of the measure.[14]

Owen arrogantly assumed that he had succeeded in his 'formidable task', and undoubtedly his ideas made some impact in London. But, as always, he gravely underestimated the strength of opposition. He was particularly unfair to Peel over the Parliamentary delay:

> Had Sir Robert Peel been so inclined, he might have speedily carried this bill, as it was, through the House of Commons, during the first session, in time for it to have passed triumphantly through the Lords. But it appeared afterwards that he was too much under the influence of his brother manufacturers; and he allowed this bill, of so much real importance to the country, the master manufacturers, and the working classes, to be dragged through the House of Commons for four sessions before it was passed, and when passed it had been so mutilated in all its valuable clauses, that it became valueless for the objects I had intended.

Owen, as he himself admitted, was 'an utter novice in the manner of conducting the business of this country in parliament'.[15] Peel had acted quickly enough in June 1815 when proposing the Bill.[16] This was, however, late in the Commons Session and, not unreasonably, the Bill was deferred. Nor was it unreasonable in Peel to accede to pressure for an inquiry, as he did on 3 April 1816, when he moved for a Select Committee. A Parliament increasingly convinced of the virtues of economic liberalism could scarcely be expected to reactivate its declining 'mercantilist' role at the whim of two industrialists. Smaller masters (and some uncritical historians) were, indeed, later inclined to ascribe industrial reform campaigns to the monopolistic ambitions of major employers.

The Select Committee sat under Peel's chairmanship from 25 April and heard forty-seven witnesses, including twenty-nine masters, before closing its investigations on 18 June. Owen

Page 107 (left) The lade looking towards the dam from No 1 mill. Note on the right No 3 mill, in the centre the end of Caithness Row and on the left the engine house and New Institution; *(right)* mill dam above Dundaff Linn first built by Dale c1785. This became a subject of dispute with the Misses Edmondstone of Corehouse. Note the unusually low water-level at midsummer 1968

Page 108 (*left*) Rear of No 1 mill. The steel reinforcing was added when the mill was cut down to stop it falling into the river Clyde; (*below*) rear of mills 2 and 3 with the School in the background and preparation rooms on the right

made five appearances, on 26 and 29 April and 6, 7 and 10 May.[17] Before giving his evidence, he had toured the factory districts with his fifteen-year-old eldest son Dale. Father and son were outraged by the conditions which they claimed to have seen in the establishments of some of their rivals: 'We found children *of ten years old worked regularly fourteen hours a day,* with but half-an-hour's interval for the mid-day meal, which was eaten in the factory', Robert Dale Owen recalled in 1874. Such work was performed often in high temperatures and in dust and fibre-polluted atmospheres. Furthermore,

> In some cases we found that greed of gain had impelled the millowners to still greater extremes of inhumanity, utterly disgraceful, indeed, to a civilised nation. Their mills were run fifteen, and in exceptional cases *sixteen* hours a day, with a single set of hands; and they did not hesitate to employ children of both sexes from the age of 8. We actually found a considerable number below that age. It need not be said that such a system could not be maintained without corporal punishment. Most of the overseers openly carried stout leather thongs, and we frequently saw even the youngest children severely beaten.

The Owens 'sought out the surgeons' who visited the children. 'Their stories haunted my dreams', wrote Robert Dale Owen:

> In some large factories, from one-fourth to one-fifth of the children were either cripples or otherwise deformed, or permanently injured by excessive toil, sometimes by brutal abuse. The younger children seldom held out more than three or four years without severe illness, often ending in death.[18]

These were recollections of over half a century later. The filial loyalty is perhaps impressive. But more careful contemporary observation would have been more valuable. Joseph Cresswell, the manager of Benjamin Gott's great Leeds woollen mills, was able to show that Owen's talk of a sixteen-hour day was untrue as far as Gott's was concerned: the undertaking worked from 6 am to 7 pm, with two hours for meals. And Adam Bogle, partner in the large Glasgow cotton firm of Henry Monteith and Bogle, asserted that many operatives had left Owen to work for his firm. Owen's system had proved irksome: one woman had stated that 'they had got a number of dancing-masters, a fiddler, a band of music; that there were drills and exercises, and that they were dancing together till they were more fatigued than if they were working'.[19] Benevolent as the New Lanark depotism might have been, it was too despotic for some.

In addition to the almost inevitable errors of an 'utter novice', Owen faced some special hazards as a large manufacturer supporting the Bill. Hostile masters sent Henry Houldsworth of Glasgow and another cotton master 'on a mission of scandal hunting' to New Lanark. They fell in with the parish minister, William Menzies, who felt slighted by Owen's patronage of dissenting ministers and considered his address at the opening of the New Institution for the Formation of Character in January 1816 to be 'of the most treasonable character against church and state'. According to Owen, the masters paraded Menzies before the Home Secretary, Lord Sidmouth, to whom the minister made charges about 'one of the most extraordinary, treasonable, and inflammatory discourses that had ever been heard in Scotland'. Menzies had not actually heard the speech, but from his wife's report insisted that 'it was most treasonable and inflammatory'. Sidmouth 'dismissed the complaint as most frivolous and uncalled for'. If Owen's account of his relationship with Sidmouth ('whom for nearly two years I had been in the habit of frequently visiting in his office') and of Sidmouth's defence of his speech is reliable, one may be led to speculate about the nature of Owen's connections with the allegedly most 'reactionary' of Home Secretaries.[20]

Owen's troubles were not yet over. 'My evidence, as an extensive mill owner, who had in his own practice adopted [a 10-hour working day] in his establishment, which at this time employed upwards of two thousand, the great majority children and young persons, had an influence not to be overcome by any ordinary or fair means', he recalled. The personal attacks were resumed in the Committee, particularly by George Philips – whose vicious examination was later expunged from the record, on the motion of Henry Brougham.[21]

In his autobiography, Owen certainly exaggerated his labours at this time. 'After attending the committee every day of its sitting during two long sessions', he tells us, 'I took less interest in a measure now so mutilated, and so unlike the bill when introduced from me: and I seldom attended the committee, or took any active part in its further progress'. The Committee, in fact, completed its work on 18 June and its 383 pages of evidence were ordered to be printed on 28 May and 19 June. Further doubt is cast on the reliability of Owen's memory by his assertion that his place at Westminster was taken in 1818 and 1819 by Nathaniel Gould, a Manchester merchant, and Richard Oastler, a Yorkshire land agent. Gould certainly financed and organised a Northern agitation; but Oastler was not to start his campaigns until 1830.[22]

Yet for all its errors and surprising vagueness over the economic and productive consequences of reduced hours even at New Lanark, Owen's evidence to the Committee had some importance. As it was obviously impossible to separate child and adult labour, he suggested that children should be employed in relays. This was a policy advanced in 1833 as a means of maintaining adults' long working hours.[23] But it was also a policy of social amelioration. Owen envisaged a half-time system for child-workers, under which they would 'be instructed one half the day, and [in] the other half . . . be initiated into the manufactories by parties employing two sets of children in the day'. Such a system was planned by Sir James Graham in 1843 and was to some extent established for 'half-timers' by his Factory Act of 1844.[24] Owen thought that productivity might rise through workers' gratitude, from

Robert Owen

the great wish to make up for any supposed or probable loss
that the proprietors might sustain in consequence of giving
this amelioration to the workpeople; such conduct to the workpeople is the most likely to make them conscientious . . .[25]

The valiant role that Owen retrospectively recorded for himself scarcely radiates from the Committee's minutes of
evidence.

4

The inconclusive nature of the 1816 evidence and Peel's ill-
health delayed further Parliamentary action, although there
was considerable agitation in the textile districts, particularly
in Lancashire.[26] Owen played some part in this campaign, after
spending much of 1817 on developing plans 'for the relief
of the poor and the emancipation of mankind'. On 19 February 1818 Peel introduced a much-weakened measure, apply-
ing only to children employed in cotton mills.[27] Opposition
rapidly rose – among others from Owen's acquaintance, Kirkman Finlay of Glasgow, who insisted that 'excepting in one
instance, in the county of Lancaster' (where seventeen girls,
locked in for nightwork, had recently been burned to death)
'there was no proof of the existence of any evils which could
justify legislative interference'. Nevertheless, Peel made considerable progress in the Commons.[28] And on 20 March Owen
published a letter to Lord Liverpool supporting reform.[29]

Presumably his experiences in 1816 had by now made Owen
wary of lashing out with unsubstantiated allegations. He carefully explained to Liverpool his understanding of the fears of
risk-taking entrepreneurs and agreed that 'the natural course
of trade, manufactures, and commerce, should not be disturbed, except when it interferes with measures affecting the
well-being of the whole community'. Factory labour provided
such an exception:

Generally speaking, the occupation which manufactures

under the existing arrangements afford, is more or less un-
healthy to those employed in them; who are called upon to
sacrifice their strength and substantial comforts for the advantage of others, and not infrequently for the benefit of
their enemies.

Owen now saw two principal evils in factory employment:

1st. – The employment of children before they possess sufficient strength for their work; before they can be initiated in
their necessary domestic duties; and before they can acquire
any fixed moral habits or knowledge that may render them
useful, or not injurious, members of the community.

2ndly, – the employment of adults, both male and female, in
situations unfavourable to health, for an excessive and unreasonable number of hours per day.

He considered Peel's Bill 'surely very inadequate' as an attempt
to deal with even the first problem.

Owen used many arguments. His paternalism shone through
the claim that the industrial workman 'was now placed under
circumstances far more unfavourable to his happiness than the
serf or villain was under the feudal system, or than the slave
was in any of the nations of antiquity'. But the evils of long
hours, low wages and child labour were remediable by 'a truly
enlightened statesman'. Indeed, 'the only safe course which
governments could now pursue, was, not to oppose, but to
lead and direct knowledge' – by regarding 'the proper training,
education, and advantageous employment of the working
classes as the primary object of government'. After en-
lightening the Prime Minister on the safety of government,
Owen condemned the 'petty, paltry relief' now proposed. He
wished for a much more comprehensive measure, and (encouraged, perhaps, by all those visits to Sidmouth and all those
jolly Lanark dinners with 'some of the first noblemen and
gentlemen of the county') urged a new policy on the Premier:

My Lord, I do hope that this important subject will be taken
up and defended by the ministers of the Crown on its broad
and true principles. I trust they will prove to the country at

large that revolution or violent reformation is not necessary
to compel them to protect the oppressed and the helpless . . .

Owen saw salvation in the extension of opportunities for
the training and education of youth. To facilitate this policy,
Peel's Bill must cover 'all manufactures whatever not carried
on in private houses'. Children should commence work at ten
(not nine) years and for the next two years should work six
(not twelve and a half) hours. No worker of any age should
work longer than twelve hours (including two hours for meals).
Owen thus proposed the ten-hour day, adding, 'I doubt whether
nine hours of regular and active employment, established as
the measure of daily labour to be required from the working
classes, would not be still more economical and profitable for
the country.' The attitudes of the Glasgow liberal bourgeoisie
alone were enough to provoke an attack on 'the blind avarice
of commerce'. But commercial greed went further, as energies
were devoted to improving 'trifling baubles and luxuries which
when perfected were of no intrinsic value whatever'; for instance,

> no real advantage has occurred from enabling our fashionable
> females to purchase fine lace and muslins at one-fourth of
> the former prices; but, to produce them at this price, many
> thousands of our population have existed amidst disease and
> wretchedness, and have been carried prematurely to their
> graves.

In all this 'my lording' to Liverpool and all this talk of the
safety valves of society there are echoes of a Robert Owen
preoccupied with his own social inadequacies. Here was the
Owen who worried that he had 'no doubt left an unpleasant
feeling of independence of courtly favour' by rejecting Grand
Duke Nicholas's 'most liberal imperial offer' to transport him
and two million other Britons to Russia. Here was the Owen
mortified by his social gaffe in trying to leave 'the Grand
Duchess of Oldenburgh, afterwards Queen of Wirtemburg'
before she had quite finished with him: he was, as he recalled,
'at this time a mere cotton-spinning manufacturer, unac-

quainted yet with the etiquette of courts, and especially with that of Imperial families'. There were other disappointments: Owen must apologise for a servant's mistake over Lord Stowell's identity; and he 'always felt that he made a very inadequate reply' to some award from the King of Saxony, as 'too much courtly favour . . . might impede his future progress' with working men ('whom he intended to instruct and direct for their good'). On the other hand, Owen seems to have enjoyed propounding his views to French royalty and nobility and certainly had some sort of relationship with their dissipated Royal Highnesses the Dukes of Kent and Sussex.[30]

Ten days after writing to Liverpool, Owen addressed an epistle 'to the British Master Manufacturers', on 30 March 1818.[31] He blamed no individual for the 'most grievous evils' of the factory system – 'the premature employment of children; and . . . the unreasonable term of daily labour now exacted from persons of all ages who are employed within our manufactories'. But again he pointed to the social dangers of allowing such abuses to continue, 'through mere indifference to the subject, or from the egregious and fatal delusion that they are connected with the prosperity of our manufactures': reform was, indeed, 'essential to the well-being of the state'. Again he drew attention to 'the unnatural circumstances in which the younger part of our operatives are now placed'. Children, he maintained,

> are permitted to be employed, almost from infancy, in our manufactures, all of which are more or less unhealthy. They are condemned to a routine of long protracted and unvarying toil within doors, at an age when their time should be exclusively divided between healthful exercises in the open air, and their school education. The utmost violence is thus offered to nature at their very outset in life. Their intellectual, as well as their physical powers, are cramped and paralysed, instead of being allowed their proper and natural development; while everything about them conspires to render their moral character depraved and dangerous. Without a vigorous constitution and good habits, children can never become

115

really useful subjects of the state, nor can their lives be rendered comfortable to themselves or uninjurious to others.

Owen restated his policy: 'no child should be employed within doors in any manufacture until he is twelve years of age'. Children of ten might perhaps be employed for five or six hours daily in order to learn manual dexterity; but Owen was convinced that 'any advantage thus procured could be obtained only by tenfold sacrifices on the part of the children, their parents, and their country'.

Like many factory reformers, Owen compared the conditions of rural and urban children:

> To mark the contrast of the two systems, look at the healthy, comparatively well-trained, Scottish peasant boy, who attends the parochial school until he is fourteen or fifteen years old, – and then turn your eyes to the feeble, pale, and wretched flax or cotton spinning children, who, at an early age are doomed all the year round to one unvarying occupation for fourteen or fifteen hours a day . . .

And like other reformers, Owen felt that 'surely it is but necessary to call your attention to these facts, and you must instantly be aware of the injustice and useless cruelty, which we thus inflict upon the most helpless beings in society'. Personally, he was 'almost ashamed to address any human being on such a subject'.

Furthermore, Owen was convinced that the so-called 'free' adult operative should be protected along with his children:

> If the operatives in our manufactures were really free, and had the option to work nine or fifteen hours a day, it might be less necessary to legislate on this subject. But what is their actual situation in this respect? Are they, in anything but appearance, free labourers? Would they not in fact be compelled to work the customary hours though they were twenty? What alternative have they – or what freedom is there in this case, but the liberty of starving?

He argued that self-interest, properly considered, should lead employers to favour shorter hours and higher wages for their principal customers – their employees. And he urged the masters to 'pour in petitions from every district' in favour of the Bill.

Peel's modified Bill passed the Commons in the spring of 1818 and was taken up by Lord Kenyon in the Lords. Further difficulties were now encountered, particularly from the Earl of Lauderdale, at this time a convinced liberal political economist. Another inquiry was ordered, by a committee of peers under Kenyon, which sat from 20 May to 5 June and examined a succession of witnesses. The most remarkable testimony came from a group of medical men employed by the cotton masters to affirm the excellent conditions of the mills and the dangers of reform.[32] In 1819 Kenyon obtained another committee which heard evidence from a succession of workers.[33] But the result of the long toil was disappointing. The Act passed on 2 July was the first real factory act, but it was a weak measure: Owen's original proposal of 1815 was indeed 'finally spoilt'. As Owen impotently sat through the Lords' debates, the Bill was 'strongly opposed, and often by the most unfair means, by almost all the cotton spinners and manufacturers in the kingdom, except Messrs Arkwright, the Strutts and the Fieldens'. The ultimate Act applied only to cotton mills, providing that children should not be employed under the age of nine and that children under sixteen should be limited to twelve hours' actual labour (excluding meal-breaks) with no night-work.[34]

Owen had undoubtedly done his best to further the original proposal. But he had already turned to other schemes. He addressed the governments of the world on 'the grand interest of society to adopt practical measures by which the largest amount of useful and valuable productions may be obtained at the least expense of manual labour and with the most comfort to the producers'. He now stressed the importance of early environment and education, inviting the allied powers assembled at Aix-la-Chapelle in 1818 to verify the results of his work at New Lanark. Again, the authoritarian paternalist streak in Owen's character stood out. 'Your Memorialist', he wrote, 'has hitherto, except in part, withheld this knowledge from the people; because he has been afraid they would act upon it, in their present neglected and unprepared state, with too much precipitancy to benefit themselves and others'.[35] The people were informed of part of the secret in 'An Address to the Working Classes' of 29 March 1819. 'The rich and the poor, the governors and the governed, have really but one interest', wrote Owen; and 'a correct knowledge of human nature will destroy all animosity and anger among men'. Humanity was at last marching towards 'the dawn of reason, and to the period when the mind of man shall be born again'.[36]

Now began the frenzied years of involvement in ever-widening schemes. New Lanark would be a model to Poor Law authorities. In 1819 a Leeds deputation found it a 'well regulated colony' with 'no quarrelsome men or brawling women': 'the moral habits of the people were . . . very exemplary; . . . although there were in the institution 1,380 females, there had been only twenty-eight illegitimate births during the last nine years and a half, and the fathers of those children had been chiefly non-resident interlopers'.[37] The Lanarkshire gentry received further tuition in the celebrated *Report to the County of Lanar*k of 1 May 1820.[38] There was the heady delight of London society headed by the dukes of Kent and Sussex, taking up 'Mr Owen's Plan'. There was an election to be fought in the burghs of Lanark, Selkirk, Peebles and Linlithgow – and lost because 'four of the old Lanark voters upon whom I had every reason to depend, had, by being feasted, kept intoxicated, and by other means known at this time to most candidates, been bribed over to my opponent'.[39] And increasingly there was the shift from philanthropy to communitarianism and ultimately to millennialism. As the vision of the new moral world gradually took shape. Owen's involvement in the down-to-earth campaign for industrial reform virtually ended.

118

5

A new generation of reformers periodically sought to improve and expand Peel's Act of 1819. John Cam Hobhouse, a radical Whig, secured minor amendments in 1825, 1829 and 1831.[40] And in 1830 Richard Oastler, a Yorkshire Tory land agent and son of one of the Leeds dignitaries who had visited New Lanark in 1819, wrote a clarion call for reform in all the textile industries in the *Leeds Mercury,* a Liberal journal edited by another of Owen's visitors, Edward Baines.[41] As a result of this celebrated attack on 'Yorkshire Slavery' a network of 'Short-Time Committees' developed throughout the textile districts of the West Riding, Lancashire and Scotland. Predominantly Tory and Radical in composition, the committees campaigned vociferously for a ten-hour day for the factory children. And they soon acquired a new Parliamentary champion in Michael Sadler, an Evangelical Tory linen merchant from Leeds. On 16 March 1832 Sadler proposed the second reading of his Bill.[42] He was forced to accept the chairmanship of a select committee of inquiry, which took a considerable volume of evidence on the horrors of child labour but which had neither completed its hearings nor issued a report when Parliament was prorogued on 16 August. At the first election under the Reform Act, in December, Sadler was defeated at Leeds and the Factory Movement had to start its militant campaign once more.[43]

Owen had played no part in Oastler's massive movement. New Harmony had dominated his American career in the mid-twenties. And when he returned to Britain in 1829 he was no longer the successful cotton magnate who could lecture to his fellow-industrialists on their mutual interests. Yet he returned to a Britain in which 'Owenism' – co-operative, 'socialist', millennial, utopian – was gaining ground. Several of his disciples had become enthusiastic 'Ten Hours' men. At Huddersfield Lawrence Pitkeithley was one of Oastler's most stalwart supporters. Manchester Owenites strongly supported Sadler during 1832, asking 'What sort of house of commons is it, either for intelligence or humanity, which requires specific evidence to show it is improper and inhuman to place children under nine years of age in the harness of fatiguing and unwholesome labour . . .?'[44] In London James Watson gave his help.[45] In the West Riding the Owenite-Oastlerite Joshua Hobson vigorously publicised the cause.[46] Above all, in Lancashire John Doherty was a redoubtable campaigner and propagandist.[47] The London Society for the Improvement of the Factory Children was presided over by Owen's friend Sussex and had as its chairman his sometime partner, William Allen.[48] Certainly, the Owenites were heavily involved in the Factory Movement.

Yet this support was far from assuring success. In January 1833 a conference at Bradford decided to send a young local Anglican priest, George Stringer Bull, to London to select a new leader in the unsympathetic new Parliament. Bull chose a young Tory Evangelical, Viscount Ashley.[49] But Ashley was defeated in the Commons and the Whig government set up a Royal Commission to re-examine the case. In the summer, largely following the Commissioners' recommendations, Lord Althorp passed the first effective Factory Act. The measure applied to cotton, woollen, worsted, hemp, flax, tow, linen and silk mills and factories. Children under nine were forbidden to work (except in silk mills) and were to be restricted to a nine-hours day or forty-eight-hours week. Young persons aged fourteen to eighteen were restricted to twelve hours daily. Children were also to receive two hours' daily education. And four inspectors were appointed to enforce the Act.[50] Outmanoeuvred and outbidden, the reformers were in despair by August: their hopes for a universal ten-hour day in the textile industries had been destroyed.

6

At this dismal period for the Factory Movement, Owen became increasingly optimistic about the imminent emergence of the new moral world, 'I rejoice in the energy and life of your proceedings', he told James Morrison, the Birmingham leader of the Operative Builders' Union in March: 'and let these be continued with judgment and our *speedy* success is certain'. The labour exchange idea was spreading, and Owen had high hopes of it:

> Last night there was a second meeting for the sections of delegates of various trades – men of business who I now plainly see will carry on these measures into successful practice. I mentioned your proceedings in Birmingham. I read your letter, it was most useful. I hope to bring with me the commencement of the correspondence between the Working Classes of London and Birmingham ... We must never allow the working men to despair again. They are beginning to know their power and strength, and all that is required is to give it a right direction.[51]

The workers alone 'could emancipate themselves from the degradation and slavery in which they had been so long held'. And they now understood this, asserted Owen:

> My object has been now accomplished and I shall have liberty to proceed in my great mission to change the condition of the Industrious Classes over the Kingdom and over the world, for this change cannot take place in one country without extending to all others. The working classes over the civilised world must now obtain their freedom, rights and privileges, or become more degraded and greater slaves than they have ever yet been ...[52]

Less optimistic reformers, who had borne the brunt of an exhausting campaign, were bitterly divided in 1833. They could not instantly change their published policies to suit the new situation. Indeed, their Factory Reformation Society, established at Birstall on 28 October, stood by the demand for a ten-hour day for all workers under twenty-one, although this would apparently involve increasing the hours of the newly-protected children.[53] It was at this time that Owen reappeared on the factory-reform scene. The equitable labour exchanges had attracted many trade unionists, and union expansion further raised Owen's hopes. 'Great changes . . . were in contemplation, . . . which should come suddenly upon society, like a thief in the night'.[54] Workers' control of industry would shortly be established. To hasten the syndicalist dawn it was necessary for all working-class organisations to federate in one vast Grand National Moral Union of the Productive and Useful Classes. And to further the progress Owen undertook a speaking tour of the North in the late autumn.

In October Owen visited Todmorden on the Yorkshire and Lancashire border. Here he met John Fielden, millionaire cotton master, determined factory reformer, Radical MP for Oldham and paternalist squire of the rugged Pennine township. The two radical philanthropists found themselves in wide agreement and planned a new organisation to demand a universal eight hours' day.[55] Owen announced the formation of the Society for Promoting National Regeneration at a rally in Manchester on 25 November. The Society's *Foundation Axioms* made its policy clear:

> Society in this country exhibits the strange anomaly of one part of the people working beyond their strength, another part working at worn-out and other employments for very inadequate wages, and another part in a state of starvation for want of employment.

> Eight hours' daily labour is enough for any human being, and under proper arrangements sufficient to afford an ample supply of food, raiment, and shelter, or the necessaries and comforts of life, and to the remainder of his time every person is entitled for education, recreation and sleep.

> The productive power of this country, aided by machinery, is so great, and so rapidly increasing, as from its misdirection to threaten danger to society by a still further fall in wages, unless some measure be adopted to reduce the hours of work, and to maintain at least the present amount of wages.

The Society's *Catechism* of thirty-one questions and answers was equally Owenite in phraseology. Even the meeting, attended by over 2,000 people, was dominated by Owen, who spoke for over a quarter of its six hours, promising the support of 150,000 trade unionists.[56]

Owen was supported by the Radical journalists John Cleave and Henry Hetherington (who apologised to Oastler for recent slanders in his *Poor Man's Guardian*). An impressive committee was formed, including such old factory reformers as Owen, John Fielden and his brothers Joshua and Thomas, George Condy, Doherty, James Turner, Philip Grant, George Higginbottom and William Clegg. The meeting resolved unanimously (among its many resolutions):

> That it is desirable that all who wish to see society improved, and confusion avoided, should endeavour to assist the working classes to obtain "for eight hours' work the present full day's wages", such eight hours to be performed between the hours of six in the morning and six in the evening; and that this new regulation should commence on the 1st day of March next.

It was soon made clear that the new eight-hour day would be enforced by widespread strikes. Furthermore, on the motion of Owen and Hetherington, it was agreed:

> That Messrs Oastler, Wood, Bull, Sadler, and others, be urgently requested to desist from soliciting parliament for a ten hours' bill, and to use their utmost exertions in aid of the measures now adopted to carry into effect, on the 1st of March next, the regulation of "eight hours' work for the present full day's wages".[57]

This was an impertinent suggestion to Oastler and his northern Tory friends, coming as it did from men who had done little if anything to help their brave campaign.

John Fielden's Parliamentary colleague at Oldham, William Cobbett, had never been enamoured of Owenism: to him, the communities were simply 'communities of paupers'. But the National Regeneration Society earned his support, as did the Owenite unions: 'The working people have long been combining in one way or another to obtain better treatment; and at last they seem to have combined for some practical purpose.'[58]

Cobbett had always supported industrial reform and now welcomed the operatives' resolution to work no more than eight hours. The man who had converted him was Fielden – who considered that while Owen had 'some very peculiar opinions or notions' he was right over the eight hours. Fielden also answered objections to the impracticability of 'National Regeneration' from such reformers as William Fitton and David Holt.[59]

Even Fielden, himself to become a close friend of Oastler, could not win over the old leaders of the Factory Movement. 'You must alter your name or you will never get on, "12 hours wages for 8 hours work" is *Unjust* – you might as well say "12d for 8d" – the poor creatures have never had 8 hours wages for 12 hours work', Oastler bluntly told Owen. With Pitkeithley and William Stocks (both prominent local Owenites) he refused to attend Owen's Manchester meeting: their presence, he argued,

> would do harm instead of good. We have no delegated Power. Our Delegate Meeting sanctioned the 10 Hour Bill and our Local Com[ees] have done the same, and the only power to alter, (as stated at Mr Bull's on Monday,) rests with the Public Meetings. If we were to turn aside from the resolutions of the Delegates and Com[ee] Meetings we wd deservedly lose the confidence of the Operatives. You know the opinion of Mr Bull, Mr Stocks and myself on the subject of the 8 hours plan, etc. Pitkeithley has the same. Nothing can be more full and candid than our avowal to you on the subject.

The fact was that Oastler had taken 'much pains . . . to explain his situation':

> I shall never argue against an 8 hour Bill, I have often declared 8 hours long enough, to the people at Public Meetings. I still think so, and that Children ought not to work at all. But the people must drive me by the Majorities at Public Meetings, from the 10 to the 8 hours Bill. I think the written memorandum you took from Mr Bull's is quite sufficient to explain ourselves. What wd the Operatives of Yorkshire say if I were to attend at Manchester and there formally

124

Page 125 The counting house at the end of Caithness Row prior to reconstruction for the New Lanark Association. This attractive building has been converted to a small museum

Page 126 (*left*) Detail of musicians' gallery in the School, showing refined workmanship characteristic of the building as a whole; (*below*) interior of No 3 mill showing the aisles of cast-iron columns and jack-arch construction. This photograph was taken during the clearing of the mills after closure in 1968

renounce the 10 Hour Bill? – Why they would instantly de-
throne me and I shd deserve to be beheaded. The question
must be left with the People as far as I am concerned. If
Lancashire takes the lead I shall rejoice – and I fancy the
Yorkshire men will not be backward in coming forward.

There was another hazard. John Wood, the great Bradford
Tory worsted master who had originally converted Oastler to
the cause and who had largely financed the Yorkshire campaign, would have nothing to do with the new agitation. 'I
don't think Mr Wood will even act with me again', Oastler told
Owen. 'I'm sure he won't if he don't act with Mr Bull also'.[60]
Within days 'Parson Bull' told Owen that although friendly
relations had been restored,

> Mr Wood has given us distinctly to understand that he will
> no more co-operate with us in this cause – will join in no
> agitation – will join no Societies but entirely confine himself
> to setting as good an example as he can in his own works.

> You therefore now see where we are. We have no Lord
> Treasurer now and the sinews of war must be found among
> those who have but little to spare . . .[61]

Oastler's Tory-Radical alliance was obviously under strain.

The stresses against Tory-Radicalism came from all sides.
Tory manufacturers like Wood might have doubts about the
viability of the alliance itself. Oastler himself certainly thought
little of Owen's new plans. When Owen invited him to a Bradford meeting in November, he refused in concert with William
Stocks, the Radical constable of Huddersfield and a supporter
of Owenite co-operation. Together, they rejoiced at Fielden's
support: 'his practical skill, joined with the benevolence of his
heart; with the undoubted confidence of the operative classes
in his sound judgement and the integrity of his Motives, would
render him a most valuable auxiliary'. But the Tory-Radical
leaders had serious doubts about Owen's campaign:

> If two such novices as ourselves might be allowed to suggest
> we should say, that the idea of calling public meetings in
> different districts at *present*, was premature and would be

more likely to *retard* than to *forward* your benevolent intentions. We feel the strongest desire to be Co-workers with yourself for the real benefit of the Working Classes – but we feel
assured that defeat would be our reward, if we were to
stand up publicly to propound and to defend a scheme,
which we are obliged to confess, we ourselves do not thoroughly understand . . .

The onus was on Owen to explain his case in detail.[62]

Other Radicals, in Yorkshire as well as in Lancashire,
quickly saw attractions in Owen's plans. Pitkeithley – subsequently a loyal Oastlerite – told Owen that the Huddersfield
reformers planned a public dinner to Fielden 'and on that day
to flog Messrs Oastler, Bull, Wood, Sadler, etc etc into the 8
hours or regeneration Society . . . The Regeneration System
will be firmly established on that day over the West Riding'.
All the same, after a brief visit to Scotland, Pitkeithley felt it
right to tell Owen that

I found at Glasgow and Edinburgh . . . persons strongly prej-
udiced against you. They have got a few crotchets in their
head, some regarding your irreligion some on account as
they insist of your advocacy of a community of women and
some prejudices are very strong in Scotland. Yet I assure you
there are hosts ready to welcome you and great good would
result from your visit there and I sincerely hope that you will
act on your intuitions and not disappoint your friends in that
country.[63]

Owen, as usual, ignored all warnings. 'National Regeneration' was part of that new moral world which he saw as imminent. The entire paraphernalia of the amorphous Owenite
movement moved into action. The 'missionaries' toured the industrial districts. The Owenite and Radical press stepped up its
propaganda. The demand for twelve hours' pay for an eight
hours' day inevitably had an appeal to northern and Midlands
operatives, especially against the contemporary background
of mounting industrial disputes. And the fact that Parliament
had rejected the reformers' case made extra-Parliamentary
action more attractive.[64]

'Regeneration' swept the textile districts. The Short-Time Committees of Lancashire rapidly fell before the attack, and from Boxing Day of 1833 (when Fielden addressed Pitkeithley's men at Huddersfield) some Yorkshire reformers joined the new campaign. At Manchester, Doherty produced a weekly paper for the Society entitled *The Herald of the Rights of Industry*. It promised to 'advocate a revolution, co-extensive with society itself, which will affect, more or less, every individual in these kingdoms'.[65] And Doherty's old connections with the National Association for the Protection of Labour led to Regeneration spreading to the Midlands – to Derby, Nottingham, Leicester, Loughborough, Mansfield and Chesterfield – in addition to the North.

For a time, Oastler and the other 'old' leaders of factory reform were largely deserted. The Tory-Radicals for once (and very briefly) had to agree with the new Liberal *Bradford Observer,* which proclaimed that Regeneration policy was 'benevolent, visionary and absurd'. Bull presided over two Regeneration meetings at Bradford, generally dampening Owenite spirits and finally explaining his views in detail. He refused to support the Society, though attracted by its eight-hour policy.[66] And he bluntly told the operatives why their latest scheme would fail:

> *You are a rope of sand*; you are jealous of each other. There are too many of you that would not give up one hour's occupation, one hour's comfort, or the price of one glass of ale to save *your own class* from distress and ruin . . . Where there are two men who will unite, there are twenty who will fawn on an oppressor and cringe to him . . . Suppose you had universal suffrage and vote by ballot and along with it the long hours and scanty wages of American operatives, what better would you be? Don't you know you might live in absolute and horrid slavery under a republic? . . . believe me, I had much rather be the Slave of some old English duke than a Factory Lord's Free-man . . . Now, therefore, do exercise a little forbearance, and keep your little political playthings still and quiet, when great practical questions are under discussion.

Even Oastler was now dismayed, claimed Bull. Therefore it was vital that operatives should

> Cast away all the self-imposed slavery of your ungodliness, your intoxicating cups, your dissolute habits, cease to rob your own families and your own breasts of comfort and peace, cease to suspect each other – be united – exercise forbearance – be steady and zealous in your own cause . . .

Peter Bussey, the local Owenite leader, sent this effusion to the Radical *Leeds Times*. 'We publish it', wrote the publican Bussey, 'although we must confess, that it contains truth not very creditable to the Operatives – yet we confess *it is true, and we only wish it were not so*'.[67]

For a few brief months the Regeneration Society flourished. The Short-Time Committees fell to the 'Eight Hours' men and new organisations were established. But from the start there were dark clouds on the horizon. Owen's arguments with his lieutenants, the Tolpuddle case, the masters' 'Document', the Owenite lack of organisation, the fall of the Derby unionists – indeed, all the factors that led to the collapse of the Grand National Consolidated Trades Union – rapidly turned the clouds into storms during the spring and summer of 1834. Optimistic Regenerationists continued their 'missionary' activity, memorialised the king, the masters and Parliament, organised a strike of Oldham spinners, addressed the labourers and operatives and held a delegate conference at Manchester in March.[68] But Regeneration perished with the other Owenite shibboleths between June and August. It dragged down with it a large part of the Factory Movement, just as the collapse of the Grand National ruined a wide spectrum of trade unionism.

Both unionism and factory agitation were to rise again. Both became more careful, more cautious and ultimately more successful, partly as a result of reacting against Owenism. But for the moment, in the summer of 1834, both were in ruins as a direct consequence of 'woolly' Owenite involvement. Holyoake once remarked that 'Robert Owen was a remarkable instance of a man at once Tory and revolutionary'.[69] In this case the combination was not successful. And there was a classic moral in the story: good intentions were not enough.

NOTES

¹ Robert Owen, 'Letter to the Governed of all Classes in All Nations' (Dec 1857), in *A Supplementary Appendix to the First Volume of the Life of Robert Owen,* Vol 1A (1858) [hereafter *Life* 1A], xv

² See, for instance, W. H. Chaloner, 'Robert Owen, Peter Drinkwater and the Early Factory System in Manchester, 1788–1800', *Bulletin of John Rylands Library,* 37 (1954–5); G. D. H. Cole, *Life of Robert Owen* (1965 edition); Lloyd Jones, *The Life, Times and Labours of Robert Owen* (1889–90); Frank Podmore *Robert Owen* (1923 edition); Sidney Pollard, *The Genesis of Modern Management* (1965); L. Urwick and E. F. L. Brech, *Making of Scientific Management* 1 (1946)

³ *The Life of Robert Owen Written by Himself* Vol 1 (1857), 112–13 [hereafter *Life* 1]

⁴ 42 Geo III, c 73 (1802)

⁵ John Aikin, *A Description of the Country from Thirty to Forty Miles round Manchester* (1795), 219

⁶ 'The putrid fever at Robert Peel's Radcliffe Mill', *Notes and Queries* 203 (1958), 26–35

⁷ *Parliamentary Papers* (1816) III, 133 [hereafter *PP*]

⁸ *Life* 1, 113

⁹ See Margaret Cole, *Robert Owen of New Lanark, 1771–1858* (1953), 94

¹⁰ Robert Owen, *Observations on the Cotton Trade of Great Britain and on the late Duties on the Importation of Cotton Wool* (Glasgow 1803); *Life* 1A, 3–9

¹¹ Robert Owen, *Observations on the Cotton Trade* (Glasgow 1815); *Life* 1A, 13–19; *Life* 1, 113–14, 120

¹² For perceptive comments on Owenite similarities and connections with squirearchic 'paternalism' see J. F. C. Harrison, *Robert Owen and the Owenites in Britain and America* (1969), 15 ff

¹³ Robert Owen, *Observations on the Effect of the Manufacturing System* . . . (1815); *Life* 1A, 33–45. The paper was reprinted in 1817 and 1818

¹⁴ *Life* 1A, 23–36; G. D. H. Cole and A. W. Filson, *British Working Class Movements. Select Documents, 1789–1875* (1951), 312–14

¹⁵ *Life* 1, 116

¹⁶ *PP* (1814–15) II, 735, 739

17 *PP* (1816) III, 20–8, 36–40, 86–8, 89–95, 113
18 R. D. Owen, *Threading My Way* (1874), 101 ; cf *Life* 1, 116
19 *PP* (1816) III, 129–31, 167
20 *Life* 1, 117–20
21 Ibid, 120–1
22 Ibid, 121 ; *PP* (1816) III, 1 ; see J. T. Ward, *The Factory Movement, 1830–1855* (1962), 22–8, 33–5
23 *PP* (1833) XX, 57
24 See J. T. Ward, *Sir James Graham* (1967), 193–7
25 *PP* (1816) III, 94
26 Ward, *Factory Movement*, 23–4 ; 'The Factory Movement in Lancashire, 1830–1855', *Transactions Lancashire and Cheshire Antiquarian Society* 75, 76 (1965–6)
27 *PP* (1818) I, 87, 91
28 See M. W. Thomas, *The Early Factory Legislation* (Leigh-on-Sea 1948), 22–3 ; 'Alfred' (Samuel Kydd), *The History of the Factory Movement* 1 (1857), passim
29 Robert Owen, *On The Employment of Children in Manufactories. To the Right Honourable the Earl of Liverpool* (n.p. 1818)
30 *Life* 1, 146–52, 193–200
31 Robert Owen, 'To the British Master Manufacturers on the Employment of Children in Manufactories' (30 Mar 1818) in *Life* 1A, 195–204 ; cf *An Address to the Master Manufacturers of Great Britain on the Present Existing Evils in the Manufacturing System* (Bolton 1819)
32 House of Lords Sessional Papers (1818) IX ; see Thomas, op cit 24–5 ; Ward, *Factory Movement*, 25–7
33 HL Sessional Papers (1819) XVI ; see 'Alfred', op cit 76–7
34 *Life* 1A, 21–32 ; 1, 225–6 ; 59 Geo III c 66 (1819)
35 Robert Owen, *Two Memorials on Behalf of the Working Classes* (1818)
36 *The Star* 15 Apr ; *The Examiner* 25 Apr 1819 ; *Life* 1A, 223–33
37 Edward Baines, Robert Oastler, John Cawood, *Mr Owen's Establishment at New Lanark a Failure!!* (Leeds 1819, 1838) ; *Life* 1A, 251–60 ; (Sir) Edward Baines, *The Life of Edward Baines* (1859 edition), 86–7
38 *Life* 1A, 261–320 ; *A New View of Society* (ed G. D. H. Cole, Everyman's Library 1927, 1949 ed), 245–98
39 *Life* 1, 230
40 6 Geo IV, c 63 (1825) ; 10 Geo IV, c 51 (1829) ; 10 Geo IV, c 63 (1829) ; 1 & 2 Will IV, c 31 (1831)
41 *Leeds Mercury* 16 Oct 1830. See Cecil Driver, *Tory Radical. The Life of Richard Oastler* (New York 1946), 42–4 ; J. T. Ward, *The Factory System* 2 (Newton Abbot 1970), 73–6
42 *Hansard*, 3S, XI, 340 ff ; *PP* (1831–2), II, 1
43 See Ward, *Factory Movement*, ch 3

44 *The Union Pilot and Co-operative Intelligencer* 10, 17, 24, 31 Mar ; 7, 14, 21, 28 Apr ; 5 May 1832

45 *The Working Man's Friend and Political Magazine* 13 July 1833

46 *The Voice of the West Riding* 1, 15, 22 June ; 6, 13, 20 July ; 17 Aug ; 12 Oct 1833

47 *The Poor Man's Advocate and People's Library* 21, 28 Jan ; 4, 11, 18, 25 Feb ; 3, 10, 17, 24, 31 Mar 1832

48 Ibid, 7 Apr 1832. On the failure of this body see Oastler's *Fleet Papers* 15 Oct 1842

49 See Sir Edwin Hodder, *Life and Work of the Seventh Earl of Shaftesbury* (1886) 1, 147–9 ; 'Alfred' op cit 344–8 ; J. C. Gill, *The Ten Hours Parson* (1959), 80–3 ; *Parson Bull of Byerley* (1963), 75

50 *PP* (1833) XX ; 3 & 4 Will IV, c 103 (1833)

51 Miss G. M. Phillips Coll, R. Owen to James Morrison 29 Mar 1833

52 Miss G. M. Phillips Coll, R. Owen to J. Morrison, n.d.

53 Ward, *Factory Movement,* 111–13 ; *Address to the Friends of Justice and Humanity* (Bradford 1833)

54 *The Crisis* 12 Oct 1833

55 See John Fielden, *The Curse of the Factory System* (1836 ; 1969 edition, introd J. T. Ward), xxii-iii ; G. D. H. Cole, *Attempts at General Union* (1953), ch 10 ; *Popular Movements, c 1830–1850,* ed J. T. Ward (1970), 68

56 *Voice of the West Riding* 6 Dec ; *Political Register* 7, 14, 21 Dec ; *The Pioneer* 7, 21 Dec ; *The Crisis* 14 Dec ; *Poor Man's Guardian* 28 Dec ; *Morning Chronicle* 7 Dec 1833

57 *Rights of Industry* (Manchester 1833) ; *Resolutions of the Society for Promoting National Regeneration* (Manchester 1833) ; *Voice of the West Riding* 8 Mar 1834

58 *Political Register* 2 Aug 1817, 7 Dec 1833. See G. D. H. Cole, *The Life of William Cobbett* (1947), 402–3

59 *Rights of Industry* (Manchester 1833) ; *Political Register* 14 Dec 1833 ; John Fielden, *National Regeneration* (1834)

60 Co-operative Union, Manchester, Owen Coll, Richard Oastler to R. Owen 22 Nov 1833. On Wood see J. T. Ward, 'Two Pioneers in Industrial Reform', *Bradford Textile Society Journal,* 1963

61 Co-operative Union Coll, G. S. Bull to R. Owen 27 Nov 1833

62 Co-operative Union Coll, William Stocks and R. Oastler to R. Owen 11 Nov 1833

63 Co-operative Union Coll, Lawrence Pitkeithley to R. Owen, 3 Dec 1833

64 *Bradford Observer* 6 Mar 1834

65 *Herald of the Rights of Industry* 8 Feb 1834

66 *Bradford Observer* 6, 13, 27 Mar 1834

⁶⁷ **G. S.** Bull, *The Late Meeting at Bradford* (Bradford 1834); *To The Friends of the National Regeneration Society* (Bradford, 1834); *Mr Bull and the Regeneration Society* (n.p 1834); *Herald of the Rights of Industry* 22 Mar, 19 Apr ; *Pioneer* 24 May 1834

⁶⁸ *Herald of the Rights of Industry* 15, 22 Feb ; 1, 22 Mar ; 26 Apr ; 3 May ; *Voice of the West Riding* 8 March 1834 ; *Pioneer*, passim

⁶⁹ **G. J.** Holyoake, *Sixty Years of an Agitator's Life* (1906 edition), 117

This paper is largely based on papers in the possession of Manchester, Leeds and Bradford City Libraries, Miss G. M. Phillips, the Co-operative Union and the Libraries of Cambridge and London Universities. I am greatly indebted to these owners of primary sources and to my colleagues in the Economic History Department of Strathclyde University, from whose conversation I have benefited. In particular, I am grateful to Professor S. G. E. Lythe, who made valuable suggestions on the script.

6

ORBISTON: A SCOTTISH OWENITE COMMUNITY 1825-28

IAN DONNACHIE

> *Ah! We shall see that glorious day,*
> *When, thron'd on Mercy's brow,*
> *The TRUTH shall rend that veil away*
> *Which blinds the nations now:*
> *When Earth no more with anxious fear*
> *In misery shall sigh;*
> *But pain shall cease – and every tear*
> *Be wip'd from every eye.*
>
> *The race of man no more shall mourn,*
> *Controll'd by Error's chain;*
> *Sweet innocence will then return,*
> *And all be new again.*
> *The fount of life shall then be quaff'd*
> *In peace by all who come;*
> *And every wind that blows shall waft*
> *Some wand'ring mortal home.*
>
> New Harmony children's hymn from
> *Orbiston Register* Vol 1 No 5

The word 'socialist', meaning one who advocated a 'social system', appeared in print in the columns of Robert Owen's *Co-operative Magazine* in 1827, the year that saw the abandonment of an historic experiment in Owenite socialism. At Orbiston, not far from New Lanark, groups of workers had come together under one roof to live and work as a community. The experiment had lasted less than three years. Although not directed by Owen in person, Orbiston was inspired by his teachings and supervised by several of his most ardent disciples.

Orbiston sprang directly from an Owenite vision. The world Owen dreamed of in the 1820s was one of communities or 'villages of unity and mutual co-operation' like Orbiston, Ralahine, Exeter and New Harmony stretching from pole to pole. For although Orbiston Community was not by any means unique, it was one of the earliest experiments in practical Owenite co-operation amongst workpeople in Britain. There the theories of *A New View of Society* were put to the test for the first time outside the confines of New Lanark by a motley collection of destitute and displaced workers, probably more interested in staying alive than in the creation of a new social order. A variety of equally personal reasons motivated the men who backed the scheme. They were neither urged on by self-interest nor by visions of a New Jerusalem. Unlike Owen they were not dreamers, but were more concerned with the horrors of contemporary social distress and with what little they could do to relieve it.

It was poverty, social distress and the powder-keg of Radicalism that provoked the landed gentry of Lanarkshire (already familiar with Owen's entrepreneurship and successful labour relations) into action in 1820. Most, no doubt, had read the view of Dr Henry Macnab that 'the great aims of the benevolent views of Mr Owen are the employment, instruction and comfort of the labouring classes and of the poor . . . the education and universal happiness of mankind'.[1] Although perhaps not in total agreement with all of these aims, the local gentry, drowning in a sea of social unrest, clutched at the straw of Owenism as a possible solution to their problems.

For his part, Owen grasped the opportunity presented by the Commissioners of Supply for the County of Lanark in the hope that it might eventually lead to a practical experiment in community building. He thus prepared his famous economic

136

thesis *Report to the County of Lanark,*[2] which was presented to the Commissioners on 1 May 1820:

> Mr Owen of New Lanark attended this meeting and communicated a plan he had formed with very much deliberation and attention, for ameliorating the condition of the working classes of Society; and in the presence of the said meeting a Memorial drawn up by him, pointing out the best practical modes of employing the working classes in order that public distress might be essentially relieved; and containing a recommendation to the Heritors and Farmers to give such employment in the meantime by the spade and otherwise to the peaceable and industrious laborers as their means might afford.[3]

The *Report* was afterwards remitted to a sub-committee under the chairmanship of Sir James Stewart-Denham of Coltness (friend and neighbour of Archibald James Hamilton of Dalzell), which 'embraced an early opportunity of hearing Mr Owen at great Length upon the nature and details of the Plan recommended by him for the relief of the distress of the country'.[4]

Further consideration was given to Owen's scheme at a general meeting in Hamilton on 16 November 1820. Stewart-Denham's report was hesitant in 'recommending a system which, in many of its prominent features, is acknowledged by Mr Owen himself to be at variance with those principles which are sanctioned by the most enlightened political economists of the age', but it concluded with a glowing report of New Lanark and Owen's achievements, 'which instead of involving any pecuniary sacrafice [sic], are found to operate beneficially in a commercial point of view'.[5] Philanthropy which paid profits (as Owen must well have realised) would interest even the least socially motivated landed gentleman.

The meeting then heard of 'a proposal by a respectable gentleman of the County, for granting a lease of ground sufficient for the purpose of making a trial of the Plan', as follows:

With a view to facilitate the formation of an Establishment

on Mr Owen's Plan, which would supersede the necessity of
erecting a Bridewell for the County, Mr A. J. Hamilton Yr
of Dalzell, submits a proposal to let 500–700 acres of land,
proper for this purpose . . . Mr Hamilton is willing, being
assisted by the Author of the Plan, to superintend the whole,
without charge to the County.[6]

A sketch map showing the proposed community by the banks
of the river Calder near Motherwell, resembled in plan the
agricultural and manufacturing villages (see opposite page)
advocated by Owen in *Relief for the Manufacturing Poor*
(1817). Although enthusiastic about Hamilton's offer, Owen,
not surprisingly, rejected any similarity between his proposed
community and the much-needed county Bridewell.

A petition to Parliament presented by the County of Lanark in favour of Owen's *Report* and *Plan* was rejected, and
(in the Commons at least) 'the quadrangular paradises' were
subjected to some ridicule. Although the Commissioners of
Supply for Lanark in turn rejected the scheme, Owen found a
staunch supporter in A. J. Hamilton, and together they resolved to try a model community on the Dalzell estate at
Motherwell. Capital to set up the community was to be raised
by 2,000 shares of £25 and as soon as 1,500 had been subscribed operations were to begin. Owen and Hamilton would
oversee a Committee of Management, but eventually, when
initial capital had been repaid, the worker-members of the
community would have full management of their own affairs.[7]

The Motherwell Scheme attracted little interest nationally
or in Lanarkshire. Accordingly, the co-sponsors in the summer
of 1822 sought the backing of the new Owenite British and
Foreign Philanthropic Society, whose main object was the im-
plementation of community building. The Society issued a
prospectus on the proposed Motherwell community, with a list
of subscribers (accounting for nearly half the £100,000 sought
by Owen) including Owen himself, A. J. Hamilton, James
Morrison of London, Henry Jones (a retired naval officer),
General Robert Brown of County Wexford, Captain Robert

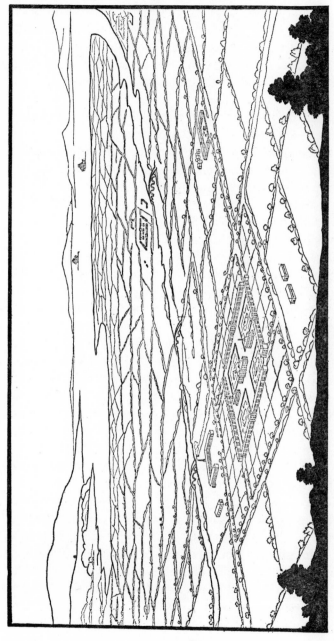

A view and plan of the agricultural and manufacturing villages of unity and mutual co-operation as devised for Owen's Report on the Poor Laws presented to the Committee of the House of Commons in 1817

O'Brien (another Irish landowner), Abram Combe, John Maxwell MP, Henry Brougham MP and William Falla (advocate of spade husbandry).[8] A distinguished gathering in London on 1 June 1822 heard Owen say that the community would form a model for others, and would train suitable individuals on the principles of the New System to act as promoters of future communities. Owen was at last convinced that the Plan would soon become a reality, but his hopes were raised only to be dashed to the ground by the failure of the British and Foreign Philanthropic Society to back their enthusiasm with action.

December 1822 found Owen in the midst of a propaganda campaign in Ireland. At that time he wrote to the President of the Edinburgh Practical Society (promoted by Scottish Owenites including Abram Combe, Captain Donald McDonald and A. J. Hamilton) saying, 'I have not for a moment lost sight of Motherwell and it is my intention to commence there at the earliest practical period. I hope this spring'.[9]

Never doubting the ultimate launching of the community, Owen purchased over 600 acres of Dalzell from the aged General Hamilton (father of Archibald James), which he later tried to sell to Abram Combe and A. J. Hamilton as the site for their community. By 1823-24 Owen was committed still further to spreading the gospel of *A New View of Society*, was involved in partnership difficulties at New Lanark, and, more significantly for the community movement in Britain, had by summer 1824 set his sights on the purchase of New Harmony. Motherwell was soon forgotten. The way was clear for Hamilton and Combe at Orbiston.

Archibald James Hamilton (1793–1834) was perhaps the most enthusiastic of the founders at Orbiston. Certainly he was well aware of the shortcomings of the experiment, but even after its failure his faith in Owenism was unshaken. Eldest son of General Hamilton, Laird of Dalzell, he was born in Edinburgh 28 October 1793. 'It was a singular coincidence', he later wrote, 'that I should be born in a year which would so determine my future feelings and opinions'.[10] He was undoubtedly a singular landed gentleman, whose 'useless' education and commissioned service with the Dragoons and Scots Greys (1812–15) in the Peninsular War and at Waterloo had left him disillusioned with the Establishment and with the accepted organisation of society. After his army service he settled at home to oversee the family estate, and began to take an increasing interest in local and national affairs.

Owen's *New View* had a profound influence on Hamilton (the two men first met in 1816) and, like Combe, he became an ardent disciple. He translated his social opinions into practical schemes aimed at relieving local unemployment in the Motherwell district, including intensive agriculture (as advocated by William Falla the horticulturalist) and cottage industries. In many ways Hamilton was the typical, paternalist Scottish landowner, with interests in his estate, parish schools and poor relief, dabbling also in economic developments, such as coalmining, turnpikes and railways. But he departed from the norm in his fervent adoption of Owenism, his rejection of the accepted social order and his criticism in 1820 of the formation of volunteer regiments to quell the Radical uprising in districts around Glasgow.[11]

Abram Combe (1785–1827) was a man of entirely different background. He was one of the seven sons of a prosperous brewer in Edinburgh, who was also a strict Calvinist. After a stringent upbringing Combe was apprenticed in the leather-tanning trade and by 1807 owned a successful tannery in Edinburgh. He quickly established himself in Edinburgh society with the help of his brothers George (advocate and widely acclaimed phrenologist) and Andrew (a highly regarded physiologist), and became well known for his satirical wit. George and another brother, William, later became involved in the affairs of Orbiston following Abram's untimely death in 1827.[12]

Combe first met Owen in 1820, visited the mills and village of New Lanark and like Hamilton before him became a firm convert to Owenism after reading the *New View*. A year later he met Hamilton who was resident in Edinburgh to attend classes in the university, a fellow disciple equally eager to put the Owenite philosophy to the test. Their first joint effort was the Edinburgh Practical Society, a co-operative group (mostly composed of skilled operatives) with an eventual membership of 500 families. Like Orbiston it had strong moral and religious undertones (its motto was 'By Our Works We Shall Be Judged') and its members had to pledge abstention from alcohol, tobacco and swearing. A society store and school were run on the lines of those at New Lanark, but within a year it had failed as a result of the misappropriation of funds by the storekeeper. According to Hamilton the personnel were badly selected, and he urged that members of future Owenite communities ought to 'be possessed of more than ordinary knowledge'.[13]

Combe himself tried community formation in his tan-yard (1822), with a profit-sharing scheme for his workers. This, too, was soon abandoned and Combe thereafter turned to writing to forward the cause of Owenism. During 1822–25 he produced numerous pamphlets advocating the adoption of community building and expounding his own economic and religious ideas.[14] Somewhat at odds with general Owenite views was his *Religious Creed of the New System with an Explanatory Catechism* (1824) which developed his own peculiar religion, 'Divine Revelation'. More interesting was a statement of his economic outlook in *The Sphere for Joint Stock Companies; or the Way to increase the Value of Land, Capital and Labour* (1825), containing details of the proposed community at Orbiston.[15]

The two key promoters of Orbiston thus emerge as men of widely different outlook and character. But, like a handful of other contemporaries from surprisingly similar backgrounds, Hamilton and Combe were swept off their feet by the freshness of the Owenite dream. Of the two, Hamilton was undoubtedly more of the realist, with a down-to-earth desire to help his fellow men. Combe, on the other hand, was motivated

Page 143 New Lanark from the end of Caithness Row with the Institution and lade in the centre and the School on the left

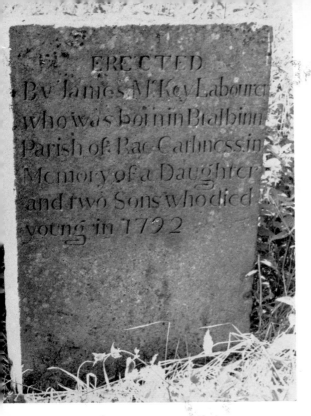

Page 144 (*left*) Headstone in New Lanark graveyard above the village, erected by a Highland emigré; (*below*) the engine house bonded onto the Institution. Built 1881–2, its doorway frustrated and annoyed the works manager on account of its narrowness

by a desire to transform 'Old Society'. The community they created was a strange mixture of paternalism, Owenism, religious and moral ideas, and reaction against urban industrialism. As far as social reform was concerned Hamilton and Combe were at one. 'They had drunk deeply of the fountain of Socialism at New Lanark', wrote Cullen, 'and the draught had acted like a magic potion'.[16]

Such was the enthusiasm of Orbiston's promoters in spring 1825 that building operations had begun before the legal and financial arrangements were completed. The site of 291 acres on the Dalzell estate near the river Calder, 'all arable and of excellent quality', was formally acquired from General John Hamilton by the Orbiston Company on 13 May 1825. The articles of agreement of the company signed earlier (18 March) set the capital at £50,000 in 200 shares of £250 and designated Abram Combe as company trustee. Several of the original subscribers to the Motherwell Scheme immediately took shares in Orbiston, and using the paid-up share capital and land as securities, Combe borrowed on bond nearly £20,000, of which the Scottish Union Insurance Company in Edinburgh loaned £12,000.[17]

The buildings of the Orbiston community, as planned, resembled the design advocated by Owen in *Relief for the Poor* and *Report to the County of Lanark,* but because so little was ever completed the similarity got no further than the drawing board (see page 146). The symmetrical, barrack-like, central block was to be four storeys high and was intended for community use, housing the kitchens, dining rooms (to accommodate 800 people), drawing rooms, ball-room, lecture halls and library. The wings on either side of the central block were to provide private living quarters for the members of the community, with special accommodation for the children. Initial construction was under way by March 1825, the first phase being the north wing. James King, a local mason, was in charge and within the month a hundred men were at work. When a workman was accidentally killed, Combe 'at once put

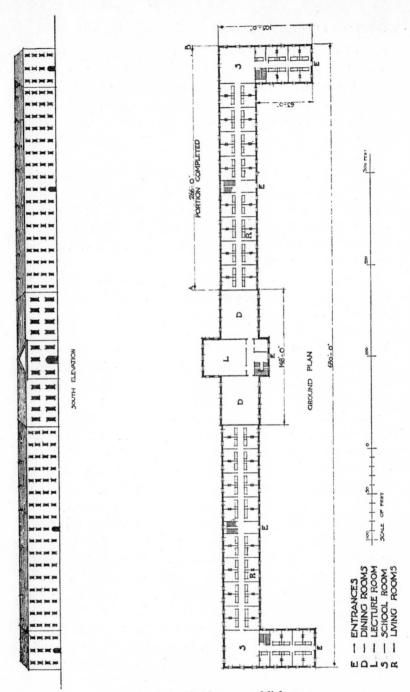

SOUTH ELEVATION

GROUND PLAN

PORTION COMPLETED

266'-0"

105'-0"

65'-0"

148'-0"

680'-0"

A

B

E — ENTRANCES
D — DINING ROOMS
L — LECTURE ROOM
S — SCHOOL ROOM
R — LIVING ROOMS

SCALE OF FEET

A plan of the Orbiston establishment

the principles of the New System into operation by making ample provision for the widow and children'.[18]

Six months later, on 17 October, a meeting of nine of the sixteen shareholders (or 'proprietors', as they were designated) was held in one of the newly finished apartments. Combe reported that 125 shares had been taken up and that expenses to date totalled over £5,000. After examining progress, several of the shareholders offered to double their investment, although they decided to postpone work on the central block of the community and concentrate efforts on building workshops nearby. 'The meeting', Combe later wrote in the *Orbiston Register*, 'expressed themselves satisfied with the way the work was conducted; and I was unanimously confirmed Trustee for the Company; and Mr Henry Jones and Mr J. Applegarth were appointed Auditors'.[19]

News of Orbiston Community spread like wildfire, and even before the north wing was completed, Combe had numerous applications. The first to arrive were a group of handloom weavers from nearby Hamilton; they were shown over the community buildings, selected their rooms and enrolled as tenants. A number of workers employed in building operations also lived in the partly completed wing during the winter of 1825–26, but large-scale occupation did not begin until the spring. Apart from the already obvious financial difficulties of the new community, the main item of discussion at the proprietors' meeting on 18 March 1826 was the selection and role of future members. The meeting agreed 'to sanction the immediate introduction of the system of Union and Mutual Co-operation' and that 'individuals who could agree to co-operate, might have management of their own affairs'. Following the shareholders' meeting, Abram Combe presided over a conference of existing and future communitarians. He undertook to become a member of the community and to supervise its affairs. In doing so, he presented the rules and regulations of the community, thirteen in number, similar to those of the Edinburgh Practical Society (and indeed many of the Friendly

147

Societies) but laying much more emphasis than before on equality and co-operation. Here at last was the basis for mutual co-operation in the first New Society.[20]

The decision to introduce co-operation was a momentous one. Much of the enthusiasm for mutual co-operation derived directly from Combe and Hamilton, who were at that stage entirely responsible for the community. Orbiston did not have the official backing of Robert Owen, and to his credit Combe pointed this out categorically in January 1826:

> Mr Owen has been the medium thro' which we have received much useful knowledge; but experience alone will determine whether or not we are mistaken. At all events Mr Owen cannot be considered responsible for any of the errors which we commit in theory or practice. He has nothing to do with our proceedings. He appears to be getting on successfully in another quarter.[21]

Owen's absence did little to encourage public enthusiasm over Orbiston, and indeed the majority of reports were hardly laudatory. Orbiston Community, like Owen's take-over of Harmony, had been planned in haste, and the same muddle and confusion seemed just as apparent.

The day after the departure of the builders and their workmen (9 April 1826) the members of the new community moved in. At once the problem of unselected personnel (so obvious at New Harmony) became clear in the New Society at Orbiston. 'A worse selection of individuals', Combe wrote, 'men, women and children, could scarcely have been made – a population made up for the most part of the worst part of Society'.[22] There were about a hundred skilled and unskilled workers, who had simply been accepted into the community as they applied. Most had come, in Combe's estimation, to avoid the evils of the Old System, 'rather than to seek the advantages of the New'.

Among the crowd of undesirables who made up the community there was confusion and disagreement from the start. Although the first week was devoted to the allocation of accommodation and generally making the building habitable, a large number of members presented themselves to Combe on the Saturday, demanding their week's wages. The ignorance of Old Society, which Owen had forecast in *Relief for the Poor* as being one of the greatest barriers to the introduction of the New, had already made itself felt at Orbiston. At a general meeting on the Monday Combe stated that 'Labour was the source of all Wealth' and attempted to explain 'other of the prevailing notions which puzzle the unlearned'. He pointed out the advantages of the New System: everyone would work to supply a common stock and the unskilled would be trained as necessary (in 'agriculture, manufacture, education or domestic economy'); each member would put a value per hour on his labour, which would be verified by an elected committee; and each member could draw from the common stock what he had earned. These proposals were 'unanimously agreed to' but, Combe remarks, 'fell to the ground like a dead letter'.[23]

During the first months there was scarcely any activity in the community that could be called mutual co-operation. Communal dining facilities were rejected by the majority of members, who 'began to look to themselves in the Old Way'. 'The New System appeared altogether inferior to the Old, that nothing but the refusal of their husbands to accompany them, prevented the wives from setting out to Old Society.'[24] Gardening around the community was more successful, and members planted fruit and vegetables, dug ditches and laid paths. Combe himself tried to set an example by spending several hours at the spade, but overcome with physical effort and worry about the community, he became ill and was forced to hurry to Edinburgh to seek medical advice. The affairs of the infant community during summer 1826 were left in the hands of Henry Jones, 'a gentleman from Devonshire', a convinced Owenite and former supporter of the British and Foreign Philanthropic Society.

While Combe was absent in Edinburgh, John Gray, the

149

Owenite theoretician, visited Orbiston. His impressions were not encouraging, as he afterwards reported to Combe:

> The Author of the Lecture on Human Happiness (who had come from London about the beginning of last year to join the Orbiston Establishment, but who had been prevented from doing so by other circumstances), went with his brother to Orbiston on some private business. He stopped two days, and on his return he gave me a lamentable account of the population who were there assembled. He said that a complete failure was now inevitable, unless we dismissed a great proportion of the present inhabitants and supplied their places with a selection of superior workmen. If we did this and provided them with capital to the extent of £10,000, he thought the concern might yet be retrieved; but without this, all such expectation must be perfectly hopeless.

Captain Robert O'Brien, one of the shareholders, expressed his views rather more strongly in a letter to Combe, which like Gray's report was also afterwards quoted in the *Register*:

> The animals at Orbiston possess neither gratitude nor good feeling. But good feeling of any kind is the result of better training than they have had; and yet there are several good persons amongst them. Dream not, my dear Sir, that this concern will regulate itself.[25]

O'Brien also insisted that the only way to improve the situation was to replace the existing community members 'with a selection of respectable and well-conditioned persons'. When Combe returned to the helm, he found things 'at sixes and sevens', but 'expressed himself as satisfied with the class of people gathered together'. The New Society had so far been a failure mainly because 'the individuals would work for wages, but they could not comprehend the idea of working for the produce of their own labour'. The members seemed unwilling to promote mutual co-operation and Combe was thus forced into taking steps to organise the community and its workforce.

Although there was general apathy in the community, there were a number of more intelligent members who were anxious to try the New System. A group of skilled workers formed a foundry company, using an old lint mill by the edge of the river Calder for their workshop. Combe was delighted with this success. Some members thought, however, that preferential treatment had been given to the foundry promoters, and seemed prepared to force the issue of Combe's interference in affairs. Combe asserted that 'he would not remain the nominal head of the experiment, and at the same time have its affairs conducted in a manner which he could not approve'.[26] The arguments were momentarily settled and the community agreed that Combe should have 'sole direction' of activities.

Increasing numbers of workers at Orbiston began to show some willingness to join in mutual co-operation and several new departments were created, including horticulture, agriculture, building and artisans. Clearly, however, there was little enthusiasm, though Combe admitted that experiment was the only path to ultimate success:

> Four months' experiment in practical measures connected with the introduction of the New System has satisfied our minds completely of the infinite superiority which such means of acquiring knowledge possess over speculation and discussion. The impressions which facts have produced on our minds compel us to consider it as a great national calamity, that the Founder of the New Society was prevented from bringing its merits to the test of demonstration ten years ago.[27]

Closing his eyes to the general disarray, Combe (as much the optimist as Owen) recorded his dreams for the future of Orbiston Community. He hoped that a house could be rented in Edinburgh or Glasgow for the benefit of members and a cottage acquired on the coast so that they could 'enjoy daily the beautiful and romantic rides for which the West Highlands are so famed'. He was even more optimistic when he wrote:

> The Community at Exeter, which is now building under the direction of Jasper Vesey, will be ready to receive any of our members, as we should certainly be to receive any of them.

The Community near Cork, of which Wm Thompson has sent us particulars, will have the same feeling. Besides those in Britain and Ireland, we have our friends of Harmony in Indiana – for a disciple of the *New System* will always be at home among his brethren.[28]

When Combe again left Orbiston in ill health (August 1826) to return to Edinburgh, the community was split into two camps – a majority in favour of co-operation and equal distribution, and a minority (mostly skilled craftsmen) who wanted to maintain the status quo. Thus Orbiston Community lost its leader at a critical stage, and this fact more than anything else forced some reorganisation of affairs on the members. During September and October A. J. Hamilton assumed nominal leadership of the community and soon found himself with a difficult situation on his hands. He was faced with growing agitation for equality and co-operation (which he himself favoured) on the one hand, and the reluctance of the foundry company and several shareholders on the other. Hamilton thought 'that the sooner the tenants acted as a body the better', and they would thus be able to take over full control of the community. After extended negotiations a meeting of the proprietors on 17 October agreed (under considerable pressure from Hamilton) to lease the land and buildings of Orbiston Community to the members. The shareholders were to be paid 5 per cent interest on their invested capital and were to have certain rights of access to accounts and influence on future capital expenditure. Each member on his part had to be re-elected to the community, agree to maintain the rules and regulations and to swear his belief in the doctrine 'that man is the creature of circumstances and that character is *formed for* and *not by the individuals,* as taught in the writings of Mr Owen'.[29] Although the legal transfer of the property had still to be concluded, the members could start to assume management of a community with ostensible equality and co-operative activity.

A provisional committee, elected earlier, was confirmed at a tenants' meeting on 19 October: President, Abram Combe; Superintendents of Departments, Miss Whitwell (formerly of New Lanark), Alexander Campbell, John Hutton, John Lambe, Edward Simpson; and Elected Representatives, Messrs Cameron, Fenner, Foster, Hamilton, Kirkpatrick, Reid, Rogers, Sheddon, Wigg and Wilson. The departments were broadly those which had developed since the start of operations and in most several trades were represented. Each of the departments for domestic arrangements, education, horticulture, agriculture, mechanics and artisans had its own superintendent, who was to keep accounts of production and expenditure and present weekly reports. The individual worker would be credited at the community store with the value of his production. Weekly meetings of the Governing Committee would likewise supervise all community affairs and examine the reports of all trades and departments.[30]

As winter drew in, it became increasingly obvious that Abram Combe was unlikely ever to see the fruits of his labours at Orbiston. In the December issue of the *Register* he wrote, 'the idea of witnessing the improvements made by the Community at Orbiston, since I left it, is now even more than I can raise a hope to'. His brother William was elected to the new office of Vice-President to act on his behalf.

Shortly after William Combe's arrival, the Governing Committee produced a detailed outline of proposals for the future of Orbiston. There were to be eight departments and every member would belong to one of them:

1 Store or bazaar
2 Domestic
3 Police
4 Lodgers
5 Education
6 Agriculture
7 Mechanics
8 Artisans

Although merely a statement of intent, the proposals envisaged a high degree of community action and co-operation, and described at length the role of each department in the life of the community. The nucleus was the Store, which was to provide every necessity, including raw materials, food and clothes. The horticultural and agricultural departments would provide the Store with grain, fruit and vegetables. The Store would function for the benefit of the whole community and members could draw goods from it to the extent of their earnings. The domestic department was responsible for day-to-day supervision of kitchens, dining-rooms, bakehouse, wash house, children's dormitories and mess-rooms. Members of the police department had 'to provide for due order throughout the building' and also prevent (if they could) 'Drunkenness, Quarrelling or Rioting'. If Orbiston had seriously expected its lodgers' department to be much of a success then it should have done something to improve its local image – for it was known throughout much of the district as 'Babylon'.[31]

The educational provision at Orbiston (for both children and adults) was modest, but successful enough considering the short life of the community. The schools were run jointly by Miss Whitwell (a former teacher at New Lanark, who went to Orbiston in summer 1826) and Alexander Campbell (an equally ardent Owenite). Subjects included the ubiquitous reading, writing and arithmetic, supplemented by history, geography, dancing and music. Discipline seems to have been rather lax and truancy was a major problem, which is surprising since at least one contemporary noted that at New Lanark 'the system was one of severe discipline, but of real and solid usefulness'.[32] Adult education at Orbiston included debating, lectures, music, dancing and drama.

The three important productive departments – Agriculture, Mechanics and Artisans – employed the majority of the workforce. Agriculture made a significant contribution to the well-being of the community and was one of the most successful ventures. The mechanics' department included the foundry company (who were nominally independent), joiners, carpenters, plumbers, glaziers, stone-cutters, masons, nailers and slaters. The artisans' department also indicated the wide variety of skills that had been attracted to Orbiston: printers, bookbinders, tailors, watch-makers, spinners and weavers, woodworkers, and also a sub-section of female needleworkers. These artisans, under the leadership of Henry Kirkpatrick (printer of the *Register*), were undoubtedly the most united in community spirit. But indeed, the minority who had opposed community of property were confined to the agricultural department and the enterprising foundry company. Both were highly independent, kept separate accounts, and attended few meetings of the Governing Committee.

There were favourable reports from various departments at the beginning of 1827. The farming operations had been fairly successful (spade husbandry employed many of the older boys usefully), the artisans and foundry were doing well, and masons, joiners and carpenters busied themselves in extending farm buildings and erecting a saw mill (driven by the foundry waterwheel). Weavers and shoemakers, printers and bookbinders undertook work for Old Society at competitive rates.[33] Some indication of the many skills available at Orbiston is well illustrated in the advertisement placard issued by the community in autumn 1826 (see pages 164–7). However, despite the successes of some of the Orbiston departments, it soon became obvious that all was not well with the community.

The growing financial difficulties were exploited by several of the shareholders who had never been firmly committed to co-operation and community action. Captain Robert O'Brien and Henry Jones both spread 'dismal forebodings' amongst members and other shareholders. Abram Combe, on the other hand, wrote with optimism from Edinburgh to A. J. Hamilton that he could not 'conceive any possible way of turning capital to better account than the one we have adopted', perhaps forgetting that Hamilton (on paper at least) had committed a large part of his personal fortune to the community.[34] Shortage of ready capital was strikingly apparent by March 1827, when

William Combe in a lengthy letter to Hamilton explained the dilemma all too clearly:

> We are sadly in want of some money just now – and if any delay takes place in getting the money from the Bank at Airdrie – the consequences may be very serious. After getting the community just on the point of doing for themselves to be obliged to retrace our steps for want of funds is very unfortunate – but an effort must be made.[35]

The community had accumulated large debts, and demands were now being made – mostly small bills and interest payments – amounting to nearly £2,000. He thought they could hold out until harvest time, when 'most of the demands would cease'. Hamilton and Abram Combe came to the rescue at once with bonds and ready cash, which temporarily saved Orbiston from bankruptcy. Affairs were still far from bright, though William Combe reported that 'a good feeling prevails among the community', and the majority of the members were anxious to be in the fields. As events turned out, this was the last harvest that was sown and reaped by Orbiston Community.[36]

Rumours and counter-rumours precipitated loss of confidence amongst community members. Many began to complain even more vociferously than before about conditions and lack of security. Even those who had continued to operate on capitalist lines began to feel the pinch, and some of the foundry operatives were first to leave (all of them consistent opponents of equal distribution).

By midsummer the financial affairs of Orbiston were desperate, and it was clear that the demise of the community was not far off. The general economic climate was such that the bondholders had been pressing for realisation of their assets for many months. In a last bid to save the community, the Governing Committee (under William Combe) investigated the running of every department to see if productivity could be improved and economies effected. The result was the abandonment of the life and soul of the New System – equal distribution and co-operation. A piece-rate system was introduced, and members were urged to make every effort to save the community.

Individual enterprise did little to retrieve the lost fortunes of Orbiston. Members continued to grumble, and many left during the summer to return to Old Society. The last hope of saving Orbiston vanished when the news of Abram Combe's death was received on 11 August. An appeal was at once made to A. J. Hamilton to take charge, but ill health prevented him from doing so. He thought in any case that his help would merely postpone the ultimate collapse of the community, for the members would do little for themselves:

> It would also be against the spirit of the System, as every individual in such a Society should feel himself interested in its success. By mutual and combined exertions they should work out their own social salvation; but this has never been exemplified in the members of Orbiston Community.[37]

Only the produce of the harvest maintained the dwindling membership during the autumn of 1827. The last edition of the *Register* (published 19 September 1827) related the sad tale of the community finances and gave a long appreciation of Abram Combe. The end came in December, when William Combe, pressed to the utmost by one of the bondholders for full repayment, was finally forced to close Orbiston. Practically all members returned to Old Society, though a handful stayed on to work the land on behalf of the shareholders, including Alexander Paul (former Secretary of Orbiston Community) who was later appointed factor and trustee on the sequestered estate. The aftermath of Orbiston was a series of protracted legal wranglings in the Court of Session, Edinburgh, but the end for the community came on that chill December day when an Owenite experiment had proved a dismal failure.

In a sad letter to Robert Owen, A. J. Hamilton outlined the tragedy of Orbiston:

> You will have heard that we have abandoned Orbiston, after

157

Abram Combe's death; none of our money supporters seemed to care anything about it, except Mrs Rathbone; and they even did us harm by representing things in a false light, as an excuse for withdrawing their support, and thus hurt us in two ways. I did all I could to animate the proprietors, of whom we had a resident company, but it would not do. They were feeble in all their exertions and could not find anyone to lend them money to go on with.[38]

Hamilton thought that too many members of Orbiston were near their friends in Old Society, and like so many of them, lazy and addicted to drink. 'The experiment at Orbiston', he later wrote, 'was no fair test of Pantisocraty [sic]'.[39]

After the collapse of the community Alexander Campbell and William Sheddon (as partners of the foundry company) were prosecuted at the instance of one of the many creditors and found themselves in Hamilton jail. Campbell wrote to Owen (who had only recently returned from America) acclaiming the virtues of the New System, 'I can only say for myself that the whole of the proceedings at Orbiston has tended to conform my mind stronger both as to the practicability and utility of your system over the present arrangement of Society.'[40] Equal distribution, he admitted, had been a failure, and Friendly Society legislation could have been used to give confidence to the members. He felt that the failure of Orbiston would 'prevent for a long time other capitalists from embarking in the like speculations', and that limited capital would similarly deter the labouring classes from forming their own communities.

Bankruptcy of both the Orbiston Company and its off-shoot, the Orbiston Foundry Company, was quickly established, but settlement of the affairs was not finally completed until 1831. The land was sold to Mrs Cecilia Douglass, who owned a neighbouring estate, for £15,050, and in the division of the assets only one creditor was paid in full. The shareholders, including the Combes, A. J. Hamilton, J. M. Morgan and Mrs Rathbone of Liverpool, lost all their investment.[41]

Of the promoters of Orbiston after the failure of the community there is little to tell. A. J. Hamilton settled down on his estate and continued to take an interest in local affairs. William Combe went to America (supposedly to join New Harmony), where his brother noted 'he displayed the same want of energy as he did on this side of the Atlantic'.[42] Alexander Campbell, who played a leading role at Orbiston, became an untiring propagandist of Owenism and later established a Bazaar in Glasgow in 1830. Alexander Paul expressed a desire to cross the Atlantic 'to find out comfort and happiness in mutual co-operation'. Many of the other confirmed Owenites (both shareholders and more prominent participants) reappeared elsewhere in trade union, radical, Owenite and Chartist circles. But the majority merged into Old Society again – as if Orbiston had never existed.

As an experiment in pantisocracy Orbiston was an utter failure. Yet its demise does not seem to have discouraged Robert Owen, for in autumn 1828 he wrote to A. J. Hamilton with his usual flowing enthusiasm:

> It will gratify you to learn that the good cause is progressing substantially in all countries, and that your exertions, although not crowned with immediate success at Orbiston, have contributed essentially to make the principles known, and to prepare the way for their practice in many places.[43]

For Owen, at least, the great experiment of Combe and Hamilton at Orbiston was only a beginning.

NOTES

[1] Henry Grey Macnab, *The New Views of Mr Owen of Lanark Impartially Examined* (1819), 125
[2] Robert Owen, *Report to the County of Lanark of a Plan for Relieving Public Distress and Removing Discontent* . . . (Glasgow 1821)
[3] Records of the County of Lanark (County Buildings, Hamilton), Commissioners of Supply Minute Book XI, 387–8, 1 May 1820

4 *Report to Lanark*, Appendix: 'Prospectus of a Plan for Establishing an Institution on Mr Owen's System in the Middle Ward of the County of Lanark', 63

5 Ibid, 65

6 Ibid, 66

7 *Parliamentary Debates* New Series V, 1316–25, 26 June 1821 ; *The Economist* (ed George Mudie) 26 Apr 1821

8 *Proceedings of the First General Meeting of the British and Foreign Philanthropic Society for the Permanent Relief of the Labouring Classes* ; held the 1st June 1822 (1822)

9 Hamilton Coll: Letters of Archibald James Hamilton Yr of Dalziel [henceforth cited as LAJH], Owen to Mr Wilson 29 Dec 1822

10 Ibid, A. J. Hamilton, *The Soldier and Citizen of the World with Reflections on Subjects of Intense Interest to the Happiness of Mankind* (MSS)

11 LAJH, Minute of a Meeting of a Special Committee of the County of Lanark 11 Mar 1820, and D. Smith to A. J. Hamilton (undated) give some indication of his interest in turnpikes and railways ; John Anderson, *Memoirs of the House of Hamilton* (Edinburgh 1825) has some useful biographical material

12 *A Biographical Dictionary of Eminent Scotsmen*, ed Thomas Thomson (Glasgow 1875), 385 ; *Dict. Nat. Biography* 4, 833–5 on George Combe and Combe family

13 Hamilton Coll, *Soldier and Citizen of the World*

14 Abram Combe, *Metaphorical Sketches of the Old and the New Systems* . . . (Edinburgh 1823) ; *Observations on the Old and New Views, and their Effects on the Conduct of Individuals, as manifested in the Proceedings of the Edinburgh Christian Instructor and Mr Owen* (Edinburgh 1823) ; *A Proposal for Commencing the Experiment of Mr Owen's System, in a Way which is not altogether opposed to the prevailing Prejudices of Mankind* (*Edinburgh Observer* 31 Jan 1824 ; reprinted in *Orbiston Register* 14 Feb and 14 Mar 1827)

15 *The Sphere for Joint-stock Companies ; or the Way to increase the Value of Land, Capital and Labour. With an Account of the Establishment at Orbiston in Lanarkshire* (Edinburgh 1825)

16 Alexander Cullen, *Adventures in Socialism: New Lanark Establishment and Orbiston Community* (Glasgow 1910), 180

17 *Sphere for Joint-stock Companies* ; List of Subscribers to Orbiston Community 27 May 1827 [see page 162] ; SRO, Court of Session, EP 58 11 Mar 1831 Ranking and Sale of Orbiston

18 *The Register for the First Society of Adherents to Divine Revelation at Orbiston in Lanarkshire. N.B.; With a circumstantial account of the rise and progress of this. The First British Community, founded on the important principles of co-operative, self-*

directed labour &c, ed A. Combe and others, 17 Nov 1825 [hereafter *OR*]

[19] *OR* 10 Nov 1825
[20] Rules and Regulations of Orbiston Community [see pages 163–4]; *OR* 30 Mar 1826
[21] *OR* 12 Jan 1826
[22] *OR* 19 Aug 1827
[23] Ibid
[24] Ibid
[25] Ibid
[26] Cullen, op cit, 232
[27] *OR* 9 Sept 1826
[28] *OR* 26 Aug 1826
[29] *OR* 7 Oct, 1 Nov 1826
[30] *OR* 1 Nov 1826
[31] *OR* 27 Dec 1826
[32] William Davidson, *History of Lanark and Guide to the Scenery* (Lanark 1828), 175, describing the New Lanark schools
[33] LAJH, W. Combe to Hamilton 4 Mar 1827; W. Falla to Hamilton 16 Aug 1826
[34] Ibid, A. Combe to Hamilton 19 Feb 1827
[35] Ibid, W. Combe to Hamilton 4 Mar 1827
[36] Ibid, W. Combe to Hamilton 14 Mar 1827
[37] Hamilton Coll, *Soldier and Citizen of the World*
[38] Co-operative Union Manchester, Owen Coll, Hamilton to Owen 8 Sept 1828
[39] *Soldier and Citizen*
[40] Co-operative Union, Owen Coll, A. Campbell to Owen 3 Oct 1828
[41] SRO, Court of Session, EP 58 11 Mar 1831, Ranking and Sale of Orbiston, Scheme of Division Among the Creditors of the Orbiston Co and State of the Interests and Order of Ranking of the Creditors 1 Apr 1830; ibid EP 78 8 July 1831, Discharge of Alex. Paul, Trustee, contains much interesting detail on legal and financial affairs
[42] LAJH, A. Paul to Hamilton 17 Aug 1829
[43] Ibid, Owen to Hamilton 14 Oct 1828

The best account of Orbiston Community and its founders is provided by Alexander Cullen, *Adventures in Socialism: New Lanark Establishment and Orbiston Community* (Glasgow 1910). J. F. C. Harrison, *Robert Owen and the Owenites in Britain and America* (1969) provides excellent fresh material on the Owenite community movement. W. H. G. Armytage, *Heavens Below: Utopian Experiments in England 1560–1960* (1961) has a short chapter on Orbiston and much useful detail on other contemporary community experiments. Manuscript sources are widely scattered but the bulk of primary material on Orbiston is available in the Hamilton Collection, Motherwell Public Library, which includes the Orbiston Letters, letters of Archibald James Hamilton, and a large collection of contemporary books and pamphlets.

I acknowledge with gratitude the help of the librarians and staff of Motherwell Public Library; Lanark County Library; Lindsay Institute, Lanark; Scottish Record Office, Edinburgh; National Library of Scotland; Mitchell Library, Glasgow; University of Glasgow Library and the Co-operative Union Ltd, Manchester. I also wish to thank the Rt Hon Lord Hamilton of Dalziel, Professor S. G. Checkland, Professor Peter Payne, Mr Anthony Slaven and Dr John Butt for their assistance and encouragement.

<h2 style="text-align:center">APPENDIX</h2>

1   *Subscribers to Orbiston Community as at 27th May 1827*

Joseph Applegarth, advanced to Abram Combe	£20	
William Falla	„	£40	
Henry Jones	„	£62	
Mrs Rathbone of Liverpool	„	£700	
Daniel Reid	„	£30 10s
George Small, Edinburgh	„	£40
James Morrison, London	„	£100
William Combe, his own account	£182 9s 10d
Robert Foster	£417 11d
Thomas Jessop, advanced to Wm Combe	£20
J. M. Morgan, advanced to Abram Combe	£200
William Brown, Manchester	„	£70
Edward Couper	„	£20
A. J. Hamilton	£12,825 15s
Abram Combe, his own account	£1,536 13s
	£16,244 8s 9d

2   *Rules and Regulations of Orbiston Community*

Introduction:—The expressed wishes of the Community should be the rule by which the conduct of members ought to be regulated; and the character of the individuals will be estimated by the alacrity or indifference which their actions shall manifest towards the wishes of the Community.

1st   It is the wish of the Community that all the individual members, male and female, shall be upon an equal footing, in point of privileges, with no other distinction than that which unavoidably attends superior habits and ideas; and that in their united capacity they shall have sole management of their own affairs.

2nd   That every individual, before joining the Society, shall carefully examine the questions put to the first applicant, and the answers thereto; and that each shall define in writing every passage in the said answers to which they are not inclined to assent.

3rd   That all members should be clean and orderly in their persons and dress when they come to the public rooms; and that they should be punctual to the hour of the public meetings, and regular in all their engagements.

4th   That a general meeting of all the members should be held regularly at 8 o'clock on Wednesday evenings for consultations on the affairs of the Society.

5th   That the division of labour should be extended to the utmost point to which experience shall prove beneficial; and that the internal and external affairs of the Society should be conducted by departments, whose duty it shall be to attend chiefly to the branches which are intrusted to their care.

6th   That the closest union shall exist among all the members in procuring all their supplies, in cooking their food, in cleaning their clothes, furniture, and appartments [sic]; and in the education and maintenance of their children.

163

7th   That no intoxicating liquors of any description shall be used, at any time, in any of the public rooms of the establishment.

8th   That the private apartments of individuals should be considered sacred and that no individual should intrude on the privacy of others.

9th   That all those who have acquired the habit of smoking tobacco, or any other habit which is injurious to themselves and offensive to others, should endeavour, while indulging such habits, to conceal their doing so as much as possible from public cognisance.

10th   That every species of force and fraud should be laid aside, and that all members of the community should cease to take advantage of the ignorance or necessity of their fellow creatures; but that, on the contrary, the kindness and attention of all should be directed to aid and to elevate the lowest to the highest point of which their nature is capable.

11th   That every individual member should have their attention directed to the affairs of the department to which they belong; and that in no case should they reiterate their application for assistance from others, until they shall have done their utmost for themselves.

12th   That all members be prepared to bear the burden of themselves and of their children.

13th   That all individuals should follow that line of conduct which experience shall prove to be best for the general interest; and they should do unto others, on all occasions, as they would that others should do unto them.

3   *Advertisement Placard Issued by Orbiston Community*

ORBISTON
October 1826

The community of operatives at this establishment, consisting of various trades, and furnished with machinery &c, requisite for performing work in the first style and at moderate prices, respectfully inform the public that the several departments into which their labour is divided are now ready to supply articles in the following branches of industry, viz:

PRINTING AND BOOKBINDING
in all their various branches, in the best style of workmanship, and at moderate prices. Handbills, cards of address, magazines, and other periodical publications, printed with accuracy and dispatch.

Books in any style and in any quantity carefully bound.

N.B.—Fancy coloured paper for stationers, and stamps for linen manufacturers, &c, &c.

BOOT AND SHOEMAKING
Ladies', gentlemens', and children's boots and shoes in the London and Edinburgh style, and much cheaper; also every description of strong articles made and repaired.

N.B.—superior blacking.

CARVING AND GILDING
Looking-glass and picture-frame-making. Old frames new gilt, glasses new polished and silvered, prints and needle-work neatly framed and glazed. Old work cleaned and repaired.

TURNING
Plain and fancy turning; lint wheels and reels made and repaired. Wooden basins of all sizes.

PAINTING AND GLAZING
House, ornamental, and sign-painting; paper-hangings, wire-work, &c. Imitations of all kinds of woods and marbles. Furniture and transparent painting.

WATCH AND CLOCK
making of every description, particularly repeating watches, musical snuff-boxes, &c. Jewellery repaired.

TAILORING
Ladies' habits and pelisses, gentlemens' naval and military uniforms and plain clothes made in the London style. Boys' dresses, with all kinds of common apparel suitable for working in.

HAIRDRESSING AND PERFUMERY

and every article connected therewith, in the most approved London methods.

UPHOLSTERY

Mattresses, fringes, tassels, window-blinds, bell-pulls, &c.

WHEEL-CARRIAGE MAKERS

Coach and cart work of all descriptions. Barrows, ploughs, and all kinds of agricultural implements. Cast-wheels always ready.

MASONS, JOINERS, &c.

House carpenters' and joiners' work. Cabinet and chair-making in all their branches.

MACHINERY MAKERS AND IRON FOUNDERS

Steam engines on the newest and most improved principles. Engine and mill work. Brass and iron castings of all descriptions. Apparatus for lighting up buildings with gas. Saws hammered and set on the shortest notice. All kinds of screw-presses, &c.

TINSMITH

Brazier and tin-plate worker. All kinds of sheet ironwork, tin goods, shower, slipper, and improved warm baths, &c.

WEAVING

Plain and fancy weaving, &c.

The Community intend very shortly to open a Bazaar for public inspection, in which a great variety of articles which they manufacture will be offered for sale. The public will perceive that the trades enumerated above will, at times, command the great advantages that a union of labour and interest can give to forward any operation required. In general society it too often occurs that an opposition of interests prevents some part of an undertaking from having the same superior skill employed in the execution of it that the rest may have; but in this Establishment the united intellegence [sic] of the whole body will be always employed, either in forwarding their respective occupations, or concentrated when necessary, to any given operation. This superiority can only be found amongst persons united for the mutual benefit of each other.

Orbiston: A Scottish Owenite Community 1825–28

The Orbiston Register, price 2d., is published once a fortnight, and reports the progress of this, the first community that has been established in Great Britain, founded on the important principles of co-operative, well-directed, useful labour &c; and will, we trust, afford considerable interest to the benevolent promoters of the happiness of their fellow-creatures.

Printed at the Orbiston Press.

7

ROBERT OWEN AS A BUSINESSMAN
JOHN BUTT

*Your false, vile, ignorant, and most wicked system compelled
me to learn the trade of buying cheap and selling dear, and I
was compelled to pursue it to support life – for under this
system to support life you must be tyrant or slave.*
    The Life of Robert Owen Written by Himself . . . 1857, xxiii

For obvious reasons biographers of Robert Owen have tended
to concentrate less on his career in business than on other
aspects of his life. Several short studies[1] have appeared, however, in which some attempt has been made to assess the significance of particular episodes in Owen's business career. The
purpose of this essay is to concentrate on certain discrete areas
of his career in business – his rise to partnership level, his
sources of capital, his dealings with his partners, his production
and marketing problems, his industrial relations and management policies, and his profits – in the hope that a consistent
measurement of his ability as a businessman may emerge.

1

A characteristic eulogy of Owen in the rags-to-riches mould is
not consistent with the facts, nor is the view that his success as
a relatively young man was exceptional during the industrial
revolution. He did not come from the lowest rank of society,
as a careful examination of his *Life* will reveal. His varied
experience in retailing[2] was likely to have improved his capac-

168

ity for assessing all market levels in society and to have encouraged his motivation towards success in business. This he soon demonstrated when he settled in Manchester and formed a partnership with John Jones, using £100 which he had borrowed from his brother William, a successful London saddler who had married his master's widow. In rented premises, with slender resources and slighter experience, Owen and Jones began making rovings which they supplied to spinners. Concentration on this preparatory process limited the integration necessary within the business, although Jones made machinery in addition, which Owen sold. Their major business problem was trading capital, particularly for wages, for they manufactured on credit in the expansive circumstances of Manchester in the late 1780s and early 1790s.[3] Thus far Owen's experience was comparable with that of many young hopefuls – the Gallovidians, McConnel, Kennedy, Murray and Douglas for instance, all of whom gravitated to Manchester and made money from cotton.

Owen then left Jones to work for Peter Drinkwater (1742–1801) of Bank Top mill. Drinkwater, the first man to build a mill in Manchester powered by a Watt rotary steam engine, was not, as Owen claimed, a 'sleeping partner' in the firm which Owen managed. As Dr Chaloner has carefully demonstrated, Drinkwater was a man of considerable practical ability and knowledge, with a reputation for innovation and well able to instruct Owen in many details of management.[4] In particular, he had installed Watt's governor in 1789 before Owen joined him; this reduced the violence and irregularity of the steam engine's stroke and, by making it more even, facilitated the production of very fine yarn counts. Owen's reputation as a fine spinner was largely gained as a result of his experience as manager of Drinkwater's mill.

In a somewhat justifiable fit of pique, probably in 1794, Owen left Drinkwater because his hopes of a partnership were sharply quashed, but in a period when managerial skills were in great demand his upward mobility continued. He began to supervise the building of a new mill which he intended to manage for a new partnership.[5] Although it is possible that there was in 1796 some reconstitution of the business, probably by the addition of further partners, the personnel changed very little.[6] In 1797 this cotton factory in Cambridge Street was insured by Robert Owen, Thomas Atkinson, Richard P. Moulson and Jonathan Scarth, 'carders and spinners', for £6,000 jointly with the Royal Exchange and Phoenix insurance companies.[7] By the end of the year their assets, excluding the mill buildings and warehouse, were valued by the Sun fire insurance company and the Phoenix at £11,000. Machinery alone accounted for £6,000, millwright's work for £300, stock and goods for £2,900, and a Boulton & Watt steam engine of 30hp for £1,800.[8] Stock and utensils in an additional warehouse in New Cannon Street were insured early in 1800 for a further £2,999 by John Atkinson, Robert Owen and Thomas Atkinson.[9]

Clearly, Owen had joined a very large organisation even by the prevailing standards in Manchester. This firm, known as the Chorlton Twist Company after 1796, also had as partners, in addition to those already named, Messrs Bartons, wholesale merchants and cotton manufacturers in Manchester.[10] The Atkinson brothers were associated with the firm of Borrodaile and Atkinson, hat manufacturers, furriers and bankers, with branches in London and Salford and extensive trade connexions with the West of Scotland and overseas.[11] In the late 1790s, therefore, Owen inevitably extended his experience, becoming increasingly concerned with buying cotton wool and marketing the firm's fine yarns. These were in great demand, especially among the muslin weavers in the West of Scotland.[12]

Among the yarn dealers in Glasgow, David Dale (1739–1806) was pre-eminent.[13] At New Lanark, Catrine, Newton Stewart and Spinningdale, his investment in the Scottish cotton-spinning industry was considerable. Although Owen's initial contact was via Dale's daughter, Ann Caroline, whom he married on 30 September 1799,[14] it seems likely that Owen's business interests would have, in any case, brought him into David Dale's circle.

2

At the time of his marriage Owen valued his capital at £3,000; David Dale offered a dowry of £3,000 provided that Owen settled £300 per annum on Caroline and any children, in case of his death. Apart from doubling his capital, Owen's marriage gave him access to extensive trading capital, since David Dale was cashier of the Royal Bank's Glasgow branch and an influential shareholder. Dale's connexions with clan Campbell, through marriage, provided Owen with other financial advantages, such as access to the surplus funds of Archibald Campbell of Jura, recently commented upon by Mr Robertson.[15]

It is well known that Owen and his partners bought the already established village and mills of New Lanark for £60,000 but less familiar that the business continued to be organised from Manchester.[16] The Manchester business – excluding buildings – was insured early in 1801 for £16,200.[17] Why should Owen want to leave Manchester for Scotland? His own explanation that he saw New Lanark as an ideal locale for his social experiments was probably devised through hindsight. His partners certainly regarded the New Lanark mills as a sound investment needing personal supervision. They hoped to supply their Scottish market from nearer at hand and thereby to safeguard it, or to complement their supply of fine yarns with medium and low counts. It became possible for them to play off yarn markets in Scotland against those in England and to trade via Glasgow and the Forth and Clyde Canal with the Baltic, especially with Russia, a developing market for British medium quality yarns.

Capital requirements for the Scottish business were limited by the fact that Dale transferred the business on very generous terms. The purchase price was to be paid over twenty years at £3,000 per annum with 5 per cent interest. Yet this loan was not at risk, since it was secured on the property of New Lanark, and repayment continued after Dale's death to his trustees. When Owen formed his next partnership in 1810, nine instalments to the Dale trustees were still due, and the new company took over this capital debt of £27,000 as part of the purchase price.[18] Even with a further change of partners in 1814, the Dale trustees still retained their financial interest in New Lanark. In November 1816 their account stood at £9,000, in June 1818 at £6,000, and the last instalment, £3,056 14s 3d, was paid on 30 June 1819.[19]

After his marriage Owen naturally became one of the trustees under the terms of Dale's trust deed.[20] When Dale died, he left Owen £2,000, but Owen owed his estate £11,007 2s 6d. Thus, the Dale trust funds became an important source of Owen's capital. According to the terms of the trust, Caroline Owen received £2,000 three years after Dale died and then equal sums with her sisters from income of the trust estate. As late as 1816 Owen still owed Dale's trust £10,556 10s 9d, indicating the continuing importance of this source of capital.[21]

When Owen took over New Lanark, he and his partners insured their property for £21,850 and placed another £4,000 on their stock in their warehouse in St Andrew's Square, Glasgow.[22] Owen took one-ninth of the share capital of £60,000 and was paid £1,000 per annum for managing the mills.[23] Because David Dale was in relatively poor health from 1800, Owen undertook many of his business commitments, especially those associated with the Royal Bank and with the settlement of Dale's outstanding capital accounts in Catrine, Spinningdale and Newton Stewart.[24] Scott Moncrieff, Dale's partner and fellow agent for the Royal Bank, clearly found Owen very congenial company: '22nd June, 1801: In comes Mr Owen to tell me the honest man [Dale] is arrived back from Lanark and is to be with me at 7. He is a clever lad, far from being sanguine or speculative'.[25] In fact, Owen's relationship with both his bankers was so intimate that any request for capital was likely to be treated with sympathy. His business ability was recognised, and, according to John Marshall, he had 'the management of the Bank of Scotland at Glasgow where he spends half his time'.[26] Owen's initial residence at Glasgow, his association with Glasgow trade pressure groups like the Chamber of Commerce and the cottonmasters' group in favour of repeal of the cotton duty, and his involvement in the cultural and social life of the city indicate that he had joined the local 'establishment' and that he was the more readily assimilated by it because of his relationship with the Dale family.[27]

Social assimilation had its financial rewards for Owen, in addition to the immeasurable advantage of bestowing creditworthiness. The most important was Owen's ability to inherit David Dale's control of the ready cash of Archibald Campbell of Jura.[28] Archibald Campbell [29] (1744–1835), JP, fifth of Jura and Heritable Keeper of Craignish Castle, was one of the numerous estate 'improvers' of that time who deposited their cash surpluses, derived principally from black cattle sold at the Falkirk and other trysts (or markets) with trusted Glasgow and Edinburgh merchants (often connexions by blood or marriage) as well as with the growing number of banks. He had succeeded to the estate of Jura at the age of seventeen and from a small initial rental had accumulated a great fortune, eventually owning the whole island, except for one farm, as well as land on the mainland. By his marriage David Dale became related to Archibald Campbell, and Dale's children had him as their godfather. Campbell banked with Dale personally and not with the Royal Bank, probably because he received a guaranteed 5 per cent no matter what the bank-rate. A few months before his death in March 1806, Dale wrote to Campbell asking him to transfer his money to the New Lanark Twist Company, explaining that Owen would continue to send him accounts of it and provide him with cash as required.[30]

Campbell agreed to Dale's suggestion, but Owen did not transfer his money to the company's account. Instead he kept Campbell's money in his own partnership account. Owen seems to have made annual statements to Campbell about the money and corresponded frequently on personal and business matters. John More, Dale's successor as the Royal Bank's Glasgow agent, kept the books of Dale's trustees and also the ledger account between Owen and Campbell. By 1 April 1810 Owen owed Campbell £13,005 19s 4d, upon which interest of £608 10s 5d was due. At the same date Dale's trustees owed Campbell £9,915 15s 10d and interest of £472 3s 7d.[31] Owen was a debtor to Dale's trustees for more than they owed Campbell.

On 17 October 1810 Owen informed Campbell that there had been 'advantageous changes' in the partnership at New Lanark.[32] The new partnership consisted of Owen, John Atkinson, Robert Dennistoun[33] and Alexander Campbell of Hallyards[34] (Archibald Campbell's two sons-in-law), and Colin Campbell (who was not related to Archibald); Owen had heard too late that Archibald's son, also named Colin, had wanted to become a partner. He, therefore, made a number of observations, all designed to secure Archibald's approval and continuing financial support, on the lines that the New Lanark mills were 'likely to be one of the most lucrative concerns in the kingdom'.[35] As a trustee of David Dale as well as Owen's creditor, Archibald Campbell's support was essential to Owen.

On 10 November 1810 Owen indicated to Archibald Campbell that his funds were placed with the new partnership and asked diplomatically that they should be left undisturbed until Martinmas 1812.[36] In fact, Campbell had signed a letter drafted by Owen which enabled Owen to use Campbell's money to meet share-calls. Despite Campbell's later protestations that he had intended Owen to deposit his money with the partnership, this certainly was not done.[37] Campbell claimed that he had been misled by Owen, but it seems possible that as long as Owen appeared to be in funds, their financial relationship was both uncomplaining and uncomplicated. Owen's direct indebtedness to Campbell gradually increased. By 1 May 1811 Owen owed him £20,702 11s 6d, but this increase of about £7,000 in a year was largely accounted for by withdrawals from Campbell's account with the Dale trustees and the transfer of these funds to Owen.[38]

Six months before the date that Owen had set for the beginning of repayment, on 1 May 1812, he was in debt to Campbell to the tune of £25,624 18s 8d.[39] Naturally, in a year of growing financial alarm, Campbell became increasingly restive about the security of his investment. Owen contributed to Archibald Campbell's apprehension in two ways. First, he sought an extension of the loan.[40] Secondly, he told John Atkinson of his indebtedness to Campbell, possibly to lay the debt off with Atkinson,[41] and Atkinson, probably in April 1812, told Robert Dennistoun and Alexander Campbell of the transactions between their father-in-law and Owen. Possibly their wrath may have originated, as Owen suggested in his *Life*, in their chagrin at not being trusted with their father-in-law's money, but it is more likely that they feared Owen could not repay, informed the family circle accordingly, and when told by Archibald Campbell that his money was deposited with the partnership and not with Owen personally, soon disabused him.

Growing fear that Owen could not pay and that his loan was not secured on the New Lanark property motivated Archibald Campbell's actions. It was not that he did not want to act reasonably. He asked Owen to repay £6,000 at the end of July 1812, and Owen agreed to find this sum 'but when trade is bad, money is hard to come by'.[42] On 29 July 1812 Archibald Campbell, in a letter of attorney, instructed his son John, a Glasgow lawyer, to act for him in collecting Owen's repayment of £6,000 and ensuring proper security for the rest of the loan. In a separate confidential note, Campbell was both less legalistic and less restrained:

> in case he [Owen] does not pay this Sum, and Grant proper Security to your Satisfaction for the remaining part of the said Debt, I hereby authorise you to Call up the whole from him, and to take all such legal measures for recovery thereof as you may see necessary.

175

It is however my Wish that all liberty shall be given to Mr Owen in the Adjustment of this Business, as is compatible with Prudence.

When John Campbell met Owen, he was offered Owen's life insurance policies as security in case of Owen's death.[43] However, it was not Owen's death but his bankruptcy that Campbell of Jura feared. Owen paid the £6,000 promised, told John Campbell that he would be seeking new partners at New Lanark, and offered a bill for the remaining sum. Alexander Campbell of Hallyards was less sanguine:[44] 'you should have no reliance on his [Owen] forming *any new* arrangement & act accordingly'. Colin Campbell wrote to his brother in equally Cassandra-like terms and was equally free with advice:

if you let Owen slip through your fingers you may regret it . . . If you accept his offer, he cannot refuse you . . . he dare not refuse to give you a Bill, if he makes the least hesitation, you must immediately proceed against him . . .[45]

John Campbell duly produced a statement of account between his father and Robert Owen, showing that the sum for which he required a bill was £20,195 0s 11d at 25 September 1812.[46] Owen supplied a promissory note due on 11 November 1812 and agreed to repay a further £1,100 but indicated that he was going to London on business.[47] On 7 November 1812 John Campbell asked his brother Colin and his partner, Andrew Clason or Clawson, to collect the £1,100 and stated that Owen had promised a new bill for £20,229 10s 0d to cover outstanding capital and interest.[48] Colin Campbell collected Owen's repayment, which was handed over reluctantly, but found Owen's partners most unco-operative in refusing to act as security for him. He began to fear that Owen might be made bankrupt by his partners, and that the action of his own brothers-in-law, Robert Dennistoun and Alexander Campbell, might put his father's money in jeopardy:

We [Colin Campbell and Andrew Clawson] have acted towards Mr O in the most amicable and friendly manner . . .

indeed his interest and ours are now much the same . . . I
intend to keep a sharp look out after him and his partners . . .[49]

Owen's absence in England did not remove the dire threats
to his business career. On the one hand, the Campbells might
proceed against him for recovery of their father's money once
his back was turned; on the other hand, his partners might
act against him, since he could not meet further calls on his
shares. His only hope was to find new sources of capital
through new partners – and this his old partners clearly appre-
ciated.

In Owen's absence, his partners struck the annual balance
at New Lanark on 31 December 1812. John Atkinson favoured
selling the mills, considering the state of the cotton trade, and
gave his proxy to Alexander Campbell of Hallyards, who was
of the same mind.[50] The other Glasgow partners agreed with
Alexander Campbell, and Owen was clearly outvoted. The
alliance against him could alter the contract of co-partnery or
seek the sequestration of his assets through judicial action.
Owen returned without new partners or fresh capital, told a
formal meeting of the co-partnery on 6 February 1813 that
he was dissatisfied with the valuations placed on all their
shares in New Lanark and suggested that deliberate undervaluation had occurred. His partners, fearful of legal action by
Campbell of Jura, could have been trying to write down the
value of his shares, in case they were compelled, under the
terms of the contract of co-partnery, to buy him out. Yet it was
customary in mercantile accounting to place capital assets at
their liquidation value, even in annual balances, to allow for
sharp fluctuations in trade. Alexander Campbell of Hallyards
probably had the quintessence of the argument: 'supposing
however any undervaluation to have taken place, it is plain
it could not have affected Mr Owen except in the event of
bankruptcy'.

Who could blame Owen for trying to secure the best bargain
for himself, particularly since Alexander Campbell and the

other partners favoured making him bankrupt? Owen was being sued on Archibald Campbell's behalf, and his partners hoped to forestall this legal action. He had also refused 'to contribute his proportion of the necessary funds for the Company's business'.

Meanwhile, in March 1813, Archibald Campbell of Jura, consulted John Clerk of Edinburgh about the best way to secure the outstanding amount of Owen's debt.[51] He believed that Owen's debts exceeded his assets but he wanted to avoid proceeding to sequestration if possible. His counsel advised him to get Owen to complete a trust disposition; this would not make Owen a bankrupt and would require sixty days to become effectual. If Owen could not find fresh guarantors, he could then be made bankrupt, and his partners would be compelled, under clause eight of their contract of co-partnery, to purchase his shares at a price of £23,000, the figure named in the balance of 31 December 1812. In turn, they were obliged to pay off Owen's creditors, in three instalments, from this purchase price.[52] Not surprisingly, Campbell of Jura and his sons decided to act on this advice. Owen was compelled to sign a trust disposition drafted by John Campbell and sent to him for revisions. John Campbell was named in it as trustee, and this clearly gave Campbell of Jura a sound chance of preferential treatment in the allocation of any funds.[53]

Owen's partners could not be expected to stand idly by while Campbell of Jura proceeded to Owen's sequestration. To avoid being compelled to purchase Owen's shares, they rescinded clause eight of their contract and they attempted by rumour and other devices to lower the value of the shares so that if they were compelled by court judgement to purchase New Lanark outright it would be at a very low price. Alexander Campbell of Hallyards justified to John Campbell their repudiation of clause eight on the grounds that a free sale would bring the highest price and this would benefit all Owen's creditors. From the balance of 30 June 1813 the partnership was dissolved.[54] John Campbell clearly thought – and this was also the opinion of John Clerk earlier – that the rescinding of clause eight was illegal. Thus if the partnership had not been formally dissolved Owen might well have become a sacrificial victim in a long legal battle between his partners and his principal creditor. Even if independent accountants appointed by the Court of Session found that his shares in New Lanark had been under-valued, a legally enforced sale would have been inevitable.

Disaster was avoided because Owen's sisters-in-law, led by Jane Maxwell Dale, on 5 July 1813 offered their security for his debt to Campbell of Jura.[55] Owen, on the following day, made arrangements for settlement with John Campbell. A bond was to be executed in Archibald Campbell's favour 'with the Misses Dale as cautioners'. This meant that Owen's sisters-in-law assigned all their property in trust to Archibald Campbell. Repayment was to begin from 11 November 1818 in five annual instalments of £4,000 each; interest calculated from 11 November 1813 was to be paid half-yearly in Glasgow. Before the bond and assignation were duly executed, Owen asked for the return of his 'vouchers' (presumably his promissory notes) from Archibald Campbell.[56]

John Campbell agreed to these arrangements and, provided the bond reached him within eight days, undertook to stop proceedings against Owen. He added:

> I have only further to observe that nothing but the urgent intreaty of the Miss Dales and the desire I have on the Part of my father to give you every accommodation consistent with prudence would have induced me to take their security or to risk their property in any respect, and your having assured me that this measure has met with the concurrence and approbation of . . . their guardians and Trustees . . .[57]

The settlement outlined by Owen duly took place on 15 July 1813 and was recognised by Dale's trustees on 20 and 24 July 1813.[58]

Owen's hope that he would gain a five years' respite as a result of this settlement proved illusory.[59] Before he had begun repayments, the bankruptcy of John More, successor to David Dale at the Royal Bank, produced another crisis. More was constantly in demand as an accountant or trustee on bankrupts' estates; he acted as agent in Glasgow for the Perth bank and also for the Caledonian insurance company. He was factor for Andrew Stirling's trustees and cashier to David Dale's trust.[60] Thus, the news of his financial embarrassment provoked hasty precautions from Campbell of Jura who wrote to his son John on 10 October 1816:

> It having lately come to my knowledge that the affairs of Mr More of the Royal Bank are in a deranged state, and that it is given out, that the Trustees appointed by the late David Dale owe a good deal of money to the Royal Bank, I desire therefore that you will lose no time in enquiring into this matter, as I am at a loss to conceive how it can be . . .

Sometime after 25 September 1816, More's ledger on behalf of Dale's trustees was duly examined,[61] and the Royal Bank, after More had revealed a deficiency to the Deputy Governor on 14 September 1816,[62] proceeded to investigate his books and affairs. In consequence, on 13 January 1817 the Bank claimed £87,285 12s 4d from More's estate (which was sequestrated on 10 December 1816).[63] Of this sum £33,186 8s 10d was in discounted but unretired bills granted on behalf of Dale's trustees by James Craig, Robert Owen and Stewart Douglas, all of whom had been involved between 1806 and 1813 in managing the Stanley cotton mills in Perthshire for the trustees.[64] Interest by 1816 accounted for a further £8,096 12s 9d. These bills, part of the trading capital for the various managers of the mills, were unknown to Dale's trustees – apart from More and Owen – and inevitably recriminations arose.[65]

The Royal Bank presented the bills to Dale's trustees and demanded payment. More's trustee also found a book debt of £9,000 due to him by the Dale trust, and this led to an examination of the affairs of the trust.[66] After taking counsel's opinion in December 1816, the trustees decided to dispute the validity of these bills, to dispose of some of Dale's capital assets, including the Stanley mills, and to stop any further payments to the Misses Dale until Owen repaid Archibald Campbell of Jura. Owen complained that it was unnecessary to penalise the Dales, whose annual receipts came only to £1,000, but he could not repay Campbell.[67] Accordingly, Campbell once more sought John Clerk's legal advice, since he was afraid that the property of the Dale trust was insufficient security for Owen's bond. Clerk advised him to ask Owen for further security and if this was not forthcoming, to adopt drastic measures against Owen and the Dale trustees.[68]

'Arrestment, Inhibition or Adjudication', the ultimate weapons favoured by Clerk, did not prove necessary. From 23 January 1817 Owen was compelled to support the Misses Dale, and the sums involved, together with other minor payments, were credited to him.[69] On 19 March 1817 he approached Campbell of Jura to relieve the Dales from their assignation and in return he offered the New Lanark Company as his security.[70] Although Owen approached his partners in May 1818 about this,[71] Campbell of Jura did not find it necessary to make the change, for when Owen finally discharged his debt to Campbell in November 1822, the Misses Dale were also released from their assignation.[72]

Fear at the thought of losing the case with the Royal Bank inevitably worsened relationships between Owen and his fellow trustees, of which his principal creditor, Campbell of Jura, already jaundiced in his opinion, was one.[73] It was Owen who had been mainly responsible for the financial transactions between More and the trustees, and since he had managed the Stanley mills for them from 20 March to 11 November 1811, many of the disputed bills had been signed by him. In the immediate crisis, when the Dale trustees met daily from 25 to 30 October 1816, Owen attempted to secure the appointment of his confidential clerk, John Wright junior, in place of More. This Archibald Campbell opposed, successfully nominating Donald Cuthbertson, a Glasgow accountant.[74] Meanwhile, in August 1816 Mary Dale had married a litigious parson, the

Reverend James Haldane Stewart of Percy Chapel, St Pancras, and he, in Owen's absence in England, was quite prepared either to make a compromise with the Royal Bank on the best terms available or to sue Owen and the other trustees for misappropriation of funds. Without proof, he later accused Owen as much as More of misappropriation, a story that appeared so incredible to Owen's biographer Podmore that he made no attempt to controvert it.[75]

3

The weaknesses of Owen's autobiography are most clearly evident when he discusses his relations with his partners, particularly in the period 1812–14.[76] They certainly did not act from jealousy and malevolence alone when they wished to end their association with him. It is far more likely that they had sound financial reasons, particularly his credit, to guide them. Profit figures for 1811 and 1812 did not inspire their confidence, and they rightly objected to spending more after, according to Owen's calculations, they had sanctioned improvements costing £30,000. They could not be expected to like Owen's use of Archibald Campbell's money as his share capital nor his refusal to meet his share-calls in 1812. They were legalistic in their treatment of him, but there is little evidence, except Owen's,[77] that they treated him unfairly.

When they began business together in October 1810,[78] they paid £80,000 (£35,600 for the mills and property and £44,400 for the machinery and equipment) but the capital stock was to be £182,000. Of twenty-six shares, Owen took ten (with a paid-up value of £70,000), John Atkinson six (£42,000), Robert Dennistoun four (£28,000), Alexander Campbell of Hallyards three (£21,000), and Colin Campbell three (£21,000). Of the total capital £30,000 was to be paid up by 1 January 1811 and £30,000 the year following. In addition, to meet the purchase price the partners agreed to pay £8,000 per annum for ten years. The remaining £42,000 was to be paid as and when the majority vote of partners decided. Profits were to relieve the partners of the annual advances whenever possible, but there was to be no distribution of profits until the capital was fully subscribed. Following contemporary mercantile custom, interest on capital at the maximum legal bank-rate of 5 per cent was to be distributed annually and was calculated first.

The manager was appointed by the majority of the partners, and according to Scots law had to continue to be acceptable to them. Owen 'from motives of friendship and attachment among the partners' undertook the management without salary but received £1,000 per annum for his expenses. Differences between the partners were to be settled by a majority vote. No partner was to have more than four votes whatever his capital holding: Owen and Atkinson had three each, and the other partners two each. Where the votes were equal, the number of partners determined the decision. Thus, Owen and Atkinson in alliance could not defeat the three Glasgow partners, and if Owen could not hold Atkinson's votes or those of two of his Glasgow partners, he was certain to lose control.

Balances had to be made annually on 1 January, and the books had to be signed by a majority of the partners by 1 July. Any partner wishing to dispose of his shares had to offer them first to his partners. Should any partner be declared bankrupt, his shares were to go to his solvent partners in proportion to their existing capital holdings. They were to pay the value of the bankrupt's shares to his creditors in three instalments, based on the computation made for the last annual balance. Thus, Owen's partners in 1812–13 acted quite properly under their contract. Owen could not expect to be allowed to withdraw funds from the firm when he was not meeting share-calls, nor could he expect to be paid expenses for management when he had ceased to manage. Indeed, it seems possible that he was dismissed from management under the terms of the contract, as the following details of his dealings with Robert Humphreys suggest.

Robert Humphreys,[79] recruited by Owen as under-manager

at New Lanark from Peter Drinkwater's Manchester mill on a twenty-year contract beginning in 1805 or 1806 at a salary of £350 per annum and 2½ per cent of profits, had 'been so unlucky as to have lent the whole of his little fortune to Mr Owen'. This amounted to £2,030 6s 0d (contained in Owen's promissory note) and £100 in cash during the difficult months of 1812 to Mrs Owen at Owen's request. Owen refused to repay after Humphreys left him in 1814.

In 1810–11 Humphreys had begun to be dissatisfied with the terms of his employment, since his share of profits fell below his expectations. He told Owen that he would prefer a fixed salary of £700 per annum from 1 January 1811. Owen agreed to take Humphreys' share of the profits and to pay him an extra £350 per annum but did not reveal this private arrangement to his partners, who objected strongly when they discovered it in June 1812. According to Humphreys, Owen was displaced by his partners 'for this and other instances of impropriety' on 30 June 1812. Humphreys was exonerated and promoted to manager at £700 per annum, since he refused to continue with the previous salary arrangement. Owen's partners quite clearly objected to his making private bargains with 'mill servants', and they also seem to have been disenchanted with Owen, whose affairs in 1812 Humphreys described as in 'disorder . . . arising from his total want of private capital and the smallness of the profits'.

Humphreys, in profit terms, proved a most successful manager, but Owen refused to re-employ him after his new partnership acquired New Lanark in 1814. In February 1814 Humphreys left for Glasgow to set up in business on his own, but Owen still refused to repay his debt. Humphreys certainly needed the money and wrote to Owen in London about it. Owen replied on 23 April 1814, assuring Humphreys that as soon as matters were settled with his former partners he would be repaid, and offered £500 on account via John Wright in Glasgow, if this would help. On 11 June 1814 Humphreys again wrote to Owen asking for repayment and explaining that he had nothing to do with Owen's differences with his former partners. Reluctantly, he threatened legal action. On 17 June 1814 Owen asked Humphreys to send in his account. Five days later Humphreys complied; his capital and interest account was for £2,287 14s 8d. But Owen did not settle the account on 30 June 1814, as he had promised, and on 6 July 1814 Humphreys peremptorily demanded payment. Owen now insisted that he would have to wait with the old company's other creditors until John Wright had made a final balance of the books up to 1 January 1814. He claimed that Humphreys had lent the money to the old company, not to Owen personally, and moreover, that Humphreys was in debt to him under his agreement to accept £350 per annum from Owen in lieu of $2\frac{1}{2}$ per cent of the profits. In court, Owen lost his case and was ordered to repay Humphreys' loan. This episode casts little credit on Owen and corroborates the evidence of the partnership dispute revealed in the Campbell of Jura affair.

Owen's relationships with his partners in the troubled period 1812–14 only become intelligible against the background of his capital accumulation and financial difficulties. His share in New Lanark in 1800 was worth £6,700 fully paid up, and £9,000 in 1810. Meanwhile he had received £10,000 in salary, and unspecified profits which were probably not less than another £10,000. But without access to considerable loan capital from 1810 he could not have met calls on a nominal capital holding of £70,000. Payments due on his shares by 1 January 1812 amounted to nearly £30,000, and these calls were undoubtedly met since this was the value which Owen claimed his shares were worth in correspondence with Campbell of Jura.[80] Yet he disregarded market forces in making this valuation; the liquidation value in 1812–13 might have been less because of the depression in trade. However, undistributed profits might have cushioned this price-fall. Capital accounting at annual balances was normally a hit-and-miss process, depending largely upon the prevailing economic circumstances.[81] Owen

185

made much of the discrepancy between the price (£40,000 to £60,000) which his partners placed on the business in 1812–13 and the price (£114,100) which his new partners paid at the auction in February 1814.[82] But New Lanark's profits boomed in 1813; this his old partners clearly knew even if he did not.

In *A Statement regarding the New Lanark Establishment,* printed by John Moir, an Edinburgh printer, in 1812, Owen outlined his plans for the village and the profit potential in the mills. This refined company prospectus was designed to secure new partners, and at the time that it was printed, the price expected for the establishment was £80,000. Owen claimed that capital additions made since 1810 had produced cost reductions averaging £6,000 per annum. His handicap was unsympathetic partners who had withdrawn their financial support through their inexperience of the practicalities of cotton spinning. Further, trade was complicated by foreign relations which made it necessary to replough profits 'to place the concern beyond the risk of similar events'. But the mills had a remarkable profit-making record. Quality had improved, and quantity of output, productivity and capacity had all progressively increased. The yarn produced was in constant demand from the clothing industry, and 'as soon as peace shall again take place, very abundant profits may be reasonably expected while immediate return of ten per cent on the capital to be advanced, may be confidently calculated upon'.

The detailed social provisions in this pamphlet did not obscure these economic points. Philanthropy was added to profit. Owen placed a capital cost of £200,000 on New Lanark, the equivalent of its turnover. At £80,000 it was a bargain for an 'association of some of the leading and most patriotic characters in the country'. His new partners presented a mixture of pietistic philanthropy and hard-headed acquisitiveness. They were attracted by Owen's obvious humanitarianism and the prospect of risking relatively small proportions of their fortunes on what might well become, on the evidence of Owen's

figures, an extremely profitable investment. Only William
Allen, a man of proven business experience, was apprehensive,
and he worried almost equally about Owen's 'peculiar' religious
views as about the profit potential of New Lanark.[83]

Owen's behaviour when New Lanark was sold by auction in
the Trades House, Glasgow, mirrored his business shrewdness.[84] He kept the identity of his future partners secret and
closeted those who accompanied him from London in a hotel.
He encouraged his old partners to believe that he was their sole
opposition. Yet his offer of £60,000 on the morning of the sale,
had it been accepted, might have embarrassed him more than
them, since his share of the purchase price would have been
£23,000 or 25 per cent less than his own valuation of 1812.
However, his old partners probably knew that the gross profit
of the mills in 1813 had been £52,953 15s 6d and, therefore,
treated his bid with derision. They were thus outmanoeuvred,
because they had to agree to a higher upset price than they had
intended to establish.

Alexander Macgregor, Owen's lawyer, acting on his client's
instructions raised the bid constantly by £100. This should not
be regarded as a pacific gesture nor, necessarily, as an attempt
to secure New Lanark for the lowest possible price. It probably
stimulated Owen's opponents to keep the auction in being. For
we only have Owen's word for the absolute discomfiture of his
old partners when they were finally beaten at £114,100, and
this represented a capital gain of £34,100 on the 1810 price.
The massive profits made in 1813, without Owen's aid or
management, may have muted any rapture felt at the capital
gain. Owen himself gained most, since the value of his paid-up
capital rose to £44,000, a gain of 50 per cent on the valuation
of 1812. His new partners, who had agreed to bid to £120,000
without seeing New Lanark, had to invest cash direct, whereas
Owen could transfer his old shareholding at a higher cash
value. Thus, his five £10,000 shares were easily paid for, and
the undistributed profits from the old partnership would put
him in clover.

4

Owen said surprisingly little about his production and marketing problems compared with the record that he left of his industrial relations and management policies. When he took over the management of New Lanark, he was depressed by the poor quality of the machinery, the labour force and the supervisory staff. John Marshall, the Leeds flax-spinner, went to see the falls of Clyde in September 1800 and passed by New Lanark:

> . . . the cotton works late Mr Dales – 4 large mills 6 stories high abt. 50 yds long each – 2 for twist and 2 for mule spinning. A number of houses are built for the workmen, & 400 or 500 apprentices are lodged in a half of one of the mills which has not yet been worked. They give them $1\frac{1}{2}$ hour's schooling each night after the usual mill hours 7 o clock. The present proprietors it is said wished to give that up, but could not because it was contracted for by Mr Dale in the indentures. Mr Dale not only taught the children reading & writing but the polite accomplishments he had singing masters & one year actually employed 2 dancing masters to teach the factory girls to dance. They weave some muslin, & employ in the whole abt 2000 hands. They are said to be under better discipline & to do more work with fewer hands than in Mr Dales time . . . [85]

Owen made clear attempts to improve the quality of the labour force which had been:

> collected hastily from any place from whence they could be induced to come, and the great majority of them were idle, intemperate, dishonest, devoid of truth and pretenders to religion, which they supposed would cover and excuse all their shortcomings and immoral proceedings . . . [86]

He also had to deal with slack managers who tolerated widespread theft and embezzlement, immorality and drunkenness.[87]

Management practices to prevent theft and to raise productivity were quickly introduced. From his earliest days at New

Lanark, in every room of the mills, he measured productivity per spindle per day and per week, the output of yarn per lb of cotton wool, the hanks per lb of yarn and the waste in every process. He costed labour in all the processes and took snap checks for weeks at a time of individual output. Mill by mill, in a monthly report, he listed the types of cotton wool by origin and by state of processing. He took stocks of yarn at the beginning and the end of the month, calculated the amount of yarn sent from the mills from dispatch books and the quantity of waste. Different cottons were used in different rooms to produce different counts, and this specialisation made detection of theft easier. Hours were carefully totalled, and even repairs were costed.[88] Supervision and delegation of powers was carefully controlled.

Everywhere hung 'silent monitors' or 'telegraphs' to offset the need for corporal punishment by supervisors – or abusive language. These were small four-sided pieces of wood, each side a different colour. The colour set to the front revealed the previous day's standard of behaviour and work effort for each employee. Black indicated bad work. Owen records that he 'passed daily through all the rooms and the workers observed me always to look at these telegraphs – and when black I merely looked at the person and then at the colour'. The standards were entered each day in a book so that the record of every man's work was readily available for Owen's inspection.[89]

Owen gradually reformed the labour force by modifying the environment. He favoured 'sobriety and correct conduct'; he destroyed the trade of the private retailers in the village, all of whom sold spirits; he encouraged temperance but could not achieve abstinence.[90] Whenever possible, he aimed at cleanliness and tidiness in the mills and houses as well as in the people. He hoped 'to give the children such habits as will enable the master of police to keep the village in a decent clean state'.[91] Through the truck shop he reduced the cost of living and supported the school.[92] Like a benevolent despot he tolerated all religions, the distillate of which he saw as charity to others.[93] Religion also had its use in the creation of that inner discipline which Owen wished to encourage. Drill, team dancing and community singing all were used to counteract incipient lawlessness. Dancing, in particular, as Dale had already discovered, had a special value for workers, in that it provided a 'change of motion from their constant occupations . . . most favourable for their spirits, and a strong source of attachment to the works'.[94]

Environmental control and education brought dignity to the labour force and economic advantages to their master. Owen hoped to recruit the best type of labour and in 1812 was certainly thinking in terms of an increase in the supply, possibly because he wanted to introduce twenty-four-hour working:

> giving a double supply of operatives for the same demand, and, of course, constituting a perpetual check against any sudden and great advance of labour, which, in its consequences, is usually as injurious to those employed as to their employers.[95]

The infant school, which admitted children from the age of one, enabled both parents to work. Thus, family incomes could be increased without raising wage-rates.[96] In fact, wage levels at New Lanark were lower *per capita* than elsewhere, but not per family.[97] Similarly, real wages could be raised without increasing unit costs by Owen's policy of bulk purchasing of food and other necessaries. Trade training and home economics played an important part in the curricula for older children and both reduced 'wage drift' and encouraged the recruitment of skilled workers. Parents with ambition and mature adults were inclined to see Owen's social schemes as a special reward for loyal service.[98]

The more intangible effects of Owen's social policies on his career as a businessman can be broadly categorised as relieving those tensions within the community that might have had untoward industrial repercussions. By making New Lanark so famous that its story became part of the tourist literature of the day, he gave the people a special pride in their village and in themselves and encouraged general motivation to work.[99] Every 10lb bundle of yarn bore a label with an idyllic picture of the mills and village upon it.[100] This brand image emphasised communal identity, just as drill and physical exercise tended to restrain anti-social aggression in the children. Output and productivity gains were likely in such an environment; and workers, their initial suspicion allayed, were likely to accept the employer's production management practices.

Owen gradually reduced the number of pauper apprentices in his labour force as a matter of deliberate policy. A monthly report book was kept of the 'boarders' in each room of the mills, with a statement of the time worked.[101] In 1801–2 there were employed in fourteen rooms in the mills:

Girls	Boys	Total
166	98	264

Probably two-thirds of this child labour was apprenticed – paupers originally indentured by the charity houses, mainly in Edinburgh, to Dale[102] – and boarded in No 4 mill, described as 'a lodging house warehouse and workshop'.[103] Significantly, girls outnumbered boys and in this group accounted for 63 per cent. Pauper apprentices met the initial need for a cheap labour force working mainly on piecing broken threads and cleaning machinery, but they presented problems of health, morality and discipline. Nor should it be assumed that they were necessarily cheaper than home-based apprentices, when costs of food, clothing and education were taken into account.

In 1807 John Marshall saw New Lanark once more:

> The present proprietors of the Lanark mills are extending the concern. They have built more houses & are nearly giving up the plan of having parish apprentices. They are said to employ 1600 people, only 100 of which live in Lanark, the rest near the works. Mr Owen is said to be a very strict man & is not popular in the neighbourhood . . .[104]

A more detailed examination of the labour force is possible

for the period 1810–15.[105] At 9 June 1810, there were 479
males, 907 females and a total of 1,386 employed. All the
women and 344 of the males were production workers:

	Male	*Female*	*Total*
No 1 mill	122	345	467
No 2	136	289	425
No 3	86	273	359

The rest of the male labour force consisted of 73 mechanics,
44 labourers, 4 sawers, 1 brassfounder, 5 managers and clerks,
6 storekeepers and 2 teachers. Testimony for the need for
machine-makers and building workers in a period of rapid
development may be found in the relatively large numbers in
the first two categories.

A local census taken on 1 January 1811 found 2,206 people
in the village, of which 328 were lodgers. 1,360 people were
employed in the mills and 846 elsewhere. At the national census taken on 29 June 1811 there were 380 families in the
village, containing 864 males and 1,313 females, a total of
2,177 including lodgers. Occupational census data exists for
the employees at 13 July 1811 and 30 November 1815 and is
summarised in Table 1 on page 208. Over the period there was
a tendency for the mills to retain most of their production
workers, to increase relatively and absolutely the female section of the labour force but to lose male workers, particularly
mechanics and labourers, who might be expected to be the
most mobile. Table 1 corroborates Owen's evidence in 1816
that the number employed by his company varied between
1,500 and 1,600.[106]

Labour problems were constantly important, and discipline
was severely enforced. In May 1813 eight workers were dismissed for 'absence without leave no pay allowed but what
they wrought for'. Mistakes were noted: 'George Williamson
mixed some rove in No 1 room'. Dismissal followed when
Owen 'discovered John Campbell in a fraudulent transaction
altering lines'. Punctual attendance and conscientious perform-
ance of duty were prized, and Owen ordered the spinning

masters in charge of rooms 'that they should inform me when any of themselves or workers wanted to leave for a couple of hours or more the first time I go through the rooms after meals'.[107]

Youthful high spirits provoked more local problems than drunkenness. Local proprietors, like the Edmondstones of Corehouse, found the factory operatives a nuisance in their woodlands.[108] On 20 May 1820 the village boys were forbidden to play 'shinty or clubs or throwing stones because they damage woods, break windows or hurt people'. In July the village boys were 'cautioned against attacking the yeomen with foul language'.[109] Labour discipline for the factory-village owner was certainly a more substantial issue than for town mill-owners.

Humdrum production problems arose principally from power supply difficulties, which led both Dale and Owen into conflict with the Edmondstone sisters about the weir across the Clyde. Possibly the Edmondstones wanted to raise their water-rent and to put political pressure on the local factory-owners. Owen, after a temporary compromise, increased the efficiency of the weir in 1804, but the Edmondstones could not agree to his terms. They complained in 1809 that 'Mr Owen, a man of the greatest acuteness and ability, may affect when it serves his purpose an ignorance of the law which would disgrace the meanest and stupidest of his spinners'. About 1810 a compromise was arranged and their water-rent was raised.[110] The notebook kept between 1813 and 1820 by Owen and his managers reveals a constant preoccupation with water-wheel revolutions. A dry summer or a cold winter could severely affect working.

Problems of lighting caused the dinner hour to be reduced by ten minutes in March 1816, after the introduction of a shorter working day the previous January. In 1818 Owen had the clocks put on thirty minutes in the summer and then put back in October. Shortages of raw material or excessive cotton wool prices also affected working. In the winter of 1814–15

M   193

weather conditions made transport difficult; in the autumn of 1814 supplies were simply inadequate.[111] The American embargo after 1807 led Owen to suspend production because of high cotton prices, but he still paid wages.[112]

No 3 mule mill, on 26 November 1819, was burned 'to the ground except a few stretching frames and mules saved from the west end'.[113] Owen, who was in London, promptly left for New Lanark after a plaintive message to Jeremy Bentham:

> I regret to inform you that I have received intelligence from Lanark that one of the large Mills & attendant buildings have been destroyed by fire. The loss of actual property is chiefly I hope indeed altogether covered but the inconveniences . . . arising from such an event cannot be Insured . . .[114]

Previously, in June 1814 for instance, there had been intermittent night work, but Owen placed No 4 mill, also a mule mill, on twenty-four-hour working from 6 December 1819 and re-deployed the labour force. By 13 and 14 December the following instructions had been relayed to supervisors by his manager who

> told all first masters and many seconds that no person would get to inside of gates till last Bell rings in morning and all masters must be in their places 10 minutes before six am, 4, 5 or 6 minutes before home time at breakfast and dinner. A master must always be along with the person who lights Lamps or Candles, none of Little stoves shall be lighted till after the workers come in.
>
> It is not expected that a master shall come within the gates in the slightest degree intoxicated particularly after New Year, Lanimer and St James Fair days or even 14 January. Altho this has been mentioned it is a fault that the villagers are very seldom guilty of. they are a temperate body of people.[115]

No matter what Owen's avowed position on religion, his manager enforced regulations which the acquisitively devout could support:

> no young women who are in a state of pregnancy can be allowed to stop in the works when unable to perform their

194

usual quantity or keep up their work as usual. those who are unfortunate cannot be admitted until they have satisfied the church where [they] keep session.

Business efficiency and good morals went hand in hand!

5

Many variables clearly affected the profitability of Owen's economic activities at New Lanark. The most important was certainly the volatile nature of the cotton-wool and yarn markets. Prices of raw cotton were affected by American government action before and during the war of 1812 and by the prevailing circumstances in the West Indies and the United States. There was, apart from seasonal fluctuations, a marked price rise after 1807 and a sharp fall after 1814 until the mid 1820s. By 1819 New Orleans cotton brought on average per lb one-third the price of 1814. There were substantial but less spectacular price falls for Bowed Georgia, Pernambuco and Demerara. Although Owen purchased fifteen different types of cotton for New Lanark, those named were most commonly used.[116]

Throughout Owen's time yarn counts were medium to low, mainly in the 20s and 30s by 1818 – with a range from 9 to 46 hanks per lb – the mule yarns being the finest.[117] Table 2 on page 209 summarises the known data on output, average counts, and labour costs per lb. Owen's concentration on lower counts and substantial European sales, especially in Russia, probably restricted the effects of downturns in prices, but the yarn market was exceedingly volatile especially after 1815. Yet because of the inadequacies of the surviving balance sheets we have no real picture of turnover to match output and cost figures. In general, it seems most likely that the business was rarely at full capacity except possibly in 1812 and 1820. Yet labour costs fell, despite gradually increasing yarn counts, except in the period 1805 to 1809.

Foreign sales were clearly geared to the Russian market

which was supplied directly, but no doubt some domestic sales to the more important Glasgow yarn brokers, like James Finlay & Company, went indirectly overseas. Small direct consignments were also sent to Smyrna and Trieste, St Petersburg was, however, the most important port in New Lanark's foreign trade.[118] According to Owen, 10,080 bundles of yarn were consigned to Russia in 1812,[119] and an important reason given for the recovery of the firm in 1812–13 was the defeat of the French.[120] After the battle of Leipzig in 1813 profits certainly increased. Table 3 on page 210 summarises the data fragments about sales to Russia from 1817 to 1823. In December 1825 John Wright gave the November yarn sales as about 9,000 bundles, of which 'country agents' (in Scotland) took 1,000 and the Russian market 3,500. Because of foreign demand, Wright explained, New Lanark was not feeling the effects of the collapse of the domestic boom.[121]

Allan Stewart & Company acted as agents for Robert Owen & Company in Russia.[122] J. H. Brink & Company in Elberfeld and William Teager & Company in Amsterdam organised yarn shipments from Holland to the Baltic in 1815–16, although Owen occasionally took charge of negotiations for shipping space at Leith. Competition from other yarn-producers was slight in Russia before that date. There were the English, of course, and some Americans selling mainly candlewick yarns. But Allan Stewart in August 1815 made clear to Owen how novel this was – 'This new competition we little thought of'.

The fortunate speculator who was well organised could make substantial profits because of sharp price changes in the Russian yarn market. For instance, in August 1815 Stewart reported:

As to cotton yarn the trade is absolutely at a stand for want of goods. Those who lately bought will not part with their goods for almost any price & therefore we have not heard of sales since our last. In Mosco prices are rising every day . . . Our anxiety to hear of further shipments from you is now raised to the highest pitch & we intreat you to bear in mind that Libau will in all probability be open for 3 months at least . . .

But Scottish and other yarn consignments rapidly saturated the market, which by the end of 1815 was very dull. However, in 1815 Stewart bought and sold 83,000 Russian poods [nearly 3 million lbs] of cotton yarn and, in addition, disposed of the surplus from 1814. The greatest demand had been for twist of counts 26 to 40 and for mule yarns from 30 to 46.

Apart from the clearly speculative nature of supplying yarn on consignment, which no doubt obtained in other foreign markets equally, there were additional difficulties in supplying the Russian market. If a chartered ship had to winter in Russia, the cost of freight zoomed. Similarly, supplying local markets in Russia was not easy in the winter. Because of the primitive nature of Russian regional economies in the interior, it was especially difficult to forecast demand. Credit facilities were bad, dealers were often short of liquid capital and, therefore, it was often necessary to give long-term credit, an exceedingly risky undertaking. Government intentions about customs duties and arbitrary interference in trade also posed difficulties. Commonly there were exchange problems which made it difficult to realise sterling or bullion for return to Scotland. Late payments from this market could account for dramatic changes in the apparent profitability of New Lanark. The balance figures in Table 3, recording receipts from sales in Russia, show marked fluctuations within and between years.

Sales of New Lanark yarn were made throughout Britain, a consequence of effective public relations as well as energetic marketing. In March 1820 accounts outstanding existed for Dublin, for Norwich and Carlisle in England, as well as for Edinburgh, Kirkcaldy, Perth and Glasgow.[123] Earlier, cases for debt in the Court of Session were raised by Owen against customers in Dysart, Fife, and Langholm near the English border.[124] A yarn order book detailing production in No 1 and No 2 mills in 1811–12 shows that Owen changed the mills

197

rapidly to suit demand but was spinning in these twist mills no count over 20 or under 9.[125] 9,000 bundles of yarn ordered for Norwich on 1 November 1811 consisted of 500 of No 17, 6,000 of No 18, 1,500 of No 19 and 1,000 of No 20. In January and February 1812, 1,760 bundles of numbers 24 to 40 were sent out. Later production records for 1818–20 show that the mule mills produced these higher counts, but supply from them was relatively inelastic, even at their most profitable, with twenty-four-hour working at full capacity.

Glasgow was the most important local market for cotton wool and yarn. There were eighteen Glasgow customers recorded in the balance sheet for the quarter ending 31 December 1820.[126] In addition, James Finlay & Company, Glasgow's most important cotton brokers and yarn dealers, and John Bartholomew & Company, shirt manufacturers, had large accounts. Glasgow sales, excluding sales to these two, for the period 1814–15 are summarised in Table 4 on page 210. The outstanding balances due from James Finlay & Company in the period 1818–23 are given in Table 5 (page 211). The personal and business relationships between Robert Owen and Kirkman Finlay were very close!

Unit freight costs to and from Glasgow were reduced by the co-ordination of raw-material supplies and yarn deliveries. Yet transport remained an important business problem for Robert Owen, particularly since the best seasons for easy transport were also peak farming periods when carriers were able to raise charges. Inventories were, therefore, often considerable, and this made accountancy and control more difficult.[127] The valuations placed on wool or yarn stocks might not be realised in practice. Price falls tended to be double-edged, but Owen preferred low cotton-wool prices, as may be gathered from a letter to his partner Jeremy Bentham on 23 October 1818:

> There has been a considerable fall in the prices of cotton lately & this effects [sic] the value of our stock on hand which on so large a scale as ours must always be considerable. Our

annual balance [will be] therefore less favourable than a few weeks ago I expected it would be. Our stocks of cotton . . . are comparatively light & the decline in prices is a temporary evil which generally produces a more permanent benefit. Cotton spinning is the best trade when the raw material is low & for the last two years, owing to speculations in the trade, it has been much above the usual peace prices – these speculators are now suffering by the fall & the article is likely to fall to its proper material value.[128]

Stocks, none the less, probably represented at least 10 per cent of turnover, and in periods of slack demand might rise much higher. The complete inventory picture depended ultimately upon stock held at the Glasgow warehouse. At 30 June 1822 total stock of cotton wool stood at 1,251 bags (315,269lbs) and was valued after discount at £11,984 8s 8d; 9,775¾ bundles of water twist (no count over 42) was worth £7,869 11s 3d, and 2,842 bundles of mule twist (no count over 44) were valued at £2,005 6s 3d. Loose cotton yarn at the mills accounted for £1,879 15s 10d, and loose cotton wool for £589 5s 4d.[129]

Profit figures for New Lanark during Owen's time there are summarised, partnership by partnership, in Table 6 on pages 211-13. John Wright who kept the books in Glasgow after 1810 could not give Owen any information (when Owen was preparing his autobiography) before that date, since earlier books were kept in Manchester. But on Wright's balance is written in Owen's hand £60,000 for profit during the years 1799–1810,[130] and this took no account of the normal 5 per cent 'interest' on capital.[131] Thus, Owen estimated gross profit at £90,000, 150 per cent on capital or an annual return of 15 per cent.

The second partnership from 1811 to 1814 made a gross profit, according to Wright, of £109,871 12s 3d (including the capital gain on the mills). This represented 137 per cent on capital or an annual return of nearly 46 per cent. The third partnership, during the period of Owen's management from 1814 to 1825, made a gross profit at New Lanark – allowing for capital depreciation and a loss made at Stanley mills in

1814 – of £192,915 11s 4d, about 169 per cent on capital, or an annual return of just over 15 per cent. Owen ceased to be managing partner officially from September 1825, although by then he was already in New Harmony.[132] Gross profit for the next three years, with Walker in charge, was only £6,558 16s, most of which came from the capital fund normally set aside to cover bad debts. Total gross profit for Owen's complete period as a partner 1799 to 1828 – he still had as much as £6,000 with the company in November 1831 – was £399,345 19s 7d.

Wright's figures have never been given before, but they can be confirmed in detail from other data fragments.[133] Table 6 follows the mercantile conventions of Owen's day, but I have added a gross profit figure which he would not have calculated, since the 'interest' of 5 per cent on capital was calculated first. The course of profit figures from 1811 follows generally the pattern of British trade cycles, although 1825 was a surprisingly bad year for New Lanark, possibly associated with Owen's departure for New Harmony.

The capital of £130,000 for Owen's last partnership was not fully paid up until 1816 – £76,548 8s 4d in 1814, £90,977 5s in 1815 – and the new partners agreed not to draw any profits until the end of 1817, when they could draw all that year's profits and one-third of those for 1816.[134] The profit accounts of the individual partners, as shown in balance sheets, are given on page 214, in Table 7. Owen's shares in New Lanark are not, of course, counted in this computation but they must have been worth at least £50,000, for his partners offered one share to John Wright in 1825 at £12,600.[135] His approximate share of gross profits was:

1799–1810	£10,000
1810–14	42,000
1814–25	74,000
1825–28	2,500
Total	£128,500

However, in the period covered by Table 7, Owen clearly ran

his profit account down. Meanwhile, John Walker's profit account tended to rise, making his family's succession to New Lanark more and more inevitable.

Significantly, William Allen's account was given separately from that of the other partners, for he and Owen constantly clashed after 1820. On 21 August 1822 he exercised his right to call an extraordinary meeting of the partners

> to take into consideration the propriety of purchasing Three of the Shares belonging to Robert Owen on such terms as may be agreed upon, and to make such regulations as shall be necessary to give effect to the said purchase. And to take *steps* into consideration the propriety of making regulations for the future conduct of the concern . . .[136]

For 31 July 1823 he arranged a meeting at which 'the question of the Continuance of Robt Owen as Manager will be brought forward'.[137] At the end of the same year Owen proposed to transfer one of his shares to Robert Dale Owen and another to William Owen.[138] As Mrs Browning has indicated, the quarrel between Allen and Owen was fundamental.[139] It was to lead to the transformation of Owen from the businessman to the harbinger of the New Moral World.

6

Sufficient has been said to answer those, including Podmore,[140] who allowed Owen's failure in later community ventures to cloud their judgement of his business capacities. It is certain that his financial shrewdness – and indeed, sharpness – his profit-making capacities and his management skills did not satisfy him, since he was essentially a visionary. Practically, however, his time at New Lanark was spent as an employing genius, the managing partner of an untypically large concern. There can be no doubt about his abilities as a businessman for in these, too, he was a precursor of the twentieth century rather than a representative of his own day.

NOTES

1 P. Gorb, 'Robert Owen as a Businessman', *Bulletin of the Business Historical Society* 25 (Sept 1951), 127–48 ; W. H. Chaloner, 'Robert Owen, Peter Drinkwater and the Early Factory System in Manchester, 1788–1800', *Bulletin of the John Rylands Library* 37 (Sept 1954), 78–102 ; A. J. Robertson, 'Robert Owen and the Campbell Debt 1810–22', *Business History* 11 (Jan 1969), 23–30 ; cf also my forthcoming introduction to reprint of *The Life of Robert Owen Written by Himself* and my 'Robert Owen at New Lanark', *Bulletin of the Robert Owen Bi-Centenary Association* 1 (May 1970), 8–10

2 *The Life of Robert Owen Written by Himself* Vol 1 (1857), 1-21 [hereafter *Life* 1]

3 Ibid, 22–6 ; F. Podmore, *Robert Owen* 1 (1906), 42–3

4 Chaloner, loc cit ; C. H. Drinkwater and W. G. D. Fletcher, *The Family of Drinkwater* (1920) ; Drinkwater's assets were insured 4 Jan 1793 by the Sun and Royal Exchange companies for £28,800 (including mills in Manchester and Northwich), London Guildhall Library MSS 11937, Sun Policy Registers, CD series 609997

5 I am grateful to Dr Jennifer Tann who drew my attention to a plan of this mill in the Boulton & Watt papers

6 This is clear from the insurance policies

7 London Guildhall Library, Royal Exchange Policy Registers 32/155197 1 Feb 1797, and 32a/157251 24 June 1797. I am most grateful to Dr S. D. Chapman for these references

8 Guildhall Library MS 11937/20, Sun Policy 671532 19 Oct 1797

9 Guildhall Library MS 11937/30, Sun Policy 698554 23 Jan 1800

10 *Life* 1, 42

11 Ibid, 43–6

12 Ibid, 47

13 G. Stewart, *Curiosities of Glasgow Citizenship* (Glasgow 1881), 45–64

14 *Life* 1, 47–50, 55

15 Robertson, loc cit

16 *Life* 1, 53 ; Co-operative Union Manchester, Owen Correspondence 2100, John Wright to Robert Owen 10 Jan 1853

17 Guildhall Library MS 11937/37, Sun Policy 713909 14 Jan 1801

18 SRO, Campbell of Jura Muniments GD64/1/247, Owen to Campbell 17 Oct 1810

[19] SRO, GD64/1/247, Memo of the estate of the late David Dale . . . 1816; Gourock Ropework Company MSS, Head Office Port Glasgow, Balance Sheets 1818–19 [hereafter Gourock MSS]

[20] Dale established his trust by a disposition dated 10 Mar 1804 and registered in the Books of Council and Session 29 Mar 1806. His will was dated 10 Nov 1804 and recorded in the Commissary Books of Lanarkshire

[21] SRO, GD64/1/247, Memo of the estate of the late David Dale 1816

[22] Guildhall Library MSS 11937/38, Sun Policy 716403 2 Mar 1801, and 11937/31 Sun Policy 701044 27 Mar 1800

[23] *Life* 1, 78

[24] Ibid, 71–7

[25] Anon, Some Glasgow customers of the Royal Bank around 1800, *Three Banks Review* 48 (Dec 1960), 38

[26] Brotherton Library Leeds, MS 200, Tour Book of John Marshall 1800, f32. I am grateful to Dr S. D. Chapman for this reference

[27] cf Stewart, op cit, 168 ; *Life* 1, Appendix E, F, 107

[28] cf Robertson, loc cit

[29] The following remarks are based on SRO, GD64/1/247 and especially GD64/1/315, Draft case for opinion by Mrs Dennistoun [née Ann Penelope Campbell, eldest daughter of Archibald] and Mrs Campbell [née Barbara Campbell, second daughter] concerning the rights of legitim. upon the estate of their deceased father, Sept 1835 ; cf also *Burkes Landed Gentry* (1962), 363

[30] Robertson, op cit, 24

[31] SRO, GD64/1/247, Annual Statement of R. Owen's account with Campbell of Jura and accompanying letter, R. Owen to A. Campbell 30 Apr 1810

[32] Robertson, op cit, 24, says that the New Lanark Twist Company was dissolved in 1809, but it seems more likely that the dissolution was in 1810, the last balance of the old company being 31 Dec 1809, and the basis for later partnership negotiations. *Life* 1, 85 may be misleading on this point. The contract of copartnery of the new company is clearly dated 5 Oct 1810 and possibly ran retrospectively from 1 Jan 1810, although balances give 1811 as the first year of this partnership

[33] SRO, GD64/1/199, Contract of Marriage, Dennistoun, a Glasgow merchant in the West Indian trade, married Ann Penelope Campbell 2 Oct 1797 ; GD64/1/235, he received £1,000 dowry

[34] SRO, GD64/1/201, Campbell of Hallyards, also in the West Indian trade, married Barbara Campbell 16 Aug 1800 ; GD64/1/243, he also received £1,000 dowry

[35] SRO, GD64/1/247, Owen to Campbell of Jura 17 Oct 1810

[36] Ibid, Owen to Campbell of Jura 10 Nov 1810

[37] Ibid, Memorial and Queries for Archibald Campbell of Jura 8 Mar 1813

38 Ibid, Owen to Campbell of Jura 1 May 1811
39 Ibid, copy letter, John Campbell to Owen, 16 Aug 1812
40 Ibid, Owen to Campbell of Jura 1 May 1812
41 *Life* 1, 87 ; certainly Campbell knew of Owen's indiscretion by 1 May 1812, since Owen, in his letter of that date stated: 'In future no one else will know anything of your account, as you request, but those to whom you may yourself wish to disclose it.'
42 SRO, GD64/1/247, Owen to Campbell of Jura 1 May 1812
43 Ibid, Owen to Campbell of Jura 29 July 1812 via John Campbell WS
44 Ibid, Campbell of Hallyards to John Campbell 16 Aug 1812
45 Ibid, Colin Campbell to John Campbell 16 Aug 1812
46 Ibid, copy letter, John Campbell to Owen 16 Aug 1812
47 Ibid, copy letter, Owen to John Campbell 8 Oct 1812
48 Ibid, John Campbell to C. Campbell and A. Clawson 7 Nov 1812
49 Ibid, C. Campbell to J. Campbell 11 Nov 1812
50 Ibid, Campbell of Hallyards to John Campbell 5 July 1813
51 cf Robertson, op cit, 26–7
52 SRO, GD64/1/247, Memorial and Queries for Archibald Campbell of Jura, 8 Mar 1813 ; copy contract of co-partnery of New Lanark Company 1810
53 Ibid, copy Trust Disposition by Robert Owen 19 Mar 1813
54 Ibid, Campbell of Hallyards to John Campbell 5 July 1813 ; cf also *Life* 1, 88
55 SRO, GD64/1/247, Jane M. Dale to Colin Campbell 5 July 1813
56 Ibid, Owen to John Campbell 6 July 1813
57 Ibid, copy letter, John Campbell to Owen 6 July 1813
58 Ibid, copy bond between R. Owen, Misses Dale and A. Campbell of Jura 15 July 1813 ; copy assignation by Misses Dale in favour of A. Campbell of Jura ; Dale Trustees to Misses Dale 20 and 24 July 1813
59 cf Robertson, op cit, 29
60 SRO, RH15/916, Sederunt Book of John More 1816–19, 95–6, 122
61 Ibid, GD64/1/247, copy minutes of Dale Trustees 25 Oct 1816
62 Ibid, RH15/916, 108–110
63 Ibid, 13
64 Ibid, GD64/1/247 copy minutes of Dale Trustees 25 Oct 1816 ; Memorial and Queries for Archibald Campbell of Jura 27 Dec 1816 ; copy Memorial relative to the action at the instance of the Royal Bank against Dale's Trustees 1818 ; Extracted Process, FSM 3 June 1819, Royal Bank of Scotland v the Trustees of the late David Dale, Esq.
65 Ibid, GD64/1/247, copy minutes of Dale Trustees 25 Oct 1816
66 Ibid, copy report regarding the bills claimed by the Royal Bank of Scotland as due to them by the Stanley Company by Alexander Dick, 1 Mar 1817 ; RH15/916, 17, 147

[67] Ibid, GD64/1/247, copy minutes of Dale Trustees, 26, 28, 29 Oct 1816; Memorial for the Trustees of the late David Dale and opinion of counsel thereon Dec 1816

[68] Ibid, Memorial and Queries for Archibald Campbell of Jura, 27 Dec 1816; cf GD64/1/301, with Memorial and Queries . . . 2 Dec 1816

[69] Ibid, copy minutes of Dale Trustees 23 Jan 1817

[70] Ibid, Owen to John Campbell 19 Mar 1817

[71] British Museum, Add MSS 33545 Bentham papers, f286, Owen to Jeremy Bentham 15 May 1818, f287 16 May 1818

[72] SRO, GD64/1/247, Draft discharge by A. Campbell of Jura to R. Owen and Misses Dale Nov 1822; as late as 28 July 1856 Dale's trust estate was valued at about £12,800 (Co-operative Union, Owen Correspondence 2659, Robert Dale Owen to Robert Owen from Naples 28 July 1856)

[73] SRO, GD64/1/247, Abstract of the statement of the sums advanced by the late Mr Dale and his trustees on Acct of the Stanley Cotton Mills to 22 Oct 1816. By 1819 capital and interest amounted to £42,996 19s 6d, and this amount was awarded by the Court of Session to the Royal Bank (Register of Acts and Decrees, FSI xxi, 23 Feb 1819). The trustees paid £17,126 19s 6d in Royal Bank stock (and interest on this in the period of the case) but still had to find £25,870 (SRO, EP FSM, 3 June 1819). But since the Royal Bank stock had only been valued by the trustees at £11,366 in Nov 1816, it is certainly possible that Dale's other assets, notably Forth & Clyde Canal stock, were similarly undervalued. Eventually, a net balance of £40,000 on the Dale Trust account was agreed as reasonable (GD64/1/247)

[74] Ibid, copy minutes of Dale Trustees 30 Oct 1816

[75] Ibid, Account of sums advanced to Miss Mary Dale, 9 Dec 1806–24 Sept 1816; copy Memorial for the Trustees of the late David Dale and opinion of counsel 7 March 1817; D. Dale Stewart, *Memoirs of James Haldane Stewart* (1856), 73; F. Podmore, *Robert Owen* 2 (1907), 643

[76] cf *Life* 1, 85–7

[77] Ibid, 87–8; GD64/1/247, state of affairs of Robert Owen as on 30 June 1813

[78] The following remarks are based on SRO, GD64/1/247, copy contract of Co-partnership of the New Lanark Company, 5 Oct 1810

[79] Chaloner, op cit, 94, 98; *Life* 1, 59, 91; Signet Library Edinburgh, Session Papers 631;17, Humphreys v Owen 1815

[80] SRO, GD64/1/247, State of the affairs of Robert Owen as on 30 June 1813

[81] S. Pollard, 'Capital Accounting in the Industrial Revolution', *Yorkshire Bulletin of Economic and Social Research* Nov 1963

[82] *Life* 1, 80–90

[83] *Life of William Allen* 1 (1846), 180, 209. But Allen remained a partner until 1829 (BM, Add MSS 33546, Bentham papers f267, Allen to Bentham 19 Mar 1829)

[84] *Life* 1, 90–1

[85] Brotherton Library Leeds, MS 200, Tour Book of John Marshall 1800, f30–2 ; I am most grateful to Dr S. D. Chapman for this reference and also to the staff of the Brotherton Library for their courteous help

[86] *Life* 1, 57

[87] Ibid

[88] Gourock MSS, Produce Books 1802–6

[89] *Life* 1, 80 ; Podmore 1, op cit, 90–1

[90] R. D. Owen, *Threading My Way* (1874) 70 ; Podmore 1, op cit, 84–6 n

[91] *A Statement regarding the New Lanark Establishment* (1812), 10–13 ; cf *The New Existence of Man upon Earth* (1854), Part V Appendix

[92] *PP* 1816 III, Select Committee on the Employment of Children in Factories, 20ff

[93] cf *A Supplementary Appendix to the First Volume of the Life of Robert Owen* Vol 1A (1858) [hereafter *Life* 1A], Appendix Q, 245 ; *The Contrast or Scotland as it was in the year 1745 and Scotland in 1819* (1825), 261

[94] *A Statement regarding the New Lanark Establishment* (1812), 15

[95] Ibid, 19

[96] *The Contrast*, 263

[97] *Life* 1A, Appendix R, 256

[98] Ibid, Appendix W, 329 ; One formerly a Teacher at New Lanark [author] *Robert Owen at New Lanark* (Manchester 1839)

[99] *A Statement regarding the New Lanark Establishment* (Edinburgh 1812), 20–1 ; *Life* 1A, 254–5, 329

[100] R. D. Owen, *Threading My Way* (1874), 243 n

[101] Gourock MSS, Boarders' Monthly Report Book, 1801–2

[102] *Life* 1, 60

[103] Guildhall Library MS 71937/38, Sun Policy 716403 2 Mar 1801

[104] Brotherton Library MS 200, Tour Book of John Marshall 1807, f67

[105] Gourock MSS

[106] PP 1816 III, Select Committee on the State of Children employed in Manufactories, 20 ff

[107] Gourock MSS, Notebook 1813–20

[108] SRO, UP Innes Mack L 14/9, Lanark Twist Company v Edmonstoun 1810

[109] Gourock MSS, Notebook 1813–20

[110] SRO, UP Innes Mack L 14/9 ; Gourock MSS, Balance Sheet 31 Mar 1820

[111] Gourock MSS, Notebook 1813–20

[112] *Life* 1, 63
[113] Gourock MSS, Notebook 1813–20
[114] BM, Add MSS 33545 Bentham Papers, f372, Owen to Bentham 1 Dec 1819
[115] Gourock MSS, Notebook 1813–20
[116] Ibid, Cotton Purchase and Order Books 1811 and 1814–20
[117] Ibid, Produce Books
[118] Gourock MSS, Balance Sheets 1818–23
[119] SRO, GD64/1/247 Campbell of Jura Muniments, Note of Errors in Valuation of Stock of the New Lanark Company by Robt Owen Esq 1813
[120] Signet Library, Court of Session Papers 631 ; 17, 8–9
[121] Holyoake House MSS Manchester, Owen Correspondence 80, J. Wright to Owen 10 Dec 1825
[122] This and subsequent paragraphs are based on Gourock MSS, copy letter book between Allan Stewart & Co and R. Owen & Co 1815–16
[123] Gourock MSS, Balance Sheet 31 Mar 1820
[124] SRO, UP Skene 07/4 v Dobie 11 Feb 1808 ; 07/3 Owen v Young 13 Feb 1808
[125] Gourock MSS, Yarn Order Book 1811–12
[126] Ibid, Balance Sheet 31 Dec 1820
[127] This is apparent from balance sheets.
[128] BM, Add MSS 33545, f338
[129] Gourock MSS, Balance Sheet 30 June 1822
[130] Co-operative Union, Owen Correspondence 2100, J. Wright to R. Owen 10 January 1853
[131] cf *Life* 1, 87 ; R. D. Owen, *Threading My Way* (1874), 78
[132] Owen Correspondence 80, J. Wright to R. Owen 10 Dec 1825
[133] BM, Add MSS 33545, f260, Owen to Bentham 8 Feb 1818 ; f392, Owen to Bentham 21 Feb 1820 ; Gourock MSS, Quarterly balance sheets 1818–23 ; Signet Library, 631 ;17, Humphreys v Owen 1815 ; Owen Correspondence 70, J. Wright to Owen 6 May 1825 ; SRO, GD64/1/247, Campbell of Jura Muniments, State of Affairs of Robert Owen as on 30 June 1813 and Excerpts from the books of the New Lanark Company as relating to the balance struck by them on 31 Dec 1812. Cf J. F. C. Harrison, *Robert Owen and the Owenites in Britain and America* (1969), 154–5 n
[134] BM, Add MSS 33545, f260, Owen to Bentham 8 Feb 1818
[135] Owen Correspondence 80, J. Wright to Owen 10 Dec 1825
[136] BM, Add MSS 33545, f590, Allen to Bentham 21 Aug 1822 ; cf W. Allen, *Life of William Allen* 1 (1846), 209, 344, 346, 363
[137] BM, Add MSS, 33545, f629, Allen to J. Mill 25 July 1823
[138] Ibid, f641, Owen to Bentham 31 Dec 1823
[139] vide infra 70
[140] Podmore, *Robert Owen* 2, 642–4

The author is grateful for help which he received from a number of individuals and organisations: the staffs of the London Guildhall Library, the Scottish Record Office, the Signet Library; Mr A. C. Dunsmore and the Gourock Ropework Company; Dr S. D. Chapman who drew his attention to relevant insurance policies and often kindly provided transcripts; W. H. Fraser for transcripts of the Owen correspondence in Manchester; J. R. Hume who worked jointly on the Gourock Ropework Company MSS; J. H. Treble for transcripts from the Bentham correspondence in the British Museum; John Robertson who drew on a number of references to Robert Owen in his own collection; the Social Science Research Council who provided generous support for this study.

APPENDIX

Table 1   Occupational Census of the Labour Force at New Lanark 1811 and 1815

	1811: Male	Female	Total	1815: Male	Female	Total
No 1 Mill: Picking	11	108	119	12	96	108
Carding	74	116	190	78	101	179
Spinning	61	140	201	45	150	195
Reeling & Sorting	4	44	48	7	39	46
Total for No 1 Mill	150	408	558	142	386	528
No 2 Mill: Picking	—	29	29	—	105	105
Carding	80	103	183	76	95	171
Spinning	74	114	188	55	143	198
Reeling & Sorting	9	37	46	7	38	45
Total for No 2 Mill	163	283	446	138	381	519
No 3 Mill: Picking	5	32	37	3	28	31
Carding	81	101	182	58	73	131
Spinning	19	116	135	16	103	119
Reeling & Sorting	7	37	44	7	38	45
Total for No 3 Mill	112	286	398	84	242	326
Mechanics	91		91	58		58
Labourers	50		50	22		22
Managers etc	8		8	7		7
Schoolmasters	2		2		2	2
Storekeepers	9		9	8		8
Extras	—	—	—	7	3	10
Grand Totals	585	977	1,562	466	1,014	1,480

Source: Gourock Ropework Company MSS

Table 2   New Lanark's Production and Labour Costs

Year	Yarn Output lbs	Average Count (hanks per lb.)	Labour Cost per lb (pence)
1801	514,750	24.5	5.5
1802	584,325	24	5.4
1803	510,175	24.4	5.4
1805	736,925	23.4	6.1
1809	1,146,842	18	9.5
1810	1,440,895	18	9.1
1811	1,620,373	18.5	8.9
1812	1,622,070	19.25	7.5
1814	1,385,390	25	4.7
1815	1,451,947	24.5	4
1816	1,339,434	26.5	5.4
1817	1,424,513	25.8	5.2
1818	1,457,096	24.2	4.9
1819	1,465,445	24.8	5.1
1820	1,459,094	27.2	5.3
1821	1,377,580	27	5.2

Sources: Gourock Ropework Company MSS Owen Correspondence, Manchester, 129

Notes:

1   1801–05 figures based on produce books have been estimated on the basis of December figures in each year. More work is in progress on this source.

2   Labour cost 1809–11 may include some element of capital cost but are Owen's own figures. Dispensing with child labour may also have raised costs.

3   Figures for output after 1809 higher because of additional mill in operation.

4   1820–21 figures include night-working costs after No 3 mill was destroyed in 1819.

Table 3   Value of Russian Sales

Date of Balance

		£	s	d
30 June 1819:	1818 sales	4,145	9	1
31 Dec 1818:	1819 sales	12,422	11	4
	1818 sales	26,188	16	3
30 June 1818:	1817 sales	24,014	3	6
	1818 sales	22,802	19	10
31 Mar 1820		2,367	19	10
30 June 1820		24,305	8	6
30 Sept 1820		39,874	0	4
31 Dec 1820		25,659	2	5
31 Dec 1821		21,299	8	6
31 Mar 1822		13,634	19	6
20 June 1822		19,121	1	8
31 Dec 1822		9,585	3	6
30 Sept 1823		14,374	7	11

Source: Gourock Ropework Company MSS, Balance Sheets 1818–23

Table 4   Glasgow Sales (£) 1814–15

	£	s	d
Sales to March 1814	9,076	16	1
April	15,154	18	2
May	14,289	15	9
June	5,843	6	0
July	13,139	11	10
August	10,410	3	6
September	10,276	0	10
October	9,486	6	10
November	14,889	1	1
December	Missing		
January 1815	3,181	13	11
February	3,916	12	8
March	9,469	5	2
April	7,818	11	5
May	14,020	15	6

Source: Gourock Ropework Company MSS, Salesbook 1814–15

Table 5   Outstanding Account with James Finlay & Company (£)

Balance Date	£	s	d
30 June 1818	12,899	12	8
31 Mar 1820	2,062	15	3
30 June 1820	21,440	11	4
30 Sept 1820	25,119	8	8
31 Dec 1820	24,658	15	0
31 Dec 1821	9,347	1	0
31 Mar 1822	8,147	2	4
30 June 1822	4,204	9	4
31 Dec 1822	4,373	14	0
30 Sept 1823	397	12	5

Source: Gourock Ropework Company MSS, Balance Sheets 1818–23

Table 6(a) Profits at New Lanark 1810–14
New Lanark Twist Company

Year	Profit/Loss			'Interest'	Gross Profit		
	£	s	d	£	£	s	d
1811	8,817	16	9	3,000	11,817	16	9
1812	8,000	0	0	3,000	11,000	0	0
1813	49,953	15	6	3,000	52,953	15	6
Totals	66,771	12	3	9,000	75,771	12	3
Capital gain from sale of mills					34,100	0	0
Total gross gain from partnership 1810–14					109,871	12	3

211

Table 6(b)   Profits at New Lanark 1814–25
Robert Owen & Company

Year ending Dec 31	Profit/Loss £	s	d	'Interest' £	s	d	Gross Profit/Loss £	s	d
1814*	–9,831	11	1	3,827	8	5	–6,004	2	8
1815	21,100	16	0	4,548	17	3	25,649	13	3
1816	12,984	12	8	6,500	0	0	19,484	12	8
1817	9,000	0	0	6,500	0	0	15,500	0	0
1818	9,000	0	0	6,500	0	0	15,500	0	0
1819	15,500	0	0	6,500	0	0	22,000	0	0
1820	–2,162	19	5	6,500	0	0	4,337	0	7
1821	–6,666	11	6	6,500	0	0	– 166	11	6
1822	13,000	0	0	6,500	0	0	19,500	0	0
1823	22,432	0	0	6,500	0	0	28,932	0	0
1824	15,015	0	0	6,500	0	0	21,515	0	0
Totals	99,371	6	8	66,876	5	8	166,247	12	4
Capital depreciation allowed							20,667	19	0
*Loss made at Stanley in 1814							6,000	0	0

Total gross gain at New Lanark	192,915	11	4

Table 6(c)   Profits at New Lanark 1825–28
Robert Owen & Company

Year ending 31 Dec	Profit/Loss £	'Interest' £	Gross Profit £	s	d
1825	—	6,500	6,500	0	0
1826	– 4,000	6,500	2,500	0	0
1827	–13,000	6,500	–6,500	0	0
Totals	–17,000	19,500	2,500	0	0
Fund for insuring debts			4,058	16	0

Total gross gain	6,558	16	0

Robert Owen as a Businessman

Table 6(d)   General Abstract of Gross Gain

	Profit £	'Interest' £	Gross Gain £	s	d
1799–1819	60,000	30,000	90,000	0	0
1810–1814			109,871	12	3
1814–1825			192,915	11	4
1825–1828			6,558	16	0
Total			399,345	19	7

Source: Owen Correspondence, Manchester, OC 2100, J. Wright to R. Owen 10 January 1853

213

Table 7 New Lanark Partners' Profit Accounts (£) 1818–23

Balance date	R. Owen			J. Walker			J. Foster			Jeremy Bentham			William Allen			J. Fox			M. Gibb		
	£	s	d	£	s	d	£	s	d	£	s	d	£	s	d	£	s	d	£	s	d
30 June 1818	20,836	12	5	10,090	11	8	7,315	18	11	3,943	18	5	7,075	2	10	2,895	10	0	1,917	11	2
31 Dec 1818	24,353	6	0	13,178	0	3	8,026	4	0	4,641	16	6	6,338	3	10	3,297	14	8	1,916	3	1
30 June 1819	24,109	18	7	14,248	11	9	7,804	2	5	4,653	7	9				2,931	7	8	2,211	12	1
31 Mar 1820	25,976	9	0	18,940	16	5	7,561	11	3	5,491	3	3	4,942	4	5	4,169	4	9	3,211	6	2
30 June 1820	24,337	19	8	20,122	10	10	7,766	9	0	5,864	11	6	4,829	1	3	4,509	13	10	2,927	15	11
30 Sept 1820	24,415	9	8	20,122	10	10	7,318	5	9	5,478	13	8	4,829	1	3	4,509	13	10	2,927	15	11
31 Dec 1820	21,255	12	9	20,886	15	4	7,568	3	9	5,702	8	7	4,881	2	11	4,709	0	9	2,586	14	5
31 Dec 1821	13,978	15	3	20,924	9	2	6,032	13	1	4,165	2	9	5,149	19	2	4,940	17	5	1,806	3	9
31 Mar 1822	13,644	7	3	20,924	9	2	4,629	1	10	3,799	11	6	5,149	19	2	4,940	17	5	1,806	3	9
30 June 1822	10,619	11	11	22,187	1	10	4,993	19	0	4,142	16	4	5,029	14	2	5,311	6	6	2,098	18	2
31 Dec 1822	7,536	3	11	19,065	3	9	5,881	9	8	5,428	0	0	3,944	14	10	6,620	1	3	3,241	16	11
30 Sept 1823	5,516	17	3	19,977	11	5	5,250	8	1	4,734	0	8	3,824	12	9	6,949	14	7	2,904	0	10

Source: Gourock Ropework Company MSS Balance Sheets 1818–23

8

THE INDUSTRIAL ARCHAEOLOGY OF NEW LANARK

JOHN R. HUME

In the immediate neighbourhood of the Mills is the most sublime scenery in Scotland, or even in Great Britain. It is almost needless to mention the magnificent Falls of the Clyde, and the stupendous Cartland Craigs with the beautiful Landscape of the Vale of Clyde. In short, Cotton Works more suited to the conducting, on an extensive scale, the Cotton Spinning Business, from the immediate application of the Water Power to the Machinery, or the capability of extending the Machinery, is not to be found in any other part of the Island.

Glasgow Herald 10 March 1851

1

The scenic attraction of the falls on the river Clyde has constantly appealed to a great number of visitors to the burgh of Lanark. The Glasgow merchant David Dale must have been familiar with the awe-inspiring sight and sound of Bonnington and Cora Linns, and with the less spectacular, but more tractable falls at Stonebyres and Dundaff. The Clyde throughout this particular stretch runs through a narrow valley, the sides of which steepen at times to form a gorge. When Richard Arkwright visited Scotland in 1784, Dale and he toured the district, and Arkwright expressed himself

> astonished at the advantages desirable from the falls of
> Clyde, and exultingly said, that Lanark would probably in

time become the Manchester of Scotland; as no place he had ever seen afforded better situations, or more ample streams of water for cotton machinery.[1]

The success of Arkwright's machinery was already proven, and he and Dale had formed a partnership to build a mill. At a time when water spinning was in its infancy, it would seem that there was a wide choice of sites available to them. However, the rivers of central Scotland were not particularly suited to a large-scale harnessing of water power, a fact clearly illustrated by the early restriction imposed on the development of a coke-smelting iron industry. The rivers are either large and slow or small and fast; and though the Black and White Cart, the Kelvin, the Endrick, the Ayr, the Teith and the Tay were all used to power cotton and other mills during the industrial revolution, supplies of water were frequently inadequate in summer. Conversely, where supplies were adequate, extensive works were necessary to tap appreciable amounts of power. An extreme case is the Forth, a river of great volume, whose slight fall renders it quite useless as a power source. Small wonder, then, that the Falls of Clyde so delighted Arkwright. Once the area had been selected, the choice of a site for a mill complex was not unduly difficult, though the spot eventually chosen, just below Dundaff Linn, was by no means ideal. A contemporary observer commented thus:

> This spot of ground was at that period [1784] almost a mere morass, situated in a hollow den, and of difficult access. Its only recommendation was the very powerful command of water, that the Clyde could be made to afford it; in other respects, the distance from Glasgow and the badness of the roads were rather unfavourable.[2]

The ground for the mills and village was obtained from Lord Braxfield, the Lord Justice Clerk, 'who influenced alone by the good of his country, very frankly feued the site . . . to the benevolent Mr David Dale, at a very moderate feuduty'.[3] He could well afford to – the land was valueless agriculturally, and the annual payment of £32 10s formed a useful addition

216

to his income.[4] Part of the land was owned by the Incorporation of Shoemakers in Lanark, and a feu duty of £17 7s 8d for the village houses was paid to this body.[5]

In respect of a rent of £5 a year, Sir John Lockhart Ross gave Dale permission to excavate a lade (or mill leat), a work that involved driving a tunnel through the hillside.[6] After the first mill had been built, Dale began the weir, which was built 95½ft out into the Clyde. In consequence of the addition of a second mill Dale wanted to build a bridge across the Clyde and complete the weir to the opposite bank. These plans were opposed by Anne, Janet and Patricia Edmondstone, three maiden sisters who owned the estate of Corehouse opposite New Lanark, but the weir was eventually completed with their acquiescence. However, at low water 'boys and idlers', despite the efforts of the mill manager, crossed to the Corehouse side along the top of the weir, and Dale, because of the complaints of his neighbours, made a break in it to stop this. When in 1799 Owen's company took over the mills, they filled this breach in the first dry season with 'a quantity of Stones, Cotton waste, Clay & Moss'. This angered the Edmondstones. Robert Owen then offered to pay £13 per annum for nineteen years, with a choice of a feu of a further £18 per annum or a *grassum,* or entry money, of £30 for the right to erect a masonry dam, which might be removed at the end of a lease timed to begin on 7 May 1802. Owen's offer was regarded as too low, and on 25 April 1804 the Edmondstones demanded that the weir should be broken in their half of the river, and threatened legal action. Owen then made a new proposal for a dam at a rent of £12 per annum, it being open to the Edmondstones to have it removed at any time after giving twelve months' notice.[7] On good authority, they later learned that the water rights were worth twenty to thirty times more than the amount paid by Owen and his partners. After abortive negotiations with Owen, they gave him notice to remove the weir (on 22 September 1807).

When this notice fell due, at Martinmas 1808, Owen pleaded

for delay, on account of the weather and the state of the water supply. For months nothing was done, and the Edmondstones eventually discovered that Owen was anxious to keep the mills in full production through the winter while he made alternative plans to do without the weir. The lade was extended and a new tailrace completed to achieve a greater fall of water. This work proceeded through two summers, while Owen used every legal device to procrastinate. For instance, the death of two of the sisters prompted Owen to demand a proper title from the survivor. Infuriating as this legal battle no doubt was to Owen, for Anne Edmondstone, the last of the three sisters, there was 'in truth . . . no advantage from the neighbourhood of the coy [company]'.[8] Ultimately Owen allowed the legal case to lapse, and paid much higher rents for the water rights. In June 1818 he was paying Anne Edmondstone £200, and in March 1820, £150.[9]

2

Arkwright and Dale seem to have planned a large investment at New Lanark from the beginning. Stone for the construction of the mills was quarried just downstream, and a substantial embankment was erected to give a level site for building. The first mill was built at the northern end of the site, athwart the lade, with the tailrace discharging directly into the river. Unfortunately we have no details of the construction of this first mill, nor of its waterwheel. Spinning started in March 1786.[10] On 14 June 1786 Dale took out an insurance policy with the Sun fire insurance company for £4,800. The mill building was valued at £2,000, the machinery and utensils at £2,500, the remaining £300 being for two houses.[11] The high valuation of the machinery indicates that the mill was fully equipped by the summer of 1786.

This mill was probably four or five storeys in height with the waterwheel or wheels situated at the building's centre, either over-shot or high-breast. The floors would certainly be

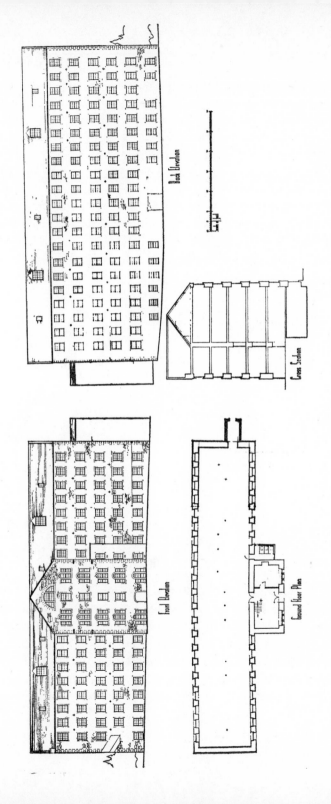

Back Elevation

Cross Section

Front Elevation

Ground Floor Plan

No 1 mill in 1945

of wood, possibly with wooden supporting columns. Fire was of course an ever-present risk in these early cotton mills, and on 9 October 1788, before the second mill was completed, Dale's first mill was burned down. Undismayed, he promptly replaced it by a new structure, completed in 1789,[12] the remains of which, cut down to three storeys and basement, still survive. This new building, known as No 1 mill, consisted of five storeys, attic and basement, 154ft long, 27ft wide and 60ft high,[13] with a projecting stair bay and three waterwheels.[14] (See illustrations on pages 72 and 108.) The design was not purely functional – there were Palladian windows in the stair bay.

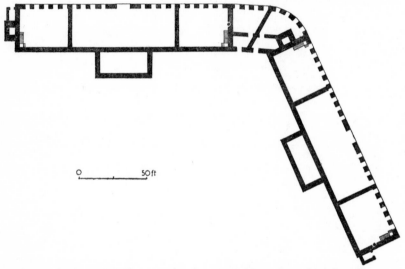

Ground plan of mills 1 and 2 in 1852. Note that the plan shows windows on one side only, since it shows the sunk storey

This feature occurs in Arkwright's earlier Masson Mill at Cromford (1783) and was repeated in several other early Scottish cotton mills, including Woodside (Aberdeen), Catrine (Ayrshire) and Spinningdale (Sutherland). Possibly this attribute indicates the hand of a single architect in the design of all these buildings, or perhaps, more likely, the widespread circulation of a common idea. The name of Robert Adam, who designed Dale's Glasgow town house has been suggested, but at present there is no firm evidence for this.[15] As mills were added in a range almost at right angles to the original block, the Palladian windows were repeated, so that on Owen's arrival in 1800 the mills presented an attractive uniformity of style.[16]

By the time of the first *Statistical Account*, building operations at New Lanark had been proceeding continuously for seven years. A force of ninety masons, carpenters and labourers had by that time erected four mills, with houses for more than 200 families.[17] Some indication of the capital sunk in the mills is given by the Sun insurance valuations of 1795. On 13 February, No 2 mill was valued at £2,200, No 3 at £2,000 and No 4 at £1,200, while part of an undistributed sum of £5,900 insured with the Phoenix should be added to give a nearer valuation.[18] No 1 mill was on 13 November valued at £2,200.[19] Millwright work (wheels and transmission shafts) was valued at £600 for each of the going mills (1, 2 and 3) and the actual spinning and preparation machinery and utensils at £3,100 each for Nos 1 and 2, and at £3,300 for No 3 mill. No 4, probably built to keep the standing labour force profitably occupied, was then and for some years later used as a lodging house for poor law apprentices, and as a warehouse and workshop. The relatively low value of £1,200 for what was the largest mill may reflect the greater fire risk in a building where cooking and metal working were in progress. Household goods in No 4 mill were in 1795 valued at £500, wearing apparel at £100, stock at £3,500 and joiners' and millwrights' tools and utensils at £1,200. Although there were slight fluctuations in valuations, in general the mills were insured for about £30,000 at least until 1801.[20]

No 2 mill was probably completed in October 1788 and was exactly the same size as the rebuilt No 1[21] (see 1852 ground plans on page 220). It remained substantially unchanged until the days of the Gourock Ropework Company. At some time during the period 1900–1914 the mill was widened by the

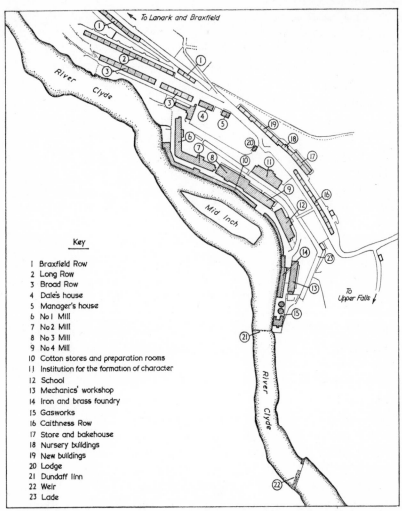

Key

1 Braxfield Row
2 Long Row
3 Broad Row
4 Dale's house
5 Manager's house
6 No 1 Mill
7 No 2 Mill
8 No 3 Mill
9 No 4 Mill
10 Cotton stores and preparation rooms
11 Institution for the formation of character
12 School
13 Mechanics' workshop
14 Iron and brass foundry
15 Gasworks
16 Caithness Row
17 Store and bakehouse
18 Nursery buildings
19 New buildings
20 Lodge
21 Dundaff linn
22 Weir
23 Lade

Plan of New Lanark, based on the first edition Ordnance Survey 25in map, 1863

demolition of the east wall nearest the lade (see plan above), and the construction of a new brick wall.[22] The original wooden floors were replaced by jack arches with columns at 7ft by 20ft centres, more than doubling the internal width (27ft to 60ft).

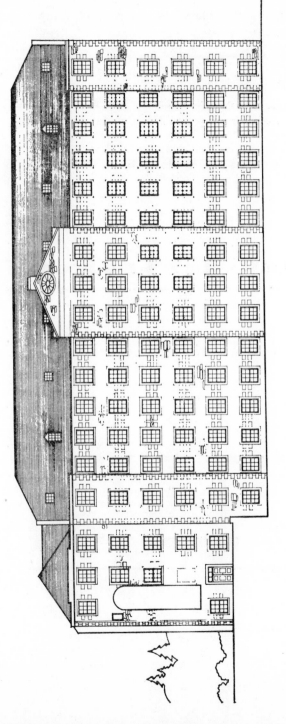

Scale of feet

Front elevation of No 3 mill in 1945

The 'jeanie house' – the original No 3 mill – was completed by the time of the *Statistical Account*. It was 130ft long, 30ft wide and 60ft high, slightly smaller than the other two but otherwise very similar.[23] On 26 November 1819 'No 3 or Mule Mill Burned to the ground except a few stretching frames and mules saved from west end', and the present No 3 (see plan below and front elevation on page 223), probably completed in

0   50 ft

Ground plan of No 3 mill in 1852

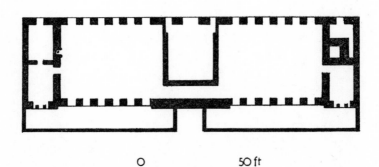

0   50 ft

Ground plan of No 4 mill in 1852

224

1826 in a plainer style, replaced it.[24] Known as the 'New Mill' as late as 1879,[25] this was the largest mill yet built and the only mill added under Owen's management. The present interior, of jack-arch construction, with cast-iron columns at 9ft 3in by 15ft centres, may well be the original, though it is possible that within the existing walls there has been much renovation – a well-documented procedure in other mills.[26] No 3 is the best preserved mill, and is a fine example from the classic period of factory architecture.

Perhaps the most handsome and certainly the largest of the early buildings was No 4 mill (ground plan on page 224). Generally similar in treatment to the first three, it had the added distinction of Palladian-windowed end bays. Completed, like No 3, in the period 1789–93 it was 156ft long, 33ft wide and 70ft high. It was used at first as a warehouse for the raw cotton and as workshops, and was also the boarding house for 275 children 'who have no parents here, and who get their maintenance, education and cloathing [sic] for their work.'[27] It still served these purposes in 1801, according to the insurance policy taken out on 2 March, at which date the number of 'boarders' was roughly the same as in 1795.[28] This mill was not fully operational until after 1813[29] – though about 1803 some tambouring was done therein.[30] Eventually it also was devoted to mule spinning. On 20 February 1883 fire broke out in the fifth room of No 4 mill:

> Two men were working there levelling up the New Mules, and were using a naked light, the flames were first seen inside the carriage of the mule they [were] working at and the course of the flames was away from them, not towards them, the mill was burned to the ground.[31]

As cotton spinning in Scotland was not particularly prosperous then, or for some years later, the building was never replaced.

Apart from the four mills, there were several other buildings in the production complex. There was a range of two-storey sheds 454ft by 20ft running along the back of mills 2, 3 and 4. Initially they were used for storage – they had a capacity of

800–1,000 bags of cotton in 1813[32] – but as pressure on mill space increased, preparation machinery was installed on one floor, the other continuing as a store.[33] At the southern end of the site a three-storey mechanics' shop, 140ft long and 29ft wide, and a single-storey brass and iron foundry, 148ft by 21ft, were built (ground plans on this page). These three buildings were certainly in existence when the mills were advertised for sale in October 1813,[34] but the actual dates of construction are unknown. At some time between 1813 and 1851 a gasworks was added, to light the mills and village. There was a small retort house with a neat octagonal stone chimney, which still survives, and two gasholders which were removed some years ago.[35]

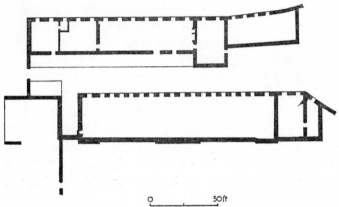

Ground plan of millwrights' shop (*below*) and foundries (*above*) in 1852

3

Very little is known about the construction of the housing in the village. The earliest houses were probably near No 1 mill; the first insurance policy of 14 June 1786 mentions two houses, one thatched and the other slated, and valued respectively at £100 and £200.[36] Caithness Row (front elevation on page 227),

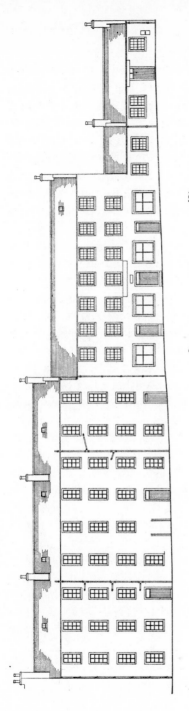

Front elevation of Nursery Buildings on the left, Store in centre, Bakehouse and Post Office on right

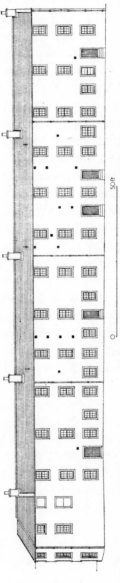

Front elevation of the north part of Caithness Row, as reconstructed for the New Lanark Association

with its elegant rounded end containing the counting house, was built to house highland immigrants, the first of whom were brought from Greenock by David Dale, after their ship bound for Maryland had been stormbound.[37] In the graveyard above the village is a tombstone 'erected by James McKey Labourer who was born in Bralbinn Parish of Rae Caithness in Memory of a Daughter and two Sons who died young in 1792'. Labour also came from Inverness and Argyllshire,[38] and later still from Ireland. By 1799 the village appeared substantially as it does today,[39] though Owen altered and rebuilt some of the houses.

The fullest description of the housing is given in a property valuation of 1881. Caithness Row consisted in fact of two blocks of four tenements of two storeys and a sunk storey; one of these blocks had rooms heated by brick flues, and these had originally been used as handloom weaving shops. Nursery Buildings (see page 71), originally planned to free No 4 mill for production, was divided into three tenements of four storeys; part was used as dwelling houses, the rest as a store for workmen's tools and potatoes. Owen built this block, perhaps the only completely new house building he undertook, about 1810. Next, on the north side, was the New Buildings (see page 54) seven tenements of four storeys used as meeting rooms and dwelling houses. It is this building, with its bellcote, which dominates the village. Probably erected by Dale, it was appropriately the meeting place of those of the Scotch Independent religion, one of the four sects represented at New Lanark. Braxfield Row (see page 230), Long Row and Double Row were alike in style, plain and uncompromising. They incorporated forty-one tenements, all with sunk storeys.[40] The complete rental of the village, according to an advertisement of 1851, was £1,400 per annum, a sum which included receipts from the store and gasworks.[41] There were also two neat houses or 'cottages' for the mill managers. In Dale's time one was occupied by the works manager, the other was used as a summer holiday home by the Dale family. When Owen

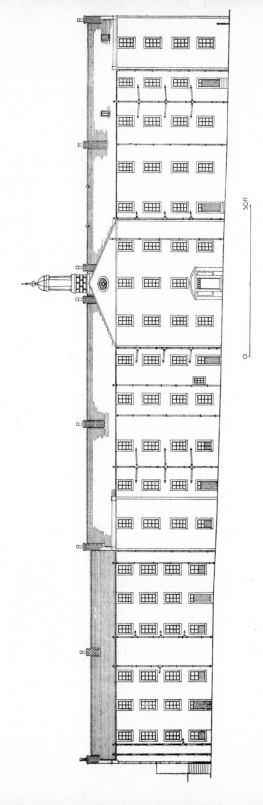

Front elevation of the New Buildings

first became manager he lived in the former, before moving to Braxfield House, a little way outside the village.[42]

Because of their connection with Owen's educational experiments, the most significant buildings in the village are perhaps the New Institution and the School. The New Institution for the Formation of Character was planned as early as 1809[43] and the structure was completed by 1813.[44] It was three storeys high, with a projecting stair bay and a neat pillared porch (ground plan on page 231). The external dimensions of the body of the building were 145ft by 45ft; internally there was a cellar 140ft long, 19ft wide and 9ft high, a first-floor room 140ft long 40ft wide and 11ft 6in high, and a second-floor room with the same length and breadth, but 21ft high, lit by two rows of windows. It was planned

> to admit of an extensive Store Cellar, a public kitchen, Eating and Exercise Room, a School, Lecture Room and Church,

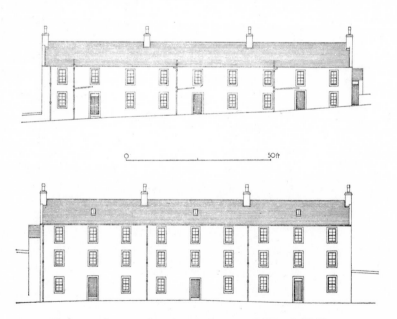

Front and rear elevations of part of Braxfield Row

all of which, it is supposed, may be fitted up in a very compleat manner, for a sum not exceeding £2500; and this arrangement may be formed so as to create permanent and substantial benefits to the inhabitants of the village and to the proprietors of the Mills.

The interior was not completed until 1816, the building being formally opened on 1 January by Owen himself. This was the occasion on which he delivered his famous 'Address to the Inhabitants of New Lanark'.[45] In his autobiography he describes how the large second floor had been arranged:

All the classes were united in one large class and lecture room . . . This room was also their class reading apartment. It was forty feet by twenty, and twenty two feet in height – with a gallery at one end to accommodate strangers . . . From this room strangers were taken into the adjoining apartment (the great writing, accounting, and lecture room,) in which were 250 or 300 children busily engaged at their respective desks,

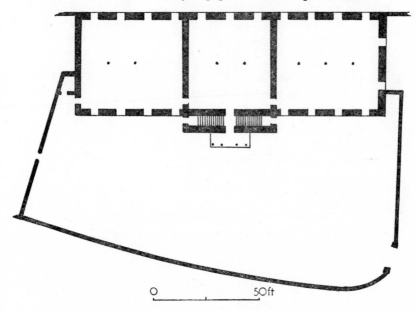

O   50ft

Ground plan of the New Institution for the Formation of Character in 1852

231

writing or accounting . . . This apartment was ninety feet long, forty wide, twenty-two high, with a gallery on three sides, and with a pulpit, from which to lecture, at one end. It was from this pulpit that I addressed an audience of about 1,200 when I opened the institution.[46]

The New Institution continued to serve as a canteen and re-creation hall for the mills until closure in 1968. The building was modified in 1881–2, when a new steam engine was installed to supplement the waterwheel driving No 3 mill. The engine house was bonded to the north end of the Institution, and is a high single-storey building, almost as tall as the Institution, with round-headed windows and a disproportionately small doorway. Its size gave concern to the works manager of the time, David Dalglish:[47]

After seeing the Engine House door up a course or two it is so awfully out of proportion small we would not allow the mason to proceed until you see it & pronounce an opinion on it. A 3 feet 6 door looks just like a narrow slit in the wall and besides it is useless for getting anything in or out of any size now or at any time – every body that sees it condemns it.

Despite this protest, the door was built as designed (see page 144). The other important addition to the Institution is a brick staircase on the south end giving access to the second floor.

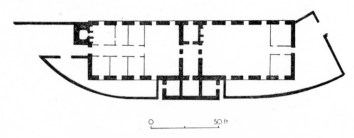

Ground plan of the School in 1852

While the New Institution is well documented, the 'School for Children' is not. The School, a three-storey building 42ft by 150ft (ground plan on page 232) was certainly in existence earlier than 1819, as it appears in undated prints showing the original No 3 mill. One of these prints has a key showing it as 'top part a School for Children, the under part a Public Kitchen',[48] and these functions continued to be accommodated until at least 1852.[49] The ground floor contained a number of small rooms, later converted to house the filter bed and pumps for the village water supply. On the first and second floors there were two large rooms, with musicians' galleries complete with neat cast-iron railings. These galleries survive, though a large hole has been cut through the floor of the northern room on the second floor. The roof of the School is in a poor state of repair.

Owen's social reforms at New Lanark were not limited to the field of education. The construction of a Store (see page 227) where goods bought in bulk were sold to the workpeople at or near cost price was another facet of his paternalism.[50] This was a three-storey building with display windows on the ground floor; the upper floors were used for the storage of goods. The Store was not in existence in 1813,[51] but appears in a print of c 1825.[52] It was described in 1851 as 'a large Store fitted up with everything necessary for the sale of Grocery Goods and Cloths, and whatever is needful for the wants of the workers'.[53] Butcher meat was supplied from a slaughterhouse at the back, and to the south a bakehouse (page 227) was added after Owen's time. The bakehouse and flour store were badly damaged by fire on 18 August 1881: 'about one o'clock managed to cut the roof & save the breadroom and back store & got out the fire by 3 o'clock. The damages are about £200'.[54] Repairs were quickly put in hand, orders being given as early as 7 September for Ballachulish or Easdale slates for the new roof.[55]

Owen's distaste for organised religion is well known; he did not, however, discourage the established tradition of religious observance at New Lanark. To supplement Dale's meeting room in New Buildings, the lecture room in the New Institution was also used as a church,[56] probably until the construction of a small Gothic Revival building just to the north of the New Buildings c1880.[57]

It was necessary to provide light, heat, water and sanitation for life in the village and mills. Before the introduction of gas, oil lighting and candles were both used in the mills, and probably in the homes of the workers. The oil in 1804–5 was bought from Pease, Wrays and Trigg of Hull, successive orders being valued at £212 12s 8d and £324 10s. These substantial sums included payment for lubricating oils as well as for fuel.[58] Candles could be had locally, as cattle slaughtered in Lanark provided tallow; in January 1805 more than 33st of candles were bought from Thomas Brown of Lanark for £21 13s 0¼d.[59] Two of the original oil lamps used in the mills are still in existence. The gasworks was certainly built before 1851, when it was described as 'an excellent Gas Work for supplying the Works and the Village'.[60] The workrooms were, in fact, only lit between October and February or March. On 5 October 1880 it was reported that 'the underflats of mills were lighted for a short time tonight for the first time this winter'. Normally two retorts were adequate, but on 20 October 'we kindled a third retort today as with that weak Coal two could not supply us'. On 28 February 1881 it was noted that 'we did without gas tonight for the first time this winter'.[61] During that period coal was being bought for gasmaking from Rigside and Douglas.[62]

Domestic heat in the village was presumably supplied by burning coal in open fires or ranges. Heating the mills was, however, a more difficult problem. The need for cheap heat had to be balanced against the risk of fire inherent in the use of both open fires and closed stoves within the buildings, and the dictates of common prudence were reinforced by the higher premiums charged by insurance companies for buildings containing stoves. Because of the coarser counts spun at New Lanark it was never necessary to heat the spinning rooms to the temperatures found in some of the Glasgow mills,[63] but a reasonable temperature was maintained by the use of ducted hot air.

William Kelly, a Lanark clockmaker appointed works manager by Dale on account of his mechanical skill, devised three methods of heating mills with safety. These he described in a report to Boulton and Watt, dated 24 March 1796. In the first, and least efficient, a stove was set in a small room adjacent to a gable wall of the mill and the air heated in this room was conducted by an iron pipe to the various floors, whence the flow was controlled by rotating sleeve valves. The defect of this method, apart from the small proportion of heat transferred from the stove room, was that the foul air from the lower room tended to be circulated. Two of these stoves installed in No 1 mill were quite inadequate.

A second and better system consisted in leading the flue from a stove set in the wall, upwards through a succession of compartments built in the thickness of the wall and separated by iron plates. Thus each compartment was warmed by the flue, and the flow of hot air was controlled by an iron valve. Kelly's third method, installed in No 3 mill, was similar in conception, but instead of internal compartments there were external chambers built onto the gable, again separated by thin iron plates. In Kelly's judgement, 'The last described stove we find answers most compleatly and *one only* at the end of the Building, is sufficient to warm a mill of 150 feet by 30 or upwards'.[64] Similar methods were employed in the New Institute where there were two stoves in the cellars with hot-air ducts terminating in the upper rooms, and also in the school, where the heating stove was at the back of the building with angled external fireholes to allow for varying wind direction.

In the early days, water was presumably drawn from the natural hillside springs or from the lade, and almost until the closure of the works an emergency fire-hydrant supply was available from the lade. About 1933 a piped water supply was introduced into the village and mills. Water was collected from springs in the hillside, allowed to run into the basement of the school, filtered through sand and gravel, and then pumped to a storage tank above Caithness Row. This system, which involved the use of steam, hydraulic and later electric pumps, was abandoned in 1968 when the storage tank was connected to the Lanark town water supply.[65] The change was welcomed in the village, as the spring water was very hard.

Sanitation in Dale's time was probably non-existent. The standard practice then was to use chamber pots and dry closets, collecting the solid excreta for sale to farmers as manure. Dung-heaps were normally close to the houses for convenience, and when streets were unmade and there were no proper dungsteads, conditions must indeed have been foul. Certainly Owen objected to the primitive sanitary arrangements in force on his arrival, and the streets were tidied up, the dung being taken to the firm's farm at Stonebyres.[66] He also installed in the New Institution 'conveniences calculated to give the children such habits as will enable the master of police to keep the village in a decent, clean state'.[67] Water-borne sewage disposal was not introduced until piped water was available, and even at the time of writing some of the houses in the village have no inside sanitation.

4

When Owen severed his connection with New Lanark in 1827 he left a village whose appearance had not greatly changed since 1800. A visitor coming down the hill into the village would pass rows of houses, with the massive bulk of the New Buildings on his left and Caithness Row with its neat rounded end in front of him, looking much the same as they had in Dale's time. When he arrived in the centre of the village, however, he would be immediately impressed with the changes. The handsome classical front of the Institution for the Formation of Character, with the children's playground in front, and the plainer, but well-proportioned school would perhaps attract his attention first. Then to the left he would see the Nursery

Buildings and a fine, well-stocked store, with handsome display windows. At first glance the mills would seem unchanged, but a closer examination would reveal that the uniformity of style had been spoiled, and that a brand new, broader, building had taken the place of No 3 mill. What would not have altered was the cheerful hum of well-maintained machinery, the roar of Dundaff Linn, and the smooth flow of the lade. A visitor today would miss the sound of machinery and note some changes in the mill buildings, but otherwise he would see the village much as Owen left it.

Not surprisingly, as New Lanark owed its layout more to physical necessity than to inspired planning, Owen did not copy New Lanark in any of his schemes, real or imaginary. New Harmony was in any case already laid out when he took it over, and his model 'villages of co-operation' were rectangular in plan with central community buildings. Orbiston, as planned, did however owe something to Owen's buildings at New Lanark, with a central block resembling the School and wings like elongated Nursery Buildings. These resemblances, however, are probably the consequence of the employment of the same architect rather than a conscious carry-over of design. The layout of New Lanark is in fact a model of compactness. Since there was no level ground, all the buildings had basements or sunk storeys, with the consequence that from one side they appear to be a storey higher than from the other. The valley is so steep that there is little room for garden ground, though in the angle made by the approach road and on the slopes above Caithness Row some allotments were laid out, and walks were made in the woods above the village. The two 'cottages' also had their own gardens. Latterly the slope below Caithness Row was used as a drying green but there is no evidence that this was always the case. What the village lacked in garden ground, however, it made up in romantic appeal. The wild woods which even today dominate the village, the Clyde with its impressive falls and its fine fishing, must have given the villagers as much pleasure as the horticultural opportunities available to the inhabitants of Catrine, Deanston or Stanley.

So far no mention has been made of changes in the ownership of the mills. Owen's takeover, and the successive partnerships with which he was involved have been described elsewhere in this volume.[68] When he finally gave up his interest in the mills they passed into the hands of the Walker family.[69] The Walkers carried on some at least of Owen's practices, and New Lanark remained in their hands until 1881, though they made an attempt to sell in 1851–2.[70] In 1881 two groups made bids for the mills. One, which proposed to set up a limited company, intended to introduce lace-curtain manufacture. The promoters, writing to ask for an extension of time before reaching an agreement, stated:

> The country as you well know is at the present time full of unemployed capital, and in another way a more favourable opportunity never occurred for taking up an investment of this nature, as any person who has recently travelled in Ayrshire, cannot but be aware, that one of the principal topics of conversation amongst all classes is the amount of profit which has been made in the Nottingham Lace Curtain Manufacture.[71]

With the introduction of machine-made lace, fortunes of £150,000 had, they claimed, been made in Nottingham, with male labour earning £2 10s to £3 10s a week; while in Scotland, where wages were 25s–30s, one Ayrshire firm with ten looms had made £11,000 profit. If their offer (not detailed) was accepted, they declared that Mr Walker 'would have the satisfaction of knowing that a very profitable business was introduced to the welfare of his present workpeople, and the general benefit of the district'. It seems likely, however, that even these glowing prospects did not attract the necessary 'unemployed capital', and on 2 April an offer from Henry Birkmyre and Provost R. S. Somerville of Port Glasgow was accepted instead. This agreement included a provision for the mills to be run by the Walkers until Whitsunday 1881, for stocks of cotton and the goods in the 'Grocery, Spirit Store & Drapery' to be bought at valuation, and for the transfer of the spirit-store licence to the purchasers.[72]

Once the Port Glasgow men had taken over, net looms were introduced without loss of time, and the netmaking business was further expanded after 1902, when some small net factories at Peel in the Isle of Man were acquired and the machines moved to New Lanark. Birkmyre and Somerville were partners in the Gourock Ropework Company, and eventually the mills were merged into that concern.[73] Throughout its tenure of the mills, which finally ended in 1970, 'the Gourock' recognised a responsibility to its heritage, and gladly and generously welcomed visitors.

5

Disappointingly little is known of the original machinery in the mills, though it is certain that in Nos 1 and 2 mills water frames on Arkwright's model were installed, with the necessary breaking and carding engines and roving frames. There were three waterwheels in each mill, grouped in the centre,[74] and driving common vertical shafts consisting of linked cast-iron sections.[75] Final drive to the machinery was from lineshafts geared to the upright shafts.[76] This 'millwright work' was insured for £600 per mill, while the spinning frames and preparing machinery were valued at £3,100.[77] By 1852 there were nine waterwheels, altogether 'equal to about 400 Horse Power'.[78] In addition to the six in Nos 1 and 2 mills, there was one set parallel to the lade, in the preparation rooms, another in No 4 mill, and one in the foundry.[79] There was no wheel in No 3 mill at that time, presumably because hand mules were in use, though later one was installed there too.[80] From 1884 the waterwheels were gradually replaced by turbines.[81] There was a Jonval turbine in No 2 mill in 1903, built by Messrs Gunter of Oldham,[82] and at closure there were three turbines, in Nos 1 and 3 mills and in the dyehouse (a conversion of the old foundry). Steam auxiliary power was also used for a time (see below).

The earliest machinery was probably made in the mills themselves, a common enough practice in the early cotton factories, though some parts may have been brought in. In 1881 John Whiteley & Sons, Cardmakers, of Brunswick Mills, Halifax, claimed that they had 'since 1780–90 done almost all the business at Lanark'.[83] Certainly in the period 1795–1804 machinery was being made at New Lanark. An ironfounder (George Wilson) and a brassfounder (David Kelly) were both employed in the village, though castings were also brought from the Omoa Foundry, including card frames. Pig iron was bought from Glenbuck, Muirkirk and Wilsontown, while Muirkirk also supplied bar iron and forgings. Swedish bar iron was obtained through the Edinburgh merchants, William and Robert Anderson. Steel spindles came from the Monkland Steel Company at 38s a gross, while wooden parts were purchased from Claud Girdwood and Company, a Glasgow firm which combined textile machinery manufacture with timber sales.[84]

In 1795 the millwrights' and mechanics' shops were situated in No 4 mill. At that time there were eighty-seven men employed in all – twenty smiths, twelve clockmakers (who were responsible for gear cutting and other fine work), nine millwrights, nineteen joiners, ten turners, two founders and fifteen hammermen and 'hagmen', or woodcutters.[85] Their working tools were valued at £1,200.[86] As well as repairing and constructing water frames and preparation machinery, the mechanics built William Kelly's patent water-powered mules – an early attempt to replace the skilled and scarce adult male spinners. Kelly started with the application of power to the mules, without a self-acting mechanism. The drive was taken from lineshafts by cotton ropes at first, and then belts were introduced. He then devised a self-acting mule that could spin coarse counts, and patented it in the summer of 1792. At the time of the *Statistical Account* there was 'a considerable number of patent jennies' in No 3 mill, as well as fifty-five 'common jennies', and it was proposed to fill No 4 mill with the new machines. But, as Kelly himself wrote in 1829, 'the size of the mules rapidly increased to 300 spindles and upwards, and two such wheels being considered a sufficient task for a man to manage, the idea of saving by spinning with boys and girls was thus superseded'. Though his patent thus enjoyed no lasting success, it had the short term effect of attracting widows with large families to the village.[87] Kelly also communicated to the Board of Trustees in 1793 the invention of a new method for erecting the 'great gear or large machinery of cotton mills'. This he reckoned would save a quarter of the water power required and would also allow parts of the mill to be shut down without alteration to the rest. The Board agreed to give him a premium of at least £20 once the invention had been applied, but there is no indication as to whether it was ever used.[88]

As implied by Kelly, improved mules were introduced, and by 1802–3 there were 6,864 mule-twist and 2,681 mule-weft spindles in No 3 mill.[89] The use of hand mules was in fact advantageous, as they required no direct water power and could thus remain in operation when water was short. By 1813 there were only 7,864 mule spindles altogether, served by 159 carding engines and the appropriate drawing, roving and stretching machinery,[90] while as late as 1851 there were 13,000 hand mule spindles in the mills, as well as 28,900 Sharp Roberts self-acting mule spindles.[91] Mules continued to be installed until at least the 1880s.[92]

Throughout the existence of the mills as a spinning unit, however, Arkwright's water frame and its more sophisticated derivatives, the throstle and the ring spinning frame were the mainstays. In 1795 there were 6,000 water spindles in No 2 and 4,500 in No 1 mill.[93] These totals rose to 8,172 and 6,144 in 1805,[94] and 11,172 and 11,676 in 1813, with 160 and 153 carding engines respectively.[95] Throstles were in use in No 2 mill in 1802 (756 spindles),[96] then appear to have gone out of use for a period. By 1851, however, water spindles had been displaced completely, and there were 22,800 throstle spindles.[97] The conversion to ring spinning is not so clearly documented, though in November 1878 a 300-spindle ring throstle frame was bought from Howard and Bullough, Globe Works, Accrington for £127 10s, and an existing 300-spindle throstle frame was converted to a Booth Sawyer ring spinning frame at a cost of £75.[98] New ring spinning machinery continued to be installed until as recently as 1963.

As the spinning process was gradually improved, so was the preparation of the rovings. New and secondhand carding engines and drawing frames were bought. In 1873, for example, William Hunter and Company of Glasgow were commissioned to purchase five intermediate frames and four drawing frames from Fintry Mills in Stirlingshire, and a further three drawing frames were obtained from Samuel Brooks of Manchester at a price of £36 each. Between 1874 and 1876, eleven 38in and six 40in carding engines were bought from John Elce & Company Limited of Manchester.[99] Modernisation continued after the Birkmyre–Somerville takeover, with new carding engines and roving frames installed in No 3 mill in 1882.[100] When the mills closed in 1968, the carding engines in No 2 mill were all by Platt Brothers of Oldham, and were dated 1904, 1905 and 1940.

After 1881 netmaking was introduced by Birkmyre and Somerville. The first looms were made by the mill mechanics, with forgings bought in. A Mr Norcross from Johnstone, Renfrewshire, was brought in to organise the net-weaving section at a wage of 27s a week. Realising his strong position as technical expert, he soon demanded a free house in addition – and got it. Bernard Ireland, a machinery maker at Buckhaven in Fife, offered to supply one loom per month, with a girl to demonstrate the working, but there is no indication that more than one was bought from him.[101] Netmaking continued until the closure of the mills, when there were twenty-two net looms in No 3 mill, twelve of them by Zang of Paris.

Though until 1881 New Lanark was primarily concerned with spinning, there seems to have been a continuing tradition of handloom weaving in the village. In 1795 there were 324 persons employed in the parish of Lanark and the neighbourhood 'in weaving and winding',[102] and when John Marshall of Leeds visited the mills in 1807 he found that 'some muslins' were being woven.[103] The weaving shops were in the basement of Caithness Row, where in 1881, as already mentioned, part of the 'sunk storey' was occupied as 'Handloom Weaving Shops, heated by brick built flues'.[104] After 1881, however, these last traces of domestic industry were swept away, and power-looms introduced to weave sailcloth and other heavy cotton fabrics. These items continued to be major products until closure.

Many problems faced the manager of a water-driven cotton mill. Apart from machine failures, about which there is no information at all at New Lanark, he had to contend with discipline of the labour force, both inside and outside the mills, and with the power supply. Owen's contribution to factory discipline, including his introduction of the silent monitor, and his careful attention to elimination of pilfering by stock and output control, is described elsewhere in this volume, as are his attempts to order life in the village.[105] Problems with the power supply, however, are properly the concern of this essay.

The power supply of any watermill inevitably presents two problems – shortage and excess of water. The former was perhaps more common and pressing. In June, July and August 1813, for example, the constant complaint was 'very short of water', while in December the mills were stopped by severe frost 'drying the river'. Even when the river was not completely frozen, the wheels themselves could freeze up, as on 3 January 1820 when the 'Teaser wheel [was] frozen to its bed and the mills stopt $1\frac{1}{2}$ hours'.[106] These were perennial problems, and though little could be done about summer drought or extremes of winter frost – except to instal auxiliary steam power – delays caused by frozen wheels were minimised by the installation of steam heating. In January 1881 there was a particularly cold spell. On the morning of Monday 17 'the frost was very intense, being 10° below zero for want of fuel to keep up steam since Saturday the old mill water wheels got frozen to the rocks, by 1 p.m. got them thawed & the steam led beneath and started'. When the thaw came, it too posed problems: on 27 January the damhead sluices were ordered to be left shut 'lest a flood should come down in the night time'. Heavy floods 'backwatered' the wheels – as on Thursday 22 April when, 'after 48 hours incessant rain, the river rose to an unusual height today. It was in at the Greasers Hole 9 inches deep, the whole of the Mid Inch was covered and the mills were all stopt. No such flood has happened since 1832'. Even when conditions were not so extreme, delays could occur. On 9 March 1881 it was reported: 'The river is so high today & the large wheel wading so, had to stop one room of self actors at Dinner Time the mill was so slow'.[107]

That there was basically an adequate supply of water is, however, indicated by the late introduction of steam power. The comparable country mills of Catrine and Blantyre had their first engines in 1800 and 1809,[108] while New Lanark's first was not purchased until 1873, when a 'Horizontal Condensing Valveless patent Steam Engine', costing £800, was delivered by William Hunter & Company of Glasgow. Steam was supplied to a cylinder of 38in diameter and 30in stroke, by a Galloway boiler 26ft long and 7ft in diameter bought for £370 from the same firm.[109] It is not clear where this engine was sited, but it was probably replaced in 1881–2 by a larger one installed in the engine house already mentioned. No details of this survive, though it was not removed until c1955. Steam was generated in two Lancashire boilers 30ft long and 7ft in diameter made by Daniel Adamson & Co of Dukinfield and delivered in July 1881 at a cost of £455 each, including transport.[110] These were housed in a brick building with a corrugated iron roof immediately to the east of the engine house and a large circular-section chimney built to provide draught. The drive from the engine was taken to No 3 mill by ropes running across the lade and a roadway.[111] This engine was apparently installed to power new carding engines and roving frames from Platts of Oldham.[112]

Occasionally, of course, the power units broke down. Normally these breakdowns were of quite a minor nature, as when gearing or shafts broke. A waterwheel pinion in No 3 mill smashed on 6 February 1881, making rooms 4, 5 and 6 idle.[113] Even apparently slight accidents could hold up production for a considerable time. On 11 June 1879, for instance, a length of shafting in the fourth room of mill No 3 'snapped at the neck behind [the] spur wheel that drives [the] upright', owing to 'torsion from too many self actors being stopped and all started again at the same moment'. Repairs were started immediately, but they involved the casting and machining of a new shaft and bushes; in spite of working round the clock it was 20 June before they were completed.[114]

Serious as these incidents were in terms of lost production, much more damaging were accidents to the wheels themselves. On 3 April 1879 the middle waterwheel in No 2 mill was severely damaged. The works manager reported that it would require 'two new centres a new set of arms for one side a new sole and one new segment and a great many bolts'. Just over a year later, on 6 May 1880:

> The water wheel of the 3rd mill broke down this forenoon between 11 & 12 o'clock, on account of one of the Keys in the East water wheel pinion having got loose & come out. The arms of the wheel as they came round struck the projecting Key & broke the neck off the shaft which fell into the body of the wheel carrying the pinion with it but all the keys dropt out and were not found, and the neck of shaft and water wheel pinion were found separate.
>
> Four arms of the wheel were broken into pieces on the East side of the wheel & some of the middle ribs of other arms broken off near the wheel sole, on the west side of wheel some of the middle ribs or feathers of the arms were also broken off near to the wheel sole and the water wheel pinion

245

had the teeth stript off and the pinion split. On the east side the plumber [sic] block, cope and both brasses were all split open by the broken neck of the shaft.

After this comprehensive smash the necessary repairs were tackled urgently. Four new arms were ordered from the Shotts Iron Company, a shaft, pinion, plummer block and cope were cast at the mills and machined, and eventually on 24 May, after working nights and Saturdays for more than a fortnight, the wheel was started at 10.30 in the morning 'although not quite finished'.[115]

Of all the reported accidents of this period, perhaps the most interesting was the stripping of drive gears in No 1 mill on 27 July 1880. The whole load had been on that side at the time,

but part of the throstles had been standing for some time past, which would make them heavier to drive, however I expected a breakdown in that mill ere long owing to the fact that hitherto the side water wheels have been driving the centre one. This arises from a blunder which had been made at one time in the Calculation of the gearing . . . the side wheels and the Centre one are all pitched into the same pinions on the upright shafts, the water wheels must make turn for turn [and] the side wheels therefore drive it one revolution in 44, and the power to do so being transmitted through the pinions on the upright shafts and the 7 foot wheels. It is not surprising these have so often broken down.[116]

Even after a turbine had been installed in 1884 there were problems. A not untypical incident occurred on 5 March 1885 when 'at 9.45 this morning the opening and shuting [sic] gearing of turbine gave way for which we had to stope the whole of the mills'. Steam power, too, had its disadvantages. In June 1887 the engine crankpin began heating badly, and after various expedients had been tried, men from Turnbull, Grant & Jack of Glasgow were called in. They found that new big-end brasses were required, and on fitting these the trouble ceased.[117]

The works managers of Lanark had to be resourceful in

dealing with problems such as these, for the isolated position of the mills made it necessary to make new parts on the spot, as far as was possible. Most of the incidents recorded in the Works Manager's Report Book are to do with mechanical problems, but there is occasionally a human touch, as in the entry for Monday 17 March 1879: 'St Patrick's Day, had to banish all green ribbons out of the mills so as to stop Cheering'.[118]

6

Too often New Lanark is seen only as Robert Owen's theatre, where the first and perhaps the most successful scenes in his social drama were acted out. But Owen had inherited from Dale a well-built and well-designed cotton complex, with a humane and progressive management; and though he made improvements in detail there was already a solid substructure without which he could have achieved little. Four large mills, with well-equipped mechanics' shops, substantial houses and an adequate labour force – the largest spinning mills in Scotland – this was Dale's achievement. Owen's contribution in building was perhaps less significant – the Institute and School, Nursery Buildings and the Store, and the replacement of No 3 mill – though the revolutionary purpose of the Institute and School must be acknowledged. His claim that he modernised the machinery is probably true, but had Dale continued to own the mill he would almost certainly have done the same, such was the rate at which innovation was taking place.

There is also a tendency to forget New Lanark after the departure of Robert Owen, and to fail to realise that the mills continued in production for a further 141 years. This is a remarkable record by any standard, and reflects great credit on the Walkers, Birkmyre & Somerville and the Gourock Ropework Company. When, after 1873, cotton spinning in Scotland entered a period of slow but steady decline many substantial firms abandoned spinning altogether. Others developed the weaving side of their activities, only to be faced with increasing competition in the years immediately before and after the First World War. Among those best able to resist competition were the owners of the few surviving large country mills; Deanston, Catrine, Stanley and New Lanark were thus able to survive into the 1960s, though only Stanley has continued into the 'seventies as a cotton spinning mill.

Since the New Lanark mills ceased production in March 1968 their future has been uncertain. The Gourock Ropework Company decided to keep the mills on a care-and-maintenance basis while a tenant was sought. Unfortunately the unattractive features of the site – poor access and distance from centres of population – made it difficult to find a firm which could take on all the buildings. Eventually Metal Extraction Ltd, a firm that makes aluminium powder from scrap, took over No 1 mill, and later purchase the whole mill complex including the Institute and School. The fate awaiting these buildings is therefore still not known.

Happily the future of at least some of the houses is reasonably secure. The Gourock Ropework Company, having maintained the village in good condition, found in 1962 that they could not afford the cost of modernising the houses and therefore offered them to Lanark Town Council for the nominal sum of £250. The Town Council declined to assume responsibility, but fortunately in 1963 the New Lanark Association was formed to modernise the houses. The pilot project was the conversion of Caithness Row, for which plans were prepared by Ian G. Lindsay and Partners of Edinburgh. The interior of the Row was completely removed and a new roof put on. This initial project was completed in 1967, and the second stage in modernisation – the Store and Nursery Buildings – was finished in 1969. The Association aims to convert the New Buildings next, and plans for this have been prepared. A pleasant feature of the renovation of Caithness Row is the use of the redecorated counting-house as a small museum.

The New Lanark Association, with financial assistance from

local and national government, as well as from private bene-
factors, has made a fine start to the preservation of at least the
external appearance of the village. It is devoutly to be hoped
that means can be found to restore Owen's historic Institute
and School and that the new owners of the mills will respect
the historical associations of this, one of the finest monuments
to the industrial revolution in the world.

NOTES

1 [Old] *Statistical Account of Scotland,* ed Sir John Sinclair, 15
  (1795), 46 [Hereafter *OSA*]
2 Ibid, 34
3 Ibid, 22–3
4 Gourock Ropework Company MSS, Head Office Port Glasgow,
  letterbook 1881–2, Alexander Lade, Writer 8 July 1881 [hereafter
  Gourock MSS]
5 Ibid, Balance Sheets, balance 31 Mar 1820
6 SRO, UP Innes Mack L/14/9, Lanark Twist Company v Edmonstoun [Edmondstone] (1810)
7 Ibid
8 Ibid
9 Gourock MSS, Balance Sheets, balance at 30 June 1818 and at
  31 Mar 1820
10 *OSA* 15, 35
11 Guildhall Library MSS, Sun Fire Insurance Policy 519065. I am
  indebted to Dr S. D. Chapman for this reference
12 *OSA* 15, 34–5
13 Ibid, 35
14 J. M. Richards, *The Functional Tradition in Early Industrial Buildings* (1958), 75
15 cf W. G. Black, 'David Dale's House in Charlotte Street', *Regality
  Club of Glasgow,* 4th series, part 2 (1902), 110–12. A photograph
  of the Old Masson Mills, showing the Palladian features, occurs
  opposite p 70 of R. S. Fitton and A. P. Wadsworth, *The Strutts
  and the Arkwrights 1758–1830* (Manchester 1958)
16 Undated print, 'A View of New Lanark from the N. West', see
  plate on p 53 ; also Frank Podmore *Robert Owen* 1 (1906), illustration facing p 48
17 *OSA* 15, 36–40
18 Guildhall Library MSS, Sun Fire Insurance Policy 638322
19 Ibid, Policy 648656

20 cf Sun Insurance Policies 664114 27 Jan 1797 ; 716403 2 March 1801

21 *OSA* 15, 34–5

22 Podmore 1, op cit, illustration facing p 80 shows No 2 mill unreconstructed

23 *OSA* 15, 35

24 Gourock MSS, Diary/Notebook of Robert Owen or mill manager 1813–20

25 Ibid, Works Manager's Report Book 1879–1904, Wednesday 11 June 1879

26 *Engineering* 2 (1866), 144, note on removal and replacement of iron columns in McConnel's mill, Manchester

27 *OSA* 15, 35–6

28 Sun Insurance Policy 11937/38 2 Mar 1801

29 *Glasgow Herald* 1 Oct 1813, Advertisement for Sale of New Lanark, No 4 mill described as 'not yet filled with machinery'

30 Gourock MSS, Produce Book 1802–6

31 Ibid, Works Manager's Report Book 1879–1904

32 *Glasgow Herald* 1 Oct 1813

33 Ibid, 10 Mar 1851, Advertisement for Sale of New Lanark: 'There is, behind the main body of the Mills, the necessary Blowing Houses. Under the roof of the back Premises is a Cotton Cellar, capable of holding upwards of 300 bales.'

34 Ibid, 1 Oct 1813

35 Glasgow City Archives, McGrigor, Donald & Co MSS, Plan of New Lanark 1852 [hereafter GCA Plan 1852]

36 Sun Insurance Policy 519065

37 *OSA* 15, 40

38 Ibid

39 A plate in T. Richardson's *Guide to Loch Lomond, Loch Long, Loch Fine and Inverary* (Glasgow 1799) shows most of the existing houses. This plate is missing from the Copies in the National Library of Scotland and the Mitchell Library Glasgow. I am indebted to Mr John Robertson for this reference

40 Gourock MSS, Letterbook 1881–2, 428

41 *Glasgow Herald,* 10 Mar 1851

42 *The Life of Robert Owen, Written by Himself* Vol 1 (1857), 71 [hereafter *Life* 1]

43 Robert Dale Owen, *Threading My Way, Twenty-seven Years of Autobiography* (1874), 77

44 *Glasgow Herald* 1 Oct 1813

45 *Life* 1, Appendix C, 333–360

46 Ibid, 144–5

47 Gourock MSS, Letterbook 1881–2, 475–6, 14 Feb 1882

48 Podmore, op cit, illustration facing 48

49 GCA Plan 1852

50 *Life* 1, 135
51 *Glasgow Herald* 1 Oct 1813. This otherwise very detailed advertisement does not mention it
52 Undated print in possession of Gourock Ropework Company
53 *Glasgow Herald* 10 Mar 1851
54 Gourock MSS, Works Manager's Report Book 1879–1904
55 Ibid, Letterbook 1881–2, 280
56 Robert Owen, *A Statement regarding The New Lanark Establishment* (Edinburgh 1812), 16–17
57 Information from Mr I. Donnachie
58 Gourock MSS, Account Book 1804–6, Dec 1804, 27 June 1805
59 Ibid
53 *Glasgow Herald* 10 Mar 1851
61 Gourock MSS, Works Manager's Report Book 1879–1904
62 Gourock MSS, Letterbook 1881–2, 375, 449
63 Parliamentary Papers 1831–2, XV, 235, average temperature in fine mills 84–86° F ; 252, temperatures in various works
64 Boulton & Watt MSS, Birmingham Reference Library, letter William Kelly to Messrs Boulton & Watt 24 Mar 1796 and accompanying report. I am indebted to Dr Jennifer Tann for this reference
65 John R. Hume, 'The Water Supply of New Lanark', *Industrial Archaeology*, 5 (1968), 384–7
66 R. D. Owen, op cit, 72
67 Robert Owen, *Statement regarding the New Lanark Establishment*, 13
68 See pages 182–7
69 *New Statistical Account of Scotland* (1845), 6, 22
70 *Glasgow Herald* 10 Mar 1851 ; GCA McGrigor, Donald & Co MSS, Plans of New Lanark
71 Gourock MSS, Letterbook 1881–2: copy letter to J. Baird Smith of Messrs McGrigor, Donald & Co, 12 Mar 1881
72 Ibid
73 George Blake *The Gourock* (Port Glasgow 1963), 110
74 GCA Plan 1852
75 Gourock MSS, Works Manager's Report Book, 1879–1904
76 Edward Baines, jr, *History of the Cotton Manufacture in Great Britain* (1835), 206
77 Sun Fire Insurance Policies 11/648656 and 8/638322, 13 Nov 1795 and 13 Feb 1795
78 *Glasgow Herald,* 10 Mar 1851
79 GCA Plan 1852
80 Gourock MSS, Works Manager's Report Book 1879–1904, Thursday 6 May 1880: 'The Water Wheel of the 3rd Mill broke down down this forenoon'
81 Ibid, 'Turbine Sucksesfuly [sic] started on Friday 7th March 1884'

82 Ibid, Monday 13 June 1903
83 Gourock MSS, Letterbook 1881–2 ; John Whiteley & Sons to R. S. Somerville 27 June 1881
84 Gourock MSS, Account Book 1804–6, 16 July 1804 to 12 April 1806
85 *OSA* 15, 36
86 Sun Insurance Policy 8/638322
87 *OSA* 15, 35–6 ; Baines, op cit, 207
88 SRO, NG1/1/28 Minutes of the Board of Trustees, 190, 210. I am indebted to Mr Norman McClain for this reference
89 Gourock MSS, Produce Book 1802–6
90 *Glasgow Herald* 1 October 1813
91 Ibid, 10 March 1851
92 Gourock MSS, Works Manager's Report Book 1879–1904, 20 Feb 1883
93 *OSA* 15, 35
94 Gourock MSS, Produce Book 1802–6
95 *Glasgow Herald* 1 Oct 1813
96 Gourock MSS, Produce Book 1802–6
97 *Glasgow Herald* 10 Mar 1851
98 Gourock MSS, Account Book Jan 1873 – May 1881, 7 and 16 Nov 1878
99 Ibid, 26 Apr 1873, 22 Aug, 3 and 19 Sept, and 1 Oct 1874 ; 8 Oct 1875 ; 13 Nov 1876
100 Ibid, Letterbook 1881–2, 9 and 11 Jan 1882
101 Ibid, 10 and 16 Nov 1881, 8 Feb 1882
102 *OSA* 15, 37
103 Brotherton Library, University of Leeds, MS 200 (Marshalls of Leeds, flax spinners) Tour book of John Marshall, Cumberland and Scotland 1807, 32
104 Gourock MSS, Letterbook 1881–2, 428
105 See pages 78, 188–95
106 Gourock MSS, Diary/Notebook of Robert Owen or mill manager 1813–20
107 Gourock MSS, Works Manager's Report Book 1879–1904
108 Boulton & Watt MSS, Birmingham Public Reference Library, Engine Book, 4–5, 76–7
109 Gourock MSS, Account Book Jan 1873 – May 1881, 5 June 1873
110 Ibid, Letterbook 1881–2, 27 June, 1 Aug 1881
111 Clearly seen in Podmore 1, op cit, illustration facing 80
112 Gourock MSS, Letterbook 1881–2, 22 Dec 1881, 9 Jan 1882
113 Ibid
114 Ibid, Works Manager's Report Book 1879–1904
115 Ibid
116 Ibid
117 Ibid
118 Ibid

The Industrial Archaeology of New Lanark

The author wishes to acknowledge his gratitude to the following people for their assistance in the preparation of this essay: Richard Dell, Glasgow City Archivist; Ian Donnachie; A. C. Dunsmore of the Gourock Ropework Company; Andrew Inglis, formerly manager of New Lanark Mills; John Robertson; the staffs of the Glagsow City Archives; the Mitchell Library, Glasgow; the National Library of Scotland; the Guildhall Library, London; the Scottish Record Office. He is particularly grateful to his colleagues John Butt, Baron Duckham and James Treble for their help and criticism, always generously given, and to Professor S. G. E. Lythe for his encouragement.

Mr John Reid of Ian G. Lindsay & Partners kindly supplied drawings from which the illustrations on pages 227, 229 and 230 were prepared, and Mrs Margaret Holmes lent the originals of the drawings on pages 219 and 223.

CHRONOLOGY

ROBERT OWEN (1771-1858)

1771	14 May born in Newtown, Montgomeryshire
1781-9	shop-boy and assistant in Stamford, London and Manchester
1789	manufacturer in partnership with John Jones in Manchester
1791	manager for Peter Drinkwater, merchant and cotton manufacturer
1793	elected member of Manchester Literary and Philosophical Society
1794	joined Chorlton Twist Company
1799	acquired New Lanark Mills, Scotland married Anne Caroline Dale
1800	January went to New Lanark and remained a partner there until 1828
1814	*A New View of Society* published
1815	leader of factory reform agitation
1817	concerned in agitation for reform of the Poor Law
1820	*Report to the County of Lanark* published
1820-30	spread of Co-operative ideas and Owenism in Britain
1825-7	Orbiston, the first Owenite community in Britain
1825-7	Owen at New Harmony, Indiana
1832	founded *The Crisis*
1832	17 September first National Equitable Labour Exchange opened
1833	leader in eight-hour agitation

1834	founded Grand National Consolidated Trades Union of Great Britain and Ireland
1834	*New Moral World* published
1839–45	Queenwood community
1844–6	Owen in USA
1848–58	spiritualist phase
1857	*Life of Robert Owen Written by Himself* published
1858	17 November died at Newtown; buried there 21 November

INDEX

References to illustrations are printed in italic

Academics, dissenting, 55
Adam, Robert, architect, 220-1
Adamson, Daniel & Co, engineers, 244
Allen, William (1770–1843), 69, 70, 120, 187, 201, 206, 207, 214
Althorp, John, Viscount (3rd Earl Spencer) (1782–1845), 120
Amsterdam, 196
Anderson, William & Robert, iron merchants, 240
Applegarth, J., 147
Apprentices, pauper, 100-1, 188, 191, 225
Archaeology, Industrial, 16, 215-53
Argyllshire, 228
Arkwright, Sir Richard (1755–1843), cottonmaster, 117, 215, 216, 218, 220
Arnold, Matthew, 67, 73
Ashley, Anthony, Viscount (7th Earl of Shaftesbury) (1801–85), 120
Association of All Classes of All Nations, 46, 95
Atkinson, John, partner in New Lanark, 170, 174, 175, 177
Atkinson, Thomas, 170
Ayr, river, 216

Baines, Edward (1774–1845), 119
Bartholomew, John & Co, shirt manufacturers, 198
Bell, Rev Andrew, 56-7
Bentham, Jeremy, 14, 32, 59-60, 62, 198, 207, 214

Birkmyre, Henry, 238-9, 242, 247
Birkmyre & Somerville, 238-9, 242, 247
Black Dwarf, 77
Blantyre, 244
Board of Trustees, 241
Bodichan, Barbara (1827–91), educationalist, 70-1
Borrodaile & Atkinson, merchants & manufacturers, 170
Boulton & Watt, engineers, 169, 170, 202
Braxfield, Lord, see MacQueen
Braxfield Row, 222, 228, 230
Brighton, 86-7
Brink, J. H. & Co, merchants, 196
British & Foreign Consolidated Association of Industry, Humanity & Knowledge, 92-3
British and Foreign School Society, 57
Brooks, Samuel, machine-maker, 242
Brougham and Vaux, Henry, 1st Lord (1778–1868), 64, 70, 111
Brown, Thomas, candle-maker (fl 1805), 234
Buchanan, James (fl 1815), teacher, 63, 64-5, 70
Buckhaven, 242
Budge, David, dancing master, 68
Bull, Rev George Stringer (1799–1864), 120, 123-4, 127, 128, 129, 130
Bussey, Peter (1805–69), 130

Caithness, *144*, 228

257

Campbell, Alexander of Hallyards (d 1817), 174, 177, 178, 182
Campbell, Alexander, Owenite, 87, 96, 153, 154, 158, 159
Campbell, Archibald (1744–1835) of Jura, 173-82, 185
Campbell, Colin, Glasgow merchant, 174, 182
Campbell, Colin, son of Archibald, 174, 176-7
Campbell, John, lawyer, 175-6, 178, 179, 180
Capital, 138, 145, 155-6, 162, 171-87
Catrine, 170, 172, 220, 238, 244, 248
Chartism, 12, 43
Child labour, 100-9, 111ff, 188, 191, 235
Chorlton Twist Company, 169-70, 171
Clason or Clawson, Andrew, merchant, 176-7
Cleave, John (1792–1847), 123
Clegg, William, 123
Clerk, John, lawyer (fl 1816), 178, 181
Clyde, Vale of, 215, 216
Cobbett, William (1763–1835), 21, 29, 77, 123-4
Cockburn, Henry, 82
Cole, G. D. H., 10, 19, 75, 84, 96, 131
Coleridge, Samuel T., 26, 32
Colquhoun, Alexander (Lord Advocate), 80
Combe, Abram (1785–1827), 140, 141-5, 147, 148, 149-50, 151-2, 153, 155, 156, 157, 159
Combe, Andrew, 141
Combe, George, 67, 141
Combe, William, 141, 153, 159
Committee, Select, on Factory Reform (1816), 106-7, 109-12, 192, 206
Communities, Owenite, 15, 29-33, 37-41, 45, 52, 70, 73, 85-7, 135-67
Competition, 196-7, 199
Condy, George (1790–1841), 123
Co-operation, 9-10, 29-31, 35, 37-8, 39-40, 44, 46, 73-4, 85-7, 93-4, 96, 135-67
Co-operative and Economical Society, 86

Co-operative societies, 10, 41, 46, 74, 85-7, 94, 135-67
Co-operators, 9, 10, 14, 15, 40, 43, 46, 74, 85-7, 94, 96, 142, 148-59
The Co-operator, 86
Corehouse, estate of, *107*, 193, 217
Cotton industry, 26, 80, 99, 169, 170, 182-201, 208-14
Craig, James, cotton-spinner, 180
Credit, 145, 150, 156, 157, 171-82, 197
Cresswell, Joseph, 109
The Crisis, 92, 98, 133

Dale, David (1739–1806), Glasgow merchant, *90*, 170-4, 179, 180, 181, 188, 203, 204, 205, 215, 216, 217, 218, 221, 228, 233, 235, 236, 247
Dale, David—trustees of, 171-82
Dalglish, David, manager (fl 1881–2), 232
Dalton, John, scientist, 55
Dalzell, *see* Hamilton, Archibald James
Dancing, 110, 145, 154, 188, 190
Deanston, 248
Dennistoun, Robert (d 1817), 174, 175, 176, 182
Derby, 92, 129-30
Discipline, factory, 78-9, 188-91, 192-3
Discipline, school, 24-5, 60, 68, 69
Doherty, John (1799–1854), 87, 120, 123, 129
Double Row, 228
Douglas, 234
Douglas, Stewart, cotton-spinner (fl 1815), 180
Drinkwater, Peter (1742–1801), 77, 169

The Economist, 85
Edinburgh, 128, 140, 141, 142, 149, 151, 152, 155, 157, 178, 186, 197
Edmondstone, Anne (fl 1820), 107, 217-18
Edmondstone, Janet (fl 1804), 107, 217
Edmondstone, Patricia (fl 1804), 107, 217
Education, 23-5, 52-75, 78, 154, 188, 190, 230-2; adult, 25, 73-4, 93, 95,

Index

154, 231; as agent of change, 23;
definition of, 23, 58-9; infant, 23,
24-5, 52, 55-6, 58-73; monitorial
system, 56-7; Owenite, 57-63, 154;
teaching methods, 66-8; visual
aids, *35*, 66-7, 73
Elce, John & Company, machine-
makers, 242
Engines, carding, 241, 242
Evans, Thomas, *Christian Policy* . . . ,
33

Factory Act: (1819), 117, 119;
(1825), 119; (1829), 119; (1831),
119; (1833), 111, 120-1; (1844),
111
Factory Bill: (1832), 119; (1843), 111
Factory Reformation Society, 121
Falla, William, 40, 140, 141
Fellenberg, Philipp Emanuel von, 75
Fielden, John (1784–1849), 91, 117,
122-4, 127-9
Fielden, Joshua (d 1847), 123
Fielden, Thomas (1790–1869), 123
Finch, John, 46, 87
Finlay, James & Co, yarn brokers,
196, 198, 211
Finlay, Kirkman (1772–1842), 82,
112, 198
Fintry Mills, 242
Fire, mill, 112, 194, 209, 220, 224,
225
Fitton, William (d 1840), 124
Foster, J., partner at New Lanark,
214
Fox, J., partner at New Lanark, 214
Frames, roving, 241, 242
Frames, water, 241
Freight, 197, 198

Gast, John, 87
General Association of Operative
Weavers in Scotland, 80, 82
Gibb, M., partner at New Lanark,
214
Girdwood, Claud & Company, tim-
ber merchants & machine-makers,
240
Glasgow, 21, 33, 73, 82, 87, 102, 104,
110, 112, 114, 128, 151, 159, 170,
171, 172, 173, 174, 175, 177, 180,
181, 184, 187, 196, 197, 198, 199,
210, 215, 216, 221, 242, 244, 246
Glasgow Herald, 215, 250, 251, 252
Glenbuck, 240
Godwin, William, 32, 57, 69
Gott, Benjamin (1862–1840) 109
Gould, Nathaniel (d 1820), 111
Gourock Ropework Company, 203,
206, 207, 208, 209, 210, 211, 214,
221, 239, 247, 248, 249, 250, 251,
252, 253
Graham, Sir James Robert George,
2nd bt (1792–1861), 111
Grand Moral Union, 91, 122
Grand National Consolidated Trades
Union, 91, 92-3, 130
Grant, Philip (d 1880), 123
Greenock, 228
Gunter, Messrs & Co, engineers, 239

Halls of Science, 74, 95
Hamilton, Archibald James (1793–
1834), 137, 138, 140-1, 142, 145,
148, 152, 155-6, 157-8, 159
Hamilton, General John, 140, 145
Harmony, New, 70, 73, 85, 119, 200
Harrison, Professor J. F. C., 9, 19,
51, 57, 74, 87, 97, 161, 207
Health and Morals of Apprentices
Act (1802), 100-1
Helvétius, Claude Adrien, 59-60
Hetherington, Henry (1792–1849),
11, 12, 16, 123
Higginbottom, George, 123
Highlanders, *144*, 228
Hill, Frederic, 14, 19
Hobhouse, Sir John Cam, 2nd bt
(1st Lord Broughton) (1786–1869),
119
Hobson, Joshua (1811–76), 120
Hole, James, 46, 51, 96
Holland, 196
Holt, David, 124
Holyoake, George Jacob (1817–
1906), 9, 42, 50, 96, 130
Houldsworth, Henry (1774–1853),
110
Housing, *54, 71,* 78, 145, 147, 188,
189, 191, 216-17, 218, 221, *222*,
226-30, 247-9
Howard & Bullough, machine-
makers, 242

259

Hull, 234
Humphreys, Robert, cotton-spinner, 183-5
Hunter, William & Company, 242

Insobriety, 22, 24, 78, 103, 129-30, 154, 188, 189
Inverness-shire, 228
Ireland, 138, 140, 152, 197, 228, 247
Ireland, Bernard, machine-maker, 242
Iron, 240

Jeffrey, Francis, 82
Johnstone, 242
Jones, Henry, 138, 147, 149, 155
Jones, John, machine-maker, 169

Kelly, William, clockmaker and manager, 235, 240-1
Kelvin, river, 216
Kent, Prince Edward, Duke of (1767–1820), 44, 84, 115, 118
Kenyon, George, 2nd Lord (1776–1856), 117
King, James, mason, 145
King, Dr William, 86-7
Kirkpatrick, Henry, Owenite printer, 153, 155

Labour; child, 100-1, 188, 191, 225; exchanges, 88-9, 121-2; note, 39, 87; theory of value, 38-42, 84-8
Lanark Town Council, 248
Lancaster, Joseph, 56
Land, 29, 40, 140, 141, 145, 155, 157
Lascelles, Henry, Viscount (2nd Earl of Harewood) (1767–1841), 105
Lauderdale, James, 8th Earl of (1759–1839), 117
Leipzig, 196
Leith, 196
Lindsay, Ian G. & Partners, architects, 227, 229, 230, 253
Liverpool, 46, 87, 158, 162
Liverpool, Robert, 2nd Earl of (1770–1828), 42, 59, 79, 83, 104, 112-15
London, 31, 56, 67, 86, 87, 105, 120, 138, 162, 169, 170

London Co-operative Society, 86
London Corresponding Society, 81
London Society for the Improvement of Factory Children, 120
Long Row, 222, 228
Lovett, William, 40-1, 43, 50, 56, 87, 94-5, 97, 98
Luddism, 80

Macgregor, Alexander, lawyer (fl 1814), 187
Maclure, William, 73
Macnab, Dr Henry, 136
Macqueen, Robert (Lord Braxfield), 81, 216
Machinery, cotton, 100, 103, 169, 170, 182, 194, 215, 216, 218, 221, 224, 225, 239-42
Machine-makers, 166, 169, 170, 238, 239-42, 244, 245, 246
Malthus, T. R., 28, 29
Manchester, 33, 55, 57, 60, 77, 101, 124, 129, 130, 169-70, 171, 199, 202, 208, 209, 213, 216, 254
Manchester, Board of Health, 101
Manchester Literary and Philosophical Society, 33, 57, 254
Manchester, Scots in, 169
Margarot, Maurice, 80-1
Markets, 195-8, 210, 211
Marshall, John, flax-spinner, 188, 191, 203, 206, 243, 252
Maryland, 228
Melbourne, Lord, 92, 94
Menzies, Rev William (fl 1815), 110
Metal Extraction Ltd, 248
Methodists, 58, 95
Mill, Masson, 220
Millennialism, 9, 15, 40, 43, 44-7, 88-93, 95-6, 128-30, 142-5, 159
Mills, cotton, 26, *53*, *72*, 100, 101, 102, 103, 105, 106, *107*, *108*, 109, 112, *126*, 169, 170, 171, 172, 177, 182, 184, 186, 187, 188-95, 199, 208-13, 215-49
'Missionaries', Owenite, 95, 128
Moir, John, printer (fl 1812), 186
Monkland Steel Company, 240
Monteith, Henry (1764–1848), 102, 110
More, Hannah, 55-6

More, John, banker (fl 1816), 174, 180, 181
Morgan, John Minter, 87
Morrison, James (d 1835), 91, 92, 121, 138, 162
Moscow, 196
Motherwell, 86, 138-40
Mudie, George (fl 1820), 85-6
Muirkirk, 240
Mules, hand, 241
Mules, Kelly's patent, 240-1
Mule spinning, 194, 198, *244*, 225, 240-1
Muslins, 170, 243

National Equitable Labour Exchange, 87, 88, 254
National Society for the Education of the Poor, 57
Neef, Joseph, 73
Net-making, 242
New Harmony, *see* Harmony
New Lanark:
accidents, 194, 225, 245-6
architectural style, *18, 53, 54, 71, 72, 107, 108, 125, 126,* 215-32
auction of, 187
bakehouse and flour-store, *227,* 233
book of character, 78, 189
building labour force, 192, 208, 221
Caithness Row, *125, 143,* 226, *227,* 228, 236, 237, 248
child labour, 188, 191; *see* Apprentices
children's accommodation, *71,* 188, 191, 221, *222, 227*
church, 228, 230, 233-4
coal-supplies, 234
communal identity, 190-1
company store, 69, 142, 189, 190, 227, 228, 233
conservation, 248-9; *see* New Lanark Association
discipline, 77-9, 188-93
dispute over weir, *107,* 193, 217-18
domestic heating, 234
engine house, *107, 144,* 232
feuing of site, 216
foundry, *222, 226,* 240
gas-works, *222,* 226, 234

graveyard, *144,* 228
handloom weaving, 243
housing, *53, 54,* 71, 78, *125,* 189, 191, 216-17, 221, *222,* 226, *227,* 228, *229, 230,* 236-7, 247, 248-9
industrial relations, 24-5, 26-9, 77-9, 188-93, 194-5
Institution for the Formation of Character, *18,* 63, 64, 66, 68, 83, *107, 143, 222,* 230-2, 233, 235, 236
insurance valuations, 172, 202, 203, 218, 221, 226, 249, 250, 252
labour force in mills, 188, 191-2, 208
lade, *107,* 143, 217, 218, *222*
Leeds, deputation to, 118, 119
lighting, 234
management practices, 182-5, 188-201
managers' housing, *222,* 228
mechanics' shop, *222, 226,* 240
Mill No 1, *72, 108,* 192, 197, 208, 218, *219, 220,* 221, *222,* 226, 235, 239, 241
Mill No 2, *72, 108,* 192, 197, 208, 220, 221, *222, 223,* 225, 239, 241
Mill No 3, *72, 107, 108,* 126, 192, 194, 208, 209, 221, *222, 223, 224,* 225, 235, 239, 240, 245
Mill No 4, 188, 194, 221, 222, *224,* 225, 239, 240
mill heating, 234-5
millwright's work, 239
New Buildings, *54, 222,* 228, *229*
Nursery Buildings, *71, 222, 227,* 228, 236-7
occupational census, 192, 208
ownership of mills, 171, 172, 174, 178, 182-7, 199-201, 216-17, 236, 238, 239, 247, 248
production problems, 188-95, 243-7
profits, 185, 186, 187, 195-201, 211-14
quarries, 218
recreation, 232, 237-8
sanitation, 236
schools, *18,* 52-75, 154, 189, 190, 230, *231, 232,* 233
site, 215-16, *222*
slaughter-house, 233

steam engine, *107*, *144*, 232, 244-5, 246
storage facilities, *222*, 225-6, 230
tailrace, 218
teachers, 64-9
water rents, 193, 217-18
water supply, 235-6
water turbines, 239, 246
waterwheels, 239, 243-4, 245-6
New Lanark Association, 248-9
New Moral World, 92
Newtown, 74, 254, 255
Nottingham Lace, 238

Oastler, Richard (1789–1861), 111, 119, 123-5, 127-30
Oberlin, Father, 63
O'Brien, James Bronterre, 43, 93
Official Gazette of the Trades' Unions, 92
Oldknow, Samuel (1756-1828), 79
Oliver 'the Spy', 81
Omoa, 240
Operative Builders Union, 91, 121
Orbiston, 15, 40, 86, 135-67
Orbiston, rules, 147, 163-4
Orbiston Register, 147, 150, 153, 155, 160-1
Output, 195, 209
Owen, Ann Caroline (née Dale), 170-1
Owen, Anne, 68
Owen, Robert:
  Address to the Inhabitants of New Lanark, 24-5, 48, 231-2, 250
  anti-clericalism, 10, 45, 47, 60, 94-5, 110
autobiography, *see Life by Himself*
  communitarianism, 15, 29-31, 37-8, 40, 43, 84-7, 135-8
  discipline, views on, 24-5, 60
  disputes with partners, 24, 70, 182-7, 201
  drunkenness, attitude to, 22, 24, 78, 188, 189
  economic thought, 14, 20-47, 84-5, 136-8
  education, 13, 23-5, 52-75, 83, 93, 190, 230-2
  environmentalism, 13, 21-5, 52, 58-9, 79-80

Factory Bills (1815–1819), 105-6, 111-17
factory reformer, 3, 27, 99-134
family, view of, 10, 45-6
'father of British Socialism', 9, 10, 41-7, 76-96
financial difficulties, 172, 174-82, 184-6
half-time system, 111
humanitarianism, 11, 16, 22, 58, 78-9, 99-131, 189-91
industrial relations, 77-9, 188-95
influences on, 31-3, 57-8, 169
as JP of Lanarkshire, 80
labour exchanges, 88-9, 121-2
and his labour force, 77-9, 188-95
labour theory of value, 38-42, 84-5, 87-8
and Malthusianism, 28-9
in Manchester, 77, 169-70
marketing problems, 195-9
marriage, views on, 45-6
opposition to political action, 10-13, 43-4, 77, 83-4, 93-4
Orbiston, 141, 145, 148, 157-8, 159
parliamentary candidature (1820), 118
partners, 169, 170, 174, 177-9, 199-201, 214
paternalism, 14, 43, 78, 93, 113, 117-18, 189-91
patronage of dissenting ministers, 110
production problems, 188-95
productivity of workers, 26-7, 111-12, 188-9
Publications:
  An Address to the Working Classes, 1819, 83-4
  A New View of Society, 20, 21, 22, 52, 57, 58, 76, 79, 140, 141
  A Statement regarding the New Lanark Establishment, 186
  Life by Himself, 10, 48, 49, 50, 96, 99, 131, 132, 168, 182, 202, 205, 206, 207, 250, 251
  Observations on the Cotton Trade, 26, 99, 102-5
  Observations on the Effect of the Manufacturing System . . ., 30, 49, 105, 131

Index

On the Employment of Children in Manufactories. To the Right Honourable the Earl of Liverpool, 48, 79-80, 96, 112-15, 132

Report to the Committee of the Association for the Relief of the Manufacturing and Labouring Poor (March 1817), 29-31, 112, 138, *139*

Report to the County of Lanark, 38-41, 46, 50, 85, 97, 118, 136-7, 145, 159, 160

To the British Master Manufacturers on the Employment of Children in Manufactories, 27, 115-17, 132

purchase of New Lanark, 171, 174, 187

reading habits, 33, 62

relationship with Humphreys, 183-5

religion, 10, 31, 44, 60, 94-5, 110, 189-90

repeal of cotton duties, 102-3

retail experience, 168-9

role of government, 22-3, 29, 38, 42-3, 99, 113

secularism, 44-5, 47, 94-5

shareholdings in New Lanark, 182, 185-7

'silent monitor', 24, 78, 79, 189

stock control, 24, 78, 188-9

syndicalism, 41, 83, 122

town planning, 236-7

and trade unionism, 88-93, 95, 96, 121-2

visits to America, 12, 70, 254-5

visits to factories, 100, 109

Owen, Robert Dale (1801–77), 33, 109, 205

Owen, William, saddler, 169

Owenism, 9, 10, 12, 13, 16, 20-47, 52, 57, 58-63, 79, 83-8, 136-7

Owenites in factory reform movement, 119-20 ff

Owenites, English, 41-2, 46-7, 67, 70, 74, 86-93, 96

Owenites, Scottish, 40, 70-1, 85-6, 135-67

Palladian windows, 220-1, 225

Parliament, 12, 80, 101, 105, 106-112, 117, 120, 139

Paul, Alexander, Owenite, 57, 158

Pease, Wrays & Trigg, oil merchants, 234

Peel, Isle of Man, 239

Peel, Sir Robert, 1st bt (1750–1830), 100, 101, 105-6, 112-14, 117, 119

Percival, Dr Thomas (1740–1804), 57, 101

Pestalozzi, Johann Heinrich, 73

Peterloo, 83

Philips, Sir George, 1st bt (1766–1847), 111

The Pioneer, 91, 92, 95

Pitkeithley, Lawrence (d 1858), 87, 119-20, 124, 128, 129

Platt Brothers, machine-makers, 242

Poor Law, 22, 28-9, 30, 100-1, 118, 139

Poor Man's Guardian, 11, 12, 16, 19

Port Glasgow, 239

Potters' Union, 95

Power, water, *107*, 155, 193, 215-16, 217-18, 220, 221, *222*, 235-6, 237, 239-40, 241, 243-4, 245-6

Prices, 192, 198-9

Production, 188-95, 209

Radicalism, 11-12, 77, 80-1, 82-3, 119, 127-9

Raikes, Robert, 56

Rathbone, William, merchant, 64

Rationalism, 24, 25, 33, 44, 45-6, 60, 85

Reform agitation, (1830-2), 11, 12, 43, 93

Regent, Prince, 43, 83

Religion and working classes, 45-6, 94-5

Richmond, Alexander, 82, 97

Rigside, 234

Ring-spinning, 242

Rivers, Scottish, 215-16

Rochdale Pioneers, 15, 46

Roebuck, Rev J. H., 34

Ross, Sir John Lockhart (fl 1784), 217

Rousseau, J. J., philosopher, 32, 57, 60

Royal Bank of Scotland, 171, 172-3, 174, 180-2
Royal Commission on factory reform (1833), 120
Russia, 171, 195-7

Sadler, Michael Thomas (1780–1835), 119, 123, 128
Sales, Yarn, 195-99, 210
Schools, *18*, 25, *35, 55-6*, 61, 65-8, *231-2*
Scott Moncrieff, Robert, banker, 172-3
Scottish Union Insurance Company, 145
Sects, religious, 190, 228
Secularism, 10, 33, 44-5, 60, 94-5
Sheddon, William, Owenite, 158
Shoemakers, Incorporation of, in Lanark, 217
Short-Time Committees, 119, 129, 130
Shortages, water, 193, 216, 217-18, 243-4
Shotts Iron Company, 246
Sidmouth, Henry, 1st Viscount (1757–1844), 42, 81, 84, 110, 113
Smith, James Elishma, 92, 95
Smyrna, 196
Socialism, scientific, 15, 40-2, 45-6, 47
Society for Promoting National Regeneration, 91, 120-30
Society for Propagation of Christian Knowledge, 55
Somerville, R. S., 238-9, 242, 247
Southey, Robert, 12, 43
Spinningdale, 170, 172, 220
Stanley, 180, 181, 205, 212, 248
Steam engines, 169, 170, 244
Steel, 240
Stewart, Allan & Co, merchants, 196-7
Stewart, Rev James Haldane, 181-2
Stocks, 198-9
Stocks, William (1782–1851), 124, 127
Stonebyres, 215, 236
Stowe, David (1793–1864), educationist, 73
St Petersburg, 196
Strike, weavers', 80, 82

Strutt, George Benson (1761–1841), 117
Sun Fire Insurance Company, 170, 202, 203, 218, 221, 226, 249, 250, 251, 252
Sussex, Prince Augustus, Duke of (1773–1843), 84, 115, 118, 120

Teager, William & Co, merchants, 196
Ten-hour agitation, 119 ff
Theology, Swedenborgian, 64
Thompson, Edward P., 11, 50, 81, 96
Throstles, 241-2
The Times, 87
Tolpuddle, 92, 130
Torrens, Robert, 37-8
Trade Unions, 46, 77, 80, 82, 87-93, 95, 96, 130
Transport, 196-7, 198
Trieste, 196
Trimmer, Sarah, 55-6
Turnbull, Grant & Jack, engineers, 246
Turner, James, 123
Tutors, private, 55

Unemployment, 27-31, 38-40, 76, 87
United Trades Association, 88
Unrest, political, 11, 42-3, 79-84, 136
Utilitarians, 14, 32, 59-60, 62

Vansittart, Nicholas (1st Lord Bexley,) (1766–), 103·
Villages, Owenite, 15, 29-31, 37, 38, 40, 44, 45, 52, 70, 73, 86, 135-67

Wages, 12, 28, 38, 39, 80, 190
Walker family, 201, 214, 238-9, 247
Walker, John (fl 1825), 201, 214
Warder, W. S., *A Brief Sketch of the Religious Society of People called Shakers*, 33
Watson, James, 120
Weavers, handloom, 80, 147, 166, 243
Whiteley, John & Sons, cardmakers, 240
Whitwill, Miss, teacher (fl 1827), 67, 154
Wilberforce, William, 43, 44, 83

Index

Wilderspin, Samuel, 60, 64
Wilsontown, 240
Wood, John (1793–1871), 123, 127-8
Woodside (Aberdeen), 220
Wooler, Jonathan, 77
Working classes, 11, 12, 14, 26, 37, 40, 41, 42, 46, 55, 77-98

Wright, John, clerk, 181, 199-200, 213

Yarn counts, 169, 195, 197-8, 209
Young, Molly (fl 1815), teacher, 64

Zang of Paris, machine-makers, 242